All Mothers Are
Working Mothers

All Mothers Are Working Mothers

Are

Working Mothers

— Laura Sabin Riley —

A Devotional for
Stay-at-Home
Moms—
and Those Who
Would Like to Be

HORIZON BOOKS

A DIVISION OF CHRISTIAN PUBLICATIONS, INC.
CAMP HILL, PENNSYLVANIA

HORIZON BOOKS

3825 Hartzdale Drive
Camp Hill, PA 17011
www.cpi-horizon.com
www.christianpublications.com

All Mothers Are Working Mothers
ISBN: 0-88965-151-5

© 1999 by Laura Sabin Riley

Printed in the United States of America

00 01 02 03 04   6 5 4 3 2

Poem "Continue On" written by Roy Lessin.
Used by permission.

May 8 story excerpted from *Lord, I Want to Know You*
© 1992 by Kay Arthur.
Reprinted by permission of Multnomah Publishers.

December 7 story excerpted from
God's Little Devotional Book For Moms.
Used by permisson of Honor Books.

Front cover photos by Jill Jongward

Unless otherwise indicated, Scripture taken from the Holy Bible:
New American Standard Version. © 1960, 1962, 1963, 1968, 1971,
1972, 1973, 1975 by The Lockman Foundation.

Whatever you do, do your work heartily,
as for the Lord rather than for men.
(Colossians 3:23)

Dedication

This book is dedicated to two of the most incredible people I know—my mother and father.

My mom has been much more than a parent to me. She has always been one of my closest friends. She sacrificed a great deal to stay home with my brothers and me and, even as a young child, I respected and admired her strong commitment to God and to our family. I credit her for my own passion toward Jesus and for my intense desire to fulfill His call for me to be a devoted wife and mother. She taught me much more than how to live; she taught me how to love and how to give.

I love you Mom, with all my heart.

My father's love and dedication to my mother provided a stable foundation for my own marriage. His commitment to his wife and children provided an atmosphere of security that enabled me to grow freely into all God has intended me to be.

Dad, this book would not be possible without your love and encouragement throughout the years to "write and write and never give up." Thank you for believing in my abilities. Your faith in me has made all the difference.

To both of you, Mom and Dad, thank you for your boundless love.

Table of Contents

October: Opportunities for Advancement
  "What's my next step up?"

November: Job Security
  "What do you mean I'm not replaceable
      if I decide to quit?"

December: The Boss
  "OK, I'll take the job—who's my supervisor?"

Introduction

---·❦·---

*W*hen our first child was born, my husband and I decided it would be best for me to stay home full time. Leaving a lucrative and rewarding career as an account coordinator for one of the nation's leading cosmetics companies for the challenging and sometimes thankless career of a mom was a rude awakening. I went from changing sales plans to changing diapers almost overnight. My suits and high heels were traded in for a pair of jeans and running shoes. The emphasis on "running" became apparent when my little cherub entered the toddler years! Out were quotas, strategy sessions and business lunches. In were laundry, bottle-washing and peanut butter sandwiches.

Five years and thousands of diapers later, I don't regret my choice. I am exactly where God wants me—and that's good enough for me. Some days I miss a career outside the home, but it pales compared to the rewards of caring for my sons full time. I'll take chubby little arms embracing me over an employer's pat on the back any day. Training forty sales consultants was gratifying, but training my children's hearts reaps eternal rewards. God's best is for my husband and me to raise our sons in biblical standards for living. He promises that my children will forever walk in those principles: "Train up a child in the way he should go, even when he is old he will not depart from it" (Proverbs 22:6).

I decided that this assignment was too important to give to someone else. Not every woman has that option, but I did. The way I see it, there was no choice to make. Research proves that the critical years in a child's development are the first seven. Values are not inherent from birth; God's Word tells us they must be taught. Respect, obedience, kindness, gentleness, patience, self-control, forgiveness—the list goes on, and so do my kids' lives. I want to be there every step of the way.

But that doesn't mean it's easy! Full-time mothering is the most difficult job I've ever had. Frustrations range from lack of affirmation and fulfillment to feelings of inadequacy to financial sacrifice. Add those to the absence of time for myself, lack of support and complete exhaustion.

My search for materials to support me as a stay-at-home mom has been disappointing. Bookstores stock many self-helps for women working outside the home, but what about women working in their homes? So I wrote this book for those of us who traded in our paychecks for toothless grins and sinks full of dishes.

I hope that this book will encourage, strengthen and inspire you as a mother. I feel compassion for the mom who drags herself to bed each night worn from the day's constant demands. I know it's tough; I've been there—still am actually. But take heart. God has heard your cry. I am confident that God wants to encourage mothers through these devotionals.

Each month focuses on something that you deal with day to day. Each day begins with the freshness of Scripture. Spending daily time in His Word enables you to maintain a biblical perspective. Following each verse is a personal reflection designed to exhort you in your role as a mother. The thoughts are as varied as the days of our lives. Each devotional is a springboard to launch your own dialogue with God. Get personal with Him. He promises to hear you, and help you: "Be anxious for nothing, but in everything by prayer and supplication with thanksgiving let your requests be made known to God. And the peace of God, which surpasses all comprehension, shall guard your hearts and minds in Christ Jesus" (Philippians 4:6-7).

You may be a mom who is currently not at home. Perhaps you want to be but cannot. In this book you may discover truths that lead to a new way of life. I have discovered that being a stay-at-home mom does not have to be exhausting and defeating. Rather, when I live a balanced life in accordance to God's statutes, meaning and purpose fill my life. My prayer is that you, too, will experience all the joy that God intends for you as a mom.

January:
The Job Description

When I say I'm a stay-at-home mom,
people say, "Oh, so you don't work?"

he comment came from a woman at a business din-
ner my husband and I attended. When I told her I
was a stay-at-home mom, she responded, "Oh, so you don't
work." I wanted to scream, "You're kidding, right?" Instead,
I smiled and replied, "Harder than you could ever imagine."
Then I turned away so I could roll my eyes. I tried not to let
her comment bother me, but it hurt. The attitude that a
woman who stays at home does "nothing" has burdened
women for decades. It leaves the mom who has chosen to
stay home and raise a family feeling insecure in her choice.

Most people have no idea how hard a stay-at-home mom
works. This job requires the skills of a teacher, counselor, maid,
short-order cook, nurse, party planner, financial analyst and
chauffeur. If stay-at-home moms were paid for these positions,
women would be standing in line to apply! Instead, however,
society has downplayed her importance. That is why the
stay-at-home mom must define her role according to the only
standard that really counts: God's Word. God holds the
"keeper of the home" in the highest esteem—just read Prov-
erbs 31. We should study and value God's attitude toward us.
After all, we serve Him, not man.

So hold your head high and know that your job matters to
God. *You* matter to God! A new year is a great time to refo-
cus your thinking, expectations and commitment to your
God-designed job.

And everyone who competes in the games exercises self-control in all things. They then do it to receive a perishable wreath, but we an imperishable. (1 Corinthians 9:25)

The new year is a great time to plan a new game strategy. We compete everyday in the marathon of life. As trainer, we teach our kids how to run so that they will not become winded and retreat to the sidelines in defeat. Every moment is potential training time.

Most topnotch athletes train many hours a day. How many hours a day do you spend with your kids? Are you training them in the ways of the Lord, in Scripture and godly values? These principles will equip them to cope with life. The time we invest in our children will enable them to run their own races. When they reach independence, we can point to the finish line and cheer them on toward the imperishable prize of eternal life. Prize athletes spend endless hours training for a medal that will end up in a dusty trophy case. Isn't it worth a few hours a day to train our kids to win an imperishable prize?

Lord, give me wisdom to adjust my schedule so that I can spend more time with my children. Show me how to instill biblical principles that will take them across the finish line and into Your kingdom.

And do not be conformed to this world, but be transformed by the renewing of your mind, that you may prove what the will of God is, that which is good and acceptable and perfect. (Romans 12:2)

What is God's will for my life? Stay-at-home moms often ask this question. The world tells us to go to work; and yet, God's Word tells us to be "workers at home" in Titus 2:5. The two messages conflict. But the only opinion that really matters is God's. We can find all the answers in His Word.

The Bible has God's will for our lives on every page. Every time I feel confused about what direction He wants me to take, the answer is in His Word. The transformation of my mind takes place as I fill it up with the Scriptures. This drives me farther away from the world's way of thinking and closer to God's way.

As Romans 12:2 states, my transformed mind proves God's will is perfect. When God's Word changes our inner nature, then our external form—the way we act, speak and treat others—is also affected. When our minds are transformed, we are a living testimony of God's will.

If you've been struggling with how to determine God's will, go to the Scriptures. Let them transform your mind. For instance, should you buy that new dining room set you want? It depends—how will you pay for it? Look at Proverbs 22:26 and Romans 13:8. Wondering about God's will in the discipline of your children? The answer is in Proverbs 13:24 and 22:15. What about the financially troubled relative who has come to you for a loan? See First Timothy 5:8. God's Word contains all the answers we need—search the Scriptures.

God, I know that Your Word contains all that I need. Help me to constantly seek You, finding the answers to my everyday concerns in the Scriptures.

January 3

See how great a love the Father has bestowed upon us, that we should be called children of God; and such we are. For this reason the world does not know us, because it did not know Him. (1 John 3:1)

You are a *child* of God! Seems ironic, doesn't it? You must work so hard to have your children respect your authority, and yet *you* are just a child! In God's beautiful web of relationships, we submit to our heavenly Father, who trains us to know, love and serve Him. We in turn teach this to our children. They are under our care, but they will always be children of God first.

This helps me understand why the world often does not acknowledge my work as a stay-at-home mom. As First John 3:1 states, "The world does not know us, because it did not know Him." The things of God don't make sense to the one who doesn't know Him. I am to keep my eyes on Him and remember that I am a child of God. He calls me His child, a term of endearment.

Part of your job description as a stay-at-home mom is to be a child of God. That includes building a relationship with your heavenly Father. By spending time with God, you teach your children that a relationship with Him is a priority. Spend time with Him daily. Be His child.

Heavenly Father, thank You for calling me Your child! How great is Your love! Just as my children desire to spend time with me, give me the desire to spend time with You.

January 4

Now it came about when Pharaoh had let the people go, that God did not lead them by the way of the land of the Philistines, even though it was near; for God said, "Lest the people change their minds when they see war, and they return to Egypt." (Exodus 13:17)

The Israelites were finally released from captivity under Pharaoh's hand. They were anxious to go home. But the quickest way was not the best way, according to Exodus 13:17. God knew that if His people took the shortcut, they would see the Philistine troops and in fear run back to Egypt. God had other plans.

He knew their faith needed bolstering, so He led them the long way with the cloud by day and the fire by night. On this route through the wilderness God demonstrated His power by parting the Red Sea, providing manna and other miracles. These acts strengthened the Israelites' faith.

There are many shortcuts to parenting—like leaving all the training to the baby-sitter or the teacher—but we must not be tempted to take them. We may not be ready for the battle that's raging just over the hill. God sees all and knows all; when it comes to navigating our families, He is the best One for the job. He often saves us from looming disaster just ahead. He knows when we are ready for the fight and the Christian faith is definitely a fight at times. Often we are called upon to defend our principles, one of them being our conviction to stay home with our children, while the world assaults our position.

Build your faith in God and in your position as a stay-at-home mom so that when you are called to battle you can defend yourself and your beliefs. Keep your eyes on God and don't try to take the shortcuts. Remember the Israelites—faster isn't necessarily better. The stronger your faith, the stronger your fight will be.

Oh God, help me to look to You for direction as I parent my children. I want to take the paths that You have mapped out for me. Help me not to be tempted by the shortcuts of the world.

January 5

Commit your works to the LORD, and your plans will be established. (Proverbs 16:3)

Your work as a mother is training hearts and shaping lives—doesn't it seem sensible to commit that important work to the Lord? My husband, Jimmy, meets weekly with a close friend to pray for their businesses. They commit their work to the Lord. I have seen God honor their prayers.

My husband's work as a general contractor is cyclical. During one slow time, a job came up that we both felt wasn't appropriate for a Christian businessman, but it paid well. Jimmy was tempted to bid it. When we discussed it, I sensed his struggle. I suggested we ask God to provide the answer. Daily, we told God our needs and asked for His direction. Within a week, we believed that God had told him not to bid on the job. Then, God provided the work we needed through a different job only one week later.

When we commit our work to the Lord, He will establish our plans. When we commit something to Him, we ask Him to help us accomplish our purpose within His guidelines and timetable. If it means compromising our integrity, then it is not His will. And if it is not His will, then it should not be a part of our plan.

Do you daily commit your work as a mother to the Lord? Raising children is hard work. We especially need His guidance because we have only one shot to do it right. Try getting together weekly with other stay-at-home moms. Pray for each other and your children. Commit your work to Him, and watch as He blesses your plans.

I commit my job as a mother to You, Lord. Help me to bring up my children in a way that pleases You. May I demonstrate Your highest standards in all I do. Bless my work and bless my children.

Whatever you do, do your work heartily, as for the Lord rather than for men. (Colossians 3:23)

A magnet on my refrigerator says, "All mothers are working mothers." How true! It makes me smile every morning as I fix breakfast for my little ones. It reminds me that what I do all day long—cooking, cleaning, washing, ironing, reading stories, playing with blocks, training little hearts—is work. A mother's work.

The world downplays caring for children; some don't even count it as work. I have found that if I focus on doing my job as a mother to please the Lord, rather than to please those around me, I feel much better about my role as a stay-at-home mom.

God holds the "keeper of the home" in high esteem. Knowing that gives my job great relevance. Cleaning sticky faces and reading the "teddy bear book" for the fourth time may not be glamorous. It's sometimes hard to see the benefits of the time we've invested in our children. For the most part, they aren't revealed until later in life. When a child decides not to cheat on a seventh-grade test, it becomes apparent our lessons about honesty did sink in. When he gives up his bus seat for an elderly person, we know he listened when we spoke of kindness and respect.

Don't listen to the negative talk around you that a woman who stays at home is lazy or doesn't want to work. Developing sensitivity, respect and integrity of character in a willful child is tough. Consider your job now as one that impacts the future. Do your work with vigor, seeking to please God. Anything worth doing for Him is worth doing well.

Thank you, Lord, for the job of caring for my precious children. Help me to concentrate on doing my job to please You, not others around me.

And when you are praying, do not use meaningless repetition, as the Gentiles do, for they suppose that they will be heard for their many words. (Matthew 6:7)

"Thank You for Mommy, Daddy, cousin Jaimee, Grandma . . . and thank You for my puppy and . . . for my Winnie-the-Pooh books. Amen," prayed three-year-old Seth at bedtime. "I pray, now Mommy pray," he said. I agreed, wondering how I could be as simple as he. Suddenly, my prayers seemed long and complicated.

As I finished the dinner dishes, I thought about Seth's prayer. His prayer was straight from the heart, genuine and full of thanksgiving. I realized how full of rhetoric and fancy-talk my prayers were at times. Listening to Seth helped me to see that I just need to say what's on my heart—no more, no less. That my son was already learning the habit of prayer blessed my heart. I sometimes worried that I wouldn't teach him the "correct way" to pray, but perhaps Seth was teaching me!

Part of my responsibility as a mother is to teach my children to pray. I grew up learning to pray about everything from my mother. She taught me that no request is too small or silly to present to God. He wanted to hear from us all the time and about anything. I now pray just that way.

A few days after my revelation about prayer, I was in the backyard with Seth when I noticed a beautiful sunset. I picked him up, pointed toward the sky and said, "Thank You God, for the pretty sunset." A few days later as he ate lunch, Seth could see the skyline through the bay window. As he munched on his raisins, I heard him say quietly, "Thank You, God, for the pretty sky." My heart swelled, and I said my own prayer of thanks for a child who was learning to pray as God intended: simply and sincerely.

Help me, Lord, to model a life of prayer to my children. Show me how to teach them to pray. May my prayers to You always be straight from my heart.

Truly I say to you, unless you are converted and become like children, you shall not enter the kingdom of heaven. (Matthew 18:3)

*I*t has been said that the best time to give your children advice is when they are young enough to believe you know what you are talking about. My children, still impressionable, hang on my every word. Their childlike faith allows them to easily believe me. What a glorious—and yet critical—position. When my children still believe I know what I am talking about, I had better make good use of that time. A good friend has three teenage boys. She has taught me that if I can win my childrens' respect when they are young, they will still listen to me when they become teenagers. I am counting on that.

My friend's teenagers still heed her advice for the most part, but they don't hang on every word like they used to. When I tell my three-year-old I don't want him to watch a television show because it is inappropriate and does not glorify God, he simply nods in understanding, and we find something else for him to watch.

When my friend tells her sixteen-year-old she'd prefer that he didn't see a movie because the content is inappropriate and does not glorify God, the case doesn't close so easily. No longer does he take everything she says at face value. That is part of growing up.

Take advantage of the window of opportunity you have to teach them everything you can while "they are young enough to believe you know what you're talking about."

Lord, thank You for the teachability of young children. Help me to make the most of this trainable time to build their childlike faith into a strong faith in You.

Give, and it will be given to you; good measure, pressed down, shaken together, running over, they will pour into your lap. For whatever measure you deal out to others, it will be dealth to you in return. (Luke 6:38)

Moms know all about giving. It is what we do best—or at least the most. Being a giver is a big part of the job for a stay-at-home mom, especially one with small children. Hitting school age provides a small reprieve from giving responsibilities. Still, housework needs to be done, meals cooked, errands run. The job of stay-at-home mom is one of a never-ending giver.

Some days I feel like I have nothing left to give. I feel as though I am pressed down, shaken together and running over—*with exhaustion*! But if we continue to give to our children, God will pour into us all that we need to keep on. The more love we give, the more love we receive. One of my favorite sayings is, "Children spell love, T-I-M-E." Soon, the days when they need all our time and attention will be gone. So when you feel you have nothing left to give, measure out your patience, press down a little and shake yourself up; soon more will pour out of you.

Lord, help me to give unselfishly to my children. Fill me up when I think I have nothing left to give. May I never say to them with my actions, "I don't have time for you!"

And being found in appearance as a man, He humbled Himself by becoming obedient to the point of death, even death on a cross. (Philippians 2:8)

Choosing to stay at home with our children sometimes means that we must give up other desires. It means dying to ourselves—which is both rewarding and painful. Imagine how Jesus must have felt as He slowly died on the cross for our sins. He was perfect and had done nothing wrong, yet He allowed soldiers to hang Him on the cross. Crucifixion is known to be an excruciating death. The body slowly suffocates. Although it was not what He wanted, Jesus humbled Himself and obeyed the Father's will—however far from His own desires.

When I feel sorry for myself, thinking that all I do is tend to the needs of others, I check myself with this verse. Yes, my job of stay-at-home mom means I have had to put some of my aspirations on the back burner. But even in my most difficult hours, I have never had to suffer the pain Jesus did. That puts things in perspective.

My job is to obey the Father's call, and that means caring for my children at home right now. Other ambitions can wait; my children cannot.

Jesus' death had a glorious finish: His resurrection. My life will have a glorious finish, too, if I continue to obey Him.

Lord, may I always put Your will first, instead of my own desires.

Then she called the name of the LORD who spoke to her, "Thou art a God who sees." (Genesis 16:13)

The Genesis story of the young servant, Hagar, fascinates me. Her plight revealed one of the names of God. When Sarai couldn't get pregnant, she used Hagar to bear Abram's child. When Hagar had conceived, Sarai reduced her again to a slave. In humiliation and fear, Hagar ran away. She found herself in the wilderness face-to-face with an angel of the Lord. He urged her to return and submit to Sarai's authority (Genesis 16:9). He promised to multiply her descendants.

The Lord told Hagar that the injustices done to her would be punished—in His way, in His time. Hagar was responsible to obey God and remember that He is *El Roi*, "the God who sees." His eyes are never shut, His back never turned. There is no hiding from God.

Like Hagar, all of us have felt used at times. As a stay-at-home mom, I may feel used by my husband, my children, even by well-meaning friends who think I have tons of extra time and volunteer me for too many projects. Yet, Hagar's situation inspires me to trust God with injustices committed against me. God says in His Word that He sees what is happening to me at every moment. I am called to love and serve, not judge and count scores.

If you have stored away unforgiveness and bitterness toward someone, let go of them right now.

Thank You, Lord, that You are El Roi, the God who sees. Help me to remember that You watch over my life at all times; You are in control. May I bring to You every wrong done to me and allow You to take care of it.

However, the spiritual is not first, but the natural; then the spiritual. (1 Corinthians 15:46)

Some days I struggle to find the redeeming qualities in picking up dirty laundry, scrubbing floors and cleaning handprints from windows. "Why am I doing this?" I wonder aloud. "I'll only have to do it again tomorrow." In the midst of wiping up yet another glass of spilled milk, I find myself grumbling instead of praising God for my work.

I doubt that I'm the only mother of young children who's been tempted to turn in her dishrag for a business suit. It's tough to see the joy in the job when you can't even see out the windows. My natural instinct is to react to my circumstances rather than respond to God's Word. The Bible tells women to be "workers at home" in Titus 2:5. So then, why is it so difficult for me to find joy when I know I'm doing what God wants me to do?

One day I looked at the sticky kitchen floor and felt overwhelmed with the never-ending task of caring for a home and family. As the boys napped, I took a Bible break. First Corinthians 15:46 spoke to my heart. I understood that my natural desires are stronger than my supernatural, because I often give in to my fleshly behavior—like grumbling and complaining. I have to consciously work to overcome the natural.

To become more positive about housework, for example, I need to ask God to replace my natural reactions with spiritual responses. I can choose to *respond* to what God's Word says about being "a worker at home." I have learned that if I respond to the Scriptures—rather than the circumstances—I can find joy even in doing the laundry.

Lord, help me to respond spiritually rather than react naturally to the circumstances of life.

And whoever exalts himself shall be humbled; and whoever humbles himself shall be exalted. (Matthew 23:12)

I remember my attempt to potty train Seth. What exasperating days. The mess, the frustration, the time. It is a round-the-clock job because you never know when an "accident" may happen. This process taught me to be humble about my children's progress, lest I be humbled myself!

Seth and I had been working on potty training for about two weeks when a few friends came over for dinner. Just after I had bragged that Seth hadn't had an accident in days, he came running and screeching about having an "accident." I, along with the rest of our company (much to my embarrassment), ran to his room to discover it was quite true. I excused myself to clean up the mess.

Fortunately, Seth's mishap didn't spoil anyone's appetite. We all got a good laugh out of the incident. But I knew I had spoken out of turn.

Humility is a necessary character quality for mothers. We will be called upon often to use it. Proverbs 18:12 says, "Before destruction the heart of man is haughty, but humility goes before honor." Most certainly our children will make us proud, but we need to be wary of arrogance. The difference is humility.

Lord, may I walk always in humility, teaching my children to do the same.

For we are His workmanship, created in Christ Jesus for good works, which God prepared beforehand, that we should walk in them. (Ephesians 2:10)

A friend of mine, a mom of three, loves to bake and concoct delicious dishes for her family. Her older son, Michael, spent a lot of time with his mother in the kitchen. He sat on the counter, first just content to observe. As he grew older, she allowed Michael to pour in ingredients and stir them up with his "special helper" spoon. His favorite treat to bake with his mom was muffins.

The Christmas that Michael was three years old, his parents deliberated over gifts. Dad wanted to get him a workshop-type bench, complete with plastic hammer, screwdriver and wrench. But his mother felt he would enjoy a play kitchen set much more. "No son of mine would want a kitchen for Christmas when he can have a workbench," exclaimed Pete. "Michael needs a workbench." Missy complied and they bought Michael the workbench.

On Christmas morning Michael stood in wide-eyed delight at the presents surrounding the tree. He ran to the workbench, examining it carefully. His father waited for Michael to swing the hammer, driving home the first plastic nail. Much to his surprise, however, Michael picked up the screwdriver and began stirring in an imaginary bowl. He turned to his mother, adorning a big smile and exclaimed, "Come on Mom, let's make muffins."

God has created each of our children special, with a variety of talents. We are wise as parents not to try to change God's workmanship, but to support each child's different endeavors—even if they are not in line with ours. As long as our children seek to serve the Lord, their works will be "good works."

Lord, help me to encourage my children's individual interests. Give me strength to avoid turning them into something they were never meant to be.

But women shall be preserved through the bearing of children.
(1 Timothy 2:15)

Many new moms feel less preserved in their early years of motherhood than at any other time. Some synonyms for preserved are protected, maintained, saved. I confess—childbirth did not leave me feeling preserved. I felt rather spent, and I don't recall that dissipating in a matter of hours, either. It often lingers for days, weeks, months, even years! Through pregnancy and the early years of rearing children, most moms feel less than desirable.

A friend with a new baby says that she wants to stay attractive for her husband. But she admits that it's difficult to feel desirable with spit-up running down her back or peanut butter and jelly stains on the front of her blouse. Sound familiar? We've all been there. The same is true of pregnancy. I remember reading about pregnant women who said it was "the best time in their lives." That's a matter of opinion. I couldn't quite make the connection between feeling as big as a whale and feeling great.

Since all Scripture is inspired by God, so First Timothy 2:15 has a thought for us from Him. God called us to bear children; that act is part of our purpose. Many stay-at-home moms get discouraged about an occupation that gives picnics in the park as a bonus instead of vacations in the Caribbean. Yet, God's Word promises that we will be preserved. What other job gives such a guarantee?

Just like the once short-lived strawberries that became a jar of sweet jam in your kitchen cupboard, with just the right ingredients, you too will be preserved.

Lord, thank You for making my job description clear in Your Word. I pray You will preserve me as a wife and mother when I feel like I'm not going to last.

From the rising of the sun to its setting
The name of the LORD is to be praised. (Psalm 113:3)

Ever have those days of total chaos in your household from the time the sun rises to the time it sets? When it seems as if everyone wakes up on the wrong side of the bed and stays there all day? Or your kids are just plain mischievous and determined to stir the pot? I know we sure have those days.

I have something to share with you that can actually turn those days into positive experiences: praise. Praising God even in the worst of circumstances seems to change things. It doesn't change the circumstances; it changes my attitude about the circumstances.

The enemy does not like to see us happy and joyful. He causes chaos in our homes because he knows this will wear us down. On days like these, I have found that praise music is a great way to change the atmosphere. I may play praise music all day long, softly in the background or loudly while the kids and I sing and dance to the music. I have discovered that when my children are rambunctious, praise music quiets them down. The tone in our house suddenly changes, and the enemy leaves. Satan cannot be present where the name of the Lord is spoken.

So the next time you need to "turn down the volume" on attitudes and actions in your household, turn up the praise music and watch God work.

Lord, I praise You for how You use music to minister to the spirits of all in my household. May my words and thoughts be full of praise to You.

For the flesh sets its desire against the Spirit, and the Spirit against the flesh; for these are in opposition to one another, so that you may not do the things that you please. (Galatians 5:17)

This Scripture vividly pictures the constant battle that rages in and around us everyday. I once saw a bumper sticker that said, "Christians aren't perfect, just forgiven." Have you ever acted out toward your kids and afterward known that you were wrong? I am easily aggravated for instance, by whiny children and can be quick to speak harshly when my patience has worn thin. Then I've kicked myself for it. That's the Spirit waging war against my flesh.

Once we ask Christ to be our Lord and Savior, the Holy Spirit comes to live in us forever. But unfortunately, our sinful nature does not just leave when the Holy Spirit shows up. Instead, they are both present and battling every day of our lives.

How true that is! I am convinced that Satan works hard to wear down moms who are trying to build a God-centered home. A house that honors the Lord threatens him. He strikes at your weakest areas. We all have different weaknesses.

The key to conquering my flesh and the enemy is allowing the Spirit to rule and reign moment by moment, day by day. Walking is a constant motion, taking one step at a time. That is how the Spirit will conquer the flesh in our lives; one day at a time, one situation at a time.

Being a soldier in God's army is part of the job as a believer; as a stay-at-home mom, you are the chief soldier and example to your children. If they see us conquering weaknesses in our life through the Spirit's power, they will march closely behind us doing the same.

Lord, I pray I will learn to yield to the power of Your Holy Spirit in my life, rather than the power of my flesh. Help me day by day, moment by moment, to walk with You.

Many are the plans in a man's heart, but the counsel of the LORD, it will stand. (Proverbs 19:21)

*I*t has been said that life without purpose is more tragic than death itself. Those who wander aimlessly through life always fall short of attaining happiness. But we don't have to search for purpose. The one who made us has determined it. God is concerned with establishing His purpose in our lives because our plans will change, but the purpose of the Lord will not. The Lord's plan leads to happiness.

In terms of your life work, God's purpose has already been determined. In Titus 2:5, he calls you a "worker at home." In choosing to be a stay-at-home mom, you have obeyed His purpose for your life. Obedience brings great blessing in this life and the one to come.

If you sometimes feel discouraged because others don't view your choice to be a stay-at-home mom as work, turn to God's Word. By choosing that path, you are on your way to fulfilling His purpose in your life. In a world of confusion and change, what could be more reassuring than the permanence of God and His Word?

Lord, thank You for revealing my purpose in life. Give me the strength to fulfill it even when others question it. Help me to rely on Your Word, not on the winds of changing opinions that whip about me. Wrap me in the surety of Your constancy.

———— ❧✿❧ ————

*Then David said to the Philistine, "You come to me with a sword,
a spear, and a javelin, but I come to you in the name of the LORD of
hosts, the God of the armies of Israel, whom you have taunted."
(1 Samuel 17:45)*

The story of David and Goliath is one of my favorites. David was not
a large man in stature, and yet he was not afraid to face the
Philistine giant from whom everyone else had fled. When Saul tried to
dress him in full armor, David couldn't even walk in it (1 Samuel 17:39).
He opted instead to go to battle with a mere slingshot and a few stones.
David knew he would be safe because he was girded with the armor of
God. What an incredible testimony of faith.

Goliath taunted David terribly about his meager stature and faith in
God, but David stood firm and trusted the Lord. At times we become our
own Goliath, intimidating ourselves with the enormity of raising our chil-
dren.

"You could never stay at home, you'll get bored," our subconscious ac-
cuses.

Or, "You've never been much of a housekeeper."

Or, "What makes you think you can raise your children in a godly
home? You didn't grow up in one."

Or, "You don't have the patience."

The lies go on and on. The enemy tries to beat us down with our weak-
nesses. Instead of listening to the giants the enemy puts before us, we need
to focus on the Lord's strength to do the job. That's what David did.

Focus on who you are in Christ. You are a child of the King, and that makes
you heir to all His strengths. David knew the Lord would enable him to de-
feat his enemy. He will do the same for you the next time you face the "Go-
liath" in your life.

*Oh God, give me the faith of David when I am feeling beaten
down. I put my trust in You.*

But all things become visible when they are exposed by the light.
(Ephesians 5:13)

*L*iving in the desert, I don't see many lightning storms. But the handful I do see each year are truly magnificent. Drawn to our porch one evening by a flicker on the horizon, I slid onto the front step, waiting. Hearing no thunder, I focused on the skyline to glimpse the impending light show, for it would come without warning. A silent streak of light soon skidded quickly across the sky, leaving behind a ribbon of pale pink. The horizon blackened again, until another bolt of light appeared. This one illumined a mountain nearby, something obscured in the black of the night. Then the lightning grew in intensity until my surroundings came alive in the light. Majestic mountains loomed in the shadowy storm, bushes danced in the wind, a jackrabbit bounded for cover. Each light display was more beautiful and more revealing.

Isn't that how God's plan for us unfolds? We are drawn to the light of His truth, and although we don't always understand, we wait on Him. Then suddenly, zap! A ray of light reveals His truth through His Word, the wisdom of a friend or in the stillness of our own hearts. We can then see more clearly around us, able to avoid the pitfalls looming in the shadows.

Are you struggling to understand God's plan for you as a stay-at-home mom? Confused about a choice or decision you need to make? Spend time in God's presence right now, waiting on Him to reveal the light of His plan.

Lord, help me to trust You even when I can't see Your plan through the darkness that sometimes surrounds me. Shine Your light little by little, guiding me as You reveal Your plan for my life.

> *They do not know nor do they understand;*
>   *They walk about in darkness;*
> *All the foundations of the earth are shaken. (Psalm 82:5)*

I listened intently as the speaker at a women's conference talked about "the purpose of a woman." One particular comment made a big impact on me. He said that the greatest enemy of the human race is ignorance. Ignorance consists of "what you don't know" and "what you do know that isn't so." He said that Satan will use ignorance to keep us from fulfilling God's purpose for our lives.

When it comes to being a stay-at-home mom, Satan has many women fooled. Some women don't know that staying home with their children is God's best for them because they have never seen or heard it in Scripture. Satan keeps them away from God's Word and Christians who can bring the Truth to them. He also uses ignorance by feeding women's minds with a lie: that a woman must hold a job outside the home to contribute to the family. The Hebrew definition of "ignorance" is darkness. The enemy aims to keep us in the dark.

This ignorance shakes the very foundations of our homes and families. If you know another woman who does not understand God's plan for her life, ask God to give you an opportunity to share it with her. Have specific Scriptures ready and share only in love, not judgment. Pray that God will break through the myth that the enemy has so successfully planted in our culture about a woman's worth.

> *Thank You, Lord, for showing me Your purpose for my life. Give*
> *me the right words to lovingly share the truth with other women.*

January 22

I fear for you, that perhaps I have labored over you in vain. (Galatians 4:11)

Ever feel like your labor is in vain? I had just finished vacuuming the carpet and scrubbing the kitchen floor when Seth came ripping in the back door with the dog chasing after him. Running to the back of the house, they tracked dirt all over my clean carpet. One look at my face told them they better make a run for it, so they did. They turned full circle, hitting every inch of carpet they had not previously soiled, finally racing across my freshly scrubbed floor.

I stood in the midst of the tiny shoe and paw prints and began to cry. I was six months pregnant, and it took all the energy I had the first time to vacuum. I headed for the vacuum to make another attempt, but not without locking the back door first.

I felt connected to Paul's frustration expressed in Galatians 4:11. He worked hard at teaching them God's laws and standards. Yet, they didn't always act like they were listening. As I teach my son respect for others and their property, I tell him that tracking mud into the house is not showing it. My son loves to play in our backyard dirt pile. I have told him countless times to wipe his shoes or even take them off before entering the house, so my frustration mounts when he doesn't heed that direction.

But no matter how many mistakes they made or how many times they failed, Paul kept working with the Galatians to help them act like children of God. Like Paul, I need to keep on laboring for the cause of Christ. Sometimes that means vacuuming twice in one day.

Lord, give me the strength to continually teach my children the right standard for living. Lift me up when I feel my labor in their lives, or in the house, is in vain. Sustain me as a mother.

Do not call to mind the former things,
  Or ponder things of the past.
Behold, I will do something new. (Isaiah 43:18-19)

Change is hard. I remember when I left a full-time corporate position to become a full-time mom. I had a promising career. Still, I knew when I had my first child that God had called me to a new field of employment. The first weeks and months of staying home full-time were difficult. I lacked the support and affirmation of a job well done. I craved the intellectual stimulation and adult companionship now gone, and I missed the paycheck. Gradually, I discovered the joy of this new job God had for me.

I began to look for the positives in my new situation, and God began to change my heart. He gave me empathy for other stay-at-home moms that would have been impossible for me to understand if I'd have stayed in the corporate world. God brought me to the point where I can encourage other moms to keep on going. When I do begin to dwell on the past, yearning for the way things "used to be," I remember God's words to the Israelites in Isaiah 43. If I am busy living in the past, God cannot do anything new in me right now. He cannot move me forward. And if there is no new growth in me, no movement, I will soon stagnate.

Don't close off the Lord from working in your life. Ask God to help you master your new situation, so that you can be all He created you to be. He has you home for many reasons—just look at a family picture and count them.

Lord, thank You for reminding me not to dwell on the past. Help me to rest in Your plan in the present and trust You with my future. Do a new work in me!

But we have this treasure in earthen vessels, that the surpassing greatness of the power may be of God and not from ourselves.
(2 Corinthians 4:7)

As a stay-at-home mom, I have had many frustrating days, when I feel that my efforts are futile and pointless. Wanting to be used by God, I wonder how folding endless loads of laundry and cleaning smashed cereal out of the carpet can be of any use to Him. The story of "The Vessel" reminds me that God most often uses those who seem to have the least to give. In the poem, the "Master" was searching for a vessel to use. He had many choices and after careful consideration, He passed up vessels most beautiful to the outer eye; vessels made of valuable gold, bright silver, elegant crystal, shiny brass and solid wood. Vessels that would seemingly serve His purposes best. These next lines from the poem are my favorite:

Then the Master looked down and saw a vessel of clay.
Empty and broken it helplessly lay.
No hope had the vessel that the Master might choose—
to cleanse, and make whole, to fill and use.
"Ah! Now this is the vessel I've been hoping to find.
I'll mend it and use it and make it all mine.
I need not the vessel with pride of itself,
Nor one that is narrow to sit on the shelf,
Nor one that is big-mouthed and shallow and loud,
Nor one that displays his contents so proud,
Nor the one who thinks he can do things just right,
But this plain earthly vessel filled with power and might."
Then gently He lifted the vessel of clay,
mended and cleansed it and filled it that day.
He spoke to it kindly—"There's work you must do . . .
Just pour out to others as I pour into you."

It is when we feel useless, that God can use us the most.

My Lord and Master, remind me daily that I am useful to You just the way I am, and that my work for my family is of worth to You.

And He was saying to them all, "If anyone wishes to come after Me, let him deny himself, and take up his cross daily, and follow Me." (Luke 9:23)

Being a disciple of Christ requires sacrifice. When we decide to follow Jesus, we are often called to give up our fleshly desires in order to do what is pleasing to Him. Following Jesus costs more than anything except *not* following Him. The price of disobedience is eternal in nature. And eternity is a long time.

Being a stay-at-home mom is also costly. It requires sacrifice—of our time, money, desires, personal goals. That is what Jesus talked about in Luke 9:23. We each have our own personal cross to bear. Just like the one Jesus carried to His death, it gets heavy at times. Caring for a family taxes your physical strength and energy. But Jesus promises to restore our strength and carry our burdens, if we will come to Him. Christ never meant for you to carry your load alone. He will lift the cross from your shoulders and place it on His. All you have to do is ask for His help.

Scripture tells us that a disciple of Christ must first count the cost (Luke 14:28). I believe the same is true for a stay-at-home mom. God has called us to this task. Yet, we must take the job seriously. Have you counted the cost of being held accountable for your child's training?

Lord, give me the fortitude to carry out my responsibilities as a stay-at-home mom. When the weight of my cross is too much to bear, I ask that You will take it and walk with me.

For such is the will of God that by doing right you may silence the ignorance of foolish men. (1 Peter 2:15)

Have you ever noticed that people who don't know what they're talking about seem to speak more loudly than those who do? I recall a discussion I had with one of my co-workers about moving from corporate career woman to stay-at-home mom. We were both pregnant for the first time. She said that she wasn't cut out for staying at home. She told everyone of her plan to return to work, making quite an issue of all the reasons why she should not stay home. I knew that she was not a Christian and would not relate to a biblical viewpoint. So when she inquired of my plans, I explained the practical benefits of staying home with the baby. I was careful not to condemn her opinion.

After Seth's birth, I continued to stay in touch with this former co-worker. When we spoke, I told her that I was happy with my choice to stay home. Over time, I noticed her enthusiasm fading about being a corporate mom. Now, several years later, she has left her job to stay home with her two children.

When we do what is right, which includes obeying God, but not judging others who don't, God has a way of bringing around those who are ignorant to His ways. Often that means holding our tongue when we would rather set someone straight. Of course we should defend our positions as Christians, but doing so only in love, not judgment. Our part is to follow His will, His part is to change hearts. When we do, we may soon see others follow.

Lord, help me to never sit in judgment of someone who is not following You. Keep me humble in word and deed.

Let no one look down on your youthfulness, but rather in speech, conduct, love, faith and purity, show yourself an example of those who believe. (1 Timothy 4:12)

The exuberance of a brand-new believer in Christ is so exhilarating. I have yet to be acquainted with someone who has just accepted Christ as Savior and is not excited about it. Most new believers seem to walk with a new spring in their step and a gleam in their eyes; they approach life with a zeal and desire for all to know their newfound joy. Commonly, however, their excitement is met with skepticism; both from unbelievers and believers alike, believers who have hardened in their own faith and lost their joy. This can be deflating for the new believer and often causes them to stifle or even question their new belief. Paul addresses this dilemma of the young Christian. In First Timothy 4:12, he refers to being young or youthful in the Christian faith.

Paul recognizes that the zeal of the new Christian is a part of everything they do. That is the testimony we should live as Christians, no matter how old we are in the faith. Similarly, when we have been at home for a while, it becomes all too easy to lose our joy. Remember the excitement you felt when you first decided to stay home with your children? You made so many plans to teach, train and just enjoy life with them. Has your enthusiasm been lost in the day-to-day monotony of your tasks?

Spend time reflecting on your experience as a believer and a stay-at-home mom. Follow your journey in both roles and see where it brings you today. If you have lost your joy in serving Christ or your family, ask God to rekindle your fire.

Oh Lord, I want to always have the zeal of a new believer and the excitement of a new mother. Keep those fires burning within my heart. May they grow stronger, not weaker, as time wears on.

January 28

I will sing of the lovingkindness of the LORD forever;
To all generations I will make known Thy faithfulness with my
mouth. (Psalm 89:1)

ach family has a unique story to tell. Tracing a family's lineage often reveals treasured family secrets. Knowledge of past generations can teach your children about their roots and heritage in Christ. One way to begin teaching children about their family roots is to start a journal for them.

Here's how: Keep a journal for each child that begins at birth, or even during your pregnancy. Write in detail how you felt when you carried him or her in your womb and at birth. Outline the highlights of each year, noting milestones in their physical, emotional, intellectual and spiritual development. Be sure to include a progression of the child's blossoming personality and insights on how God will use him or her. Include a family tree, and give as much information as you can find on every member. Don't forget to journal any special prayers you have said for each child, noting God's answers. Write specifics on how you have seen God work in their lives as their faith has matured. Note special spiritual dates, such as dedication, receiving Christ as Savior and baptism.

You can create your own journal or buy one from a bookstore. I recommend *A Mother's Journal—A Collection of Family Memories* by Mary Engelbreit. It includes an outline for the complete family tree and sections on the backgrounds of each parent. It follows the child's heritage from conception through the college years, offering fill-in-the-blanks and plenty of empty pages to record your thoughts and feelings about your child. It is never too late to begin a journal for your child.

Keeping a detailed journal of your child's life and family history is a priceless treasure to pass on. As they read how uniquely God fashioned them, it will encourage their walk with the Lord. Start your journal today. Make known the lovingkindness of the Lord in your family.

Thank You, Lord, for Your faithfulness and lovingkindness to our
family. Help me to diligently record Your goodness to us so that I
can someday share it with my children.

And, fathers, do not provoke your children to anger; but bring them up in the discipline and instruction of the Lord. (Ephesians 6:4)

Although Paul addressed this instruction to fathers, I believe it applies to mothers, too. The command was specific to men because they are to be honored as heads of the household. All instruction is to trickle down from them. So, what does it mean to provoke someone? Generally, it refers to agitating someone to the point of action or feeling— usually anger!

Parents provoke their children to anger in many ways. One is by expecting too much from them. I recently read a story about a mom whose eight-year-old son loved soccer, so she signed him up to play in the community sports program. She attended all the practices and games. After a while however, her support turned into provocation when she began critiquing her son's performance. She took notes and pointed out his errors. Her intentions were good, but her method provoked him to frustration and anger. Finally, he quit.

We often provoke our children to anger because we are not in tune with their wants, needs or sensitivities. If your teen is sensitive about his acne-prone skin, don't harass him about caring for his face. If your son is naturally gifted in football but wants to pursue baseball, let him try out. If your toddler wants to put together a puzzle by herself, resist the temptation to do it for her.

So many times we rush in when we see our children struggle. What they really need is for us to be available when they are ready to seek our help. When we know our children feel passionately or sensitively about certain matters, we can avoid provoking them. When in doubt, don't push—pray.

Lord, help me not to provoke my children to anger. Make me sensitive to their needs and desires, and show me how to support them without being pushy.

January 30

Blessed are the peacemakers, for they shall be called sons of God.
(Matthew 5:9)

Seth and Emily, both two year olds, happily played—until Emily got something my son wanted. When she opened a musical book, he ran with the speed of light and ripped the book from Emily's hands. "Mine!" he screamed. She jumped to her feet and latched on to the book with both hands, "No, Mine!" she hollered.

After discussing the benefits of sharing, coupled with some required quiet time to think about it, Emily and Seth decided to play harmoniously, each with a pile of musical books. Unfortunately, that was not the last time that day I played referee. I learned that moms are frequently called to the battlefront.

Why is it so hard for toddlers to play peacefully together? Human nature, I suppose. Even some adults don't play well with others. But I believe we can train our children to be peacemakers, no matter what the situation. With so much time to practice, children eventually learn—repetition, after all, is the mother of learning.

Help me, Lord, to teach my children to be peacemakers. Lead me as
I train them up in the way You would have them go.

But prove yourselves doers of the word, and not merely hearers who delude themselves. (James 1:22)

Any woman who chooses to stay at home and raise her children is a busy woman. She is constantly doing—doing things for the members of her household! Unfortunately, there are still many in our society who think that a woman who stays at home is doing absolutely nothing. At least nothing of real value.

I was having a conversation with a friend of mine one day who is a mother of two boys, as well as a full-time elementary teacher. She was picking up her neighbor's mail for the summer while they were away vacationing and when I asked if her neighbor was a teacher also, my friend replied, "No, she's just a housewife. She doesn't do anything." At her comment, I felt my eyebrows raise and my mouth start to twitch, so I bit my tongue. It took her a few moments to realize what she had said to me, a stay-at-home mom, and she quickly stammered out, "Well, uh, you know what I mean."

To be honest, I'm not quite sure what she meant. I do know, however, that her view of a stay-at-home mom is painfully common. The misconception that a mother who is at home managing her family is not doing anything of worth, can be cleared up with a quick glance into the Bible. Scripture communicates again and again the value of training children. Today's verse, in fact, verifies that a mother dedicated to the task of raising a loving family is actually a "doer of the Word." And I'd rather be a "doer of the Word" than a doer of the world.

When I determine my actions based on God's Word, not on the world's belief system, I am always doing something of real value. Eternal value. And actions speak louder than words.

Lord, show me constantly how to be a doer of Your Word and not just a hearer. May I follow Your commands in every area of my life, beginning in my home. I pray that I may be a humble example to others that they may desire to set Your Word into action in their lives. May all that I do, from the dishes to the training of little hearts, glorify You.

February:
Job Qualifications

I thought they said no experience was needed.

It's the most demanding job there is, yet requires no prior experience and carries no pre-qualification requirements. Anyone can become a parent—anyone at all. That's a scary thought. The job of shaping and molding a life is the most honorable occupation there is. So why do I feel so overwhelmed by the task at times? A little insecurity in my abilities is good because it causes me to run to God. I will rely on His strength, His power, His wisdom more if I am inexperienced. I will depend on Him and not my own abilities, which often fail. God never fails.

I need only one qualification to be a good parent—a heart for God. A heart for God seeks after Him and does what He requires. It doesn't mean I'll be perfect, but it does mean I'll trust Him to lead me. Having a heart for God means I can experience such things as unconditional love and acceptance, grace and mercy. Once I have encountered these treasures, I can pass them on to my children. Many of the devotionals this month focus on qualities that flow from our hearts once we focus on God's heart.

So, take heart in your abilities, or rather God's abilities within you. Rest assured He will equip you with all you need to do the job right!

. . . through love serve one another. (Galatians 5:13)

A friend shared with me how God had touched her heart with a special thought one day. Kathy was earnestly pursuing God's wisdom in becoming a better mother. Like many of us, she used to wake up every morning focused on the tasks of the day. She felt the gentle nudge of the Holy Spirit one morning telling her that she began each day with an incorrect focus. Rather than dwelling on what she could accomplish, she felt compelled to instead think of how she could serve her little girl each day. *How can I minister to my daughter, teach her and disciple her?* she began to ponder.

God teaches us to put the needs of others above our own. Serving our children is one way to accomplish this. For the stay-at-home mom with a heart for God, servanthood is definitely a big part of the job. Jesus was the ultimate Servant. With Him as a role Model, we can find comfort and strength in the job of serving our children, our husbands, our friends and our community. This new focus of thinking changed Kathy's relationship with her daughter. Every minute spent with her little girl became an opportunity to serve her rather than a distraction from her to-do list.

Serving manifests itself in many forms: loving, teaching, disciplining, giving and forgiving. Our days are filled with opportunities to serve our children: hugs and kisses, encouraging words, teaching a new skill or craft, playing a favorite game, helping with homework, going for a walk and praying together. Ask God to show you some special ways you can serve your family.

Heavenly Father, thank You for sending Your Son as a Model of servanthood. Help me to learn from His example. Show me how I can better serve those around me, especially my children.

February 2

But Ruth said, "Do not urge me to leave you or turn back from following you; for where you go, I will go, and where you lodge, I will lodge. Your people shall be my people, and your God, my God."
(Ruth 1:16)

Ruth made this statement to her mother-in-law in the wake of family death and tragedy. It is said to be one of the most beautiful statements of commitment in all literature. Understand that Ruth's husband had died, leaving her in a strange land. So when Naomi urges Ruth to go back to her native land, to her own mother, she makes an astonishing choice. Her reply to Naomi's suggestion is in Ruth 1:16. Talk about commitment and loyalty! Ruth has it. She recognizes that this poor woman, her mother-in-law, has been through great hardship. Within ten years, Naomi lost her husband and both sons. Her heart must have been empty and broken. Ruth vows to stand by Naomi until the day she dies.

Ruth's devotion to Naomi is a great example for us as mothers. What kind of relationship are you building with your children? Is it one that will invoke loyalty and commitment? Will they stand by your side when times are tough? The answers lie in your commitment to them.

Dear Lord, help me to raise my children according to Your standards, including loyalty. I pray that they will know I love them and am committed to them, no matter what.

February 3

Love . . . does not seek its own. (1 Corinthians 13:4-5)

I slammed down the phone receiver. A salesperson had just told me our furniture's arrival would be four to five weeks late. And I had found out only when I called to check the status on our order. I ranted and raved for five minutes about my rights.

After I calmed down God began to convict me about my behavior. My mind drifted back to the conversation. What had my unforgiving words communicated about God's love to that unsuspecting salesgirl? I was still angry, so I tried to shrug off God's Spirit of conviction by shoving those thoughts into the back of my mind and busied myself with housework.

A few days later at a women's church breakfast the speaker began, "Love does not seek its own." I shrank in my seat as I felt the Spirit gently tapping on my shoulder. I knew God was talking to me. I repented from my selfish attitude, realizing that I had been "seeking my own" in my response to our delayed furniture. Whether or not I was treated wrongly was not the issue. It is how *I* respond that matters. When Jesus was wronged, how did He respond? Did He demand His rights? Never. He always responded in love, and He always put others' needs above His own. How do you respond when you are treated wrongly by others, including your children? Do you immediately retaliate, demanding your rights or do you respond in love, putting others first?

> *Oh God, there are many times when I respond to a situation out of selfishness, rather than love. Help me to put others first, and when I am wronged, show me how I can lift others up, rather than seeking my own rights and what is best for me.*

But Jesus said, "Let the children alone, and do not hinder them from coming to Me; for the kingdom of heaven belongs to such as these." And after laying His hands on them, He departed from there. (Matthew 19:14-15)

We have lavished our children with affection since their births. We are a family of huggers. Anyone who knows me personally cannot greet me without receiving a hug! Our bedtime routine includes gathering in our sons' rooms to say prayers. Then, in a circular embrace, we throw our arms around each other and shout, "Family hug!" Then we squeeze each other as hard as we can. Our children love it.

We have also prayed with our boys from the time they each began to babble. While we're praying, we try to hold hands. The touch is important. In *The Blessing*, Gary Smalley and John Trent point out five elements necessary in imparting "the blessing" to our children. One is meaningful touch. Many interesting statistics support their claim. One is that the laying on of hands when we pray has "tremendous physiological benefits." They also cite a recent study at UCLA that concludes men and women need eight to ten meaningful touches a day just to maintain emotional and physical health.

Today's Scripture passage shows that Jesus also emphasized the importance of touch. He gathered the children around Him, laid hands on them and prayed for them. He could have just whispered a prayer in passing or held His hands to the heavens while the children gathered at His feet. Instead, He chose to touch them. Time and time again when Jesus ministered to people, He touched them.

Are you teaching your children the value of meaningful touch? Even if you aren't huggy by nature, learn for your children's sake. Stay-at-home moms have an advantage in this area; we can hug and kiss our children all day long! There is no assurance that a baby-sitter will give this affirmation. It is up to us, as mothers, to let our children know we love and bless them.

Lord, thank You for the value of a hug, a kiss, a touch. Show me the life-giving power that meaningful touch can bring to my family. May I follow Your example as I seek to bless my children.

Not that we are adequate in ourselves to consider anything as coming from ourselves, but our adequacy is from God.
(2 Corinthians 3:5)

When my children are sick I feel so inadequate. I lack experience in nursing and great medical knowledge. In fact, I barely got through the anatomy and physiology course I took in college.

Knowing how to care for the physical health of our children comes partially from experience. For example, when my firstborn was sixteen months old, he developed a severe case of diarrhea. Fearing dehydration I pumped him with liquids, particularly his favorite apple juice. His condition worsened so I called his pediatrician. The doctor asked a few questions, and then he explained that the acidity in apple juice made it one of the worst things Seth could drink with his condition. I was thankful he couldn't see my red face on the other end of the telephone. You can bet I never made that mistake again. I thanked God for giving me the wisdom to call the doctor before poor Seth drank one more cup of apple juice.

I am thankful that God gives me wisdom to care for my son's physical well-being. Caring for a sick child can be exhausting, and lack of rest can impair a mother's otherwise good judgment. If we look to God for wisdom and power, we do better than drawing only on our knowledge and strength.

Dear Lord, thank You for reminding me that my adequacy comes from You. Help me to remember that I don't have to be experienced in every area of knowledge. I just have to look to You for the answers, and Your grace will meet my needs.

Not that I speak from want; for I have learned to be content in whatever circumstances I am. (Philippians 4:11)

I fell into a trap during my firstborn's toddler years. I compared his performance, the milestones he reached, to that of his peers. When other children in the nursery walked and he didn't, I worried. When Seth's cousin, who is only six weeks older, ate table foods and Seth didn't, I worried. When a friend's little girl spoke in two-word sentences, and Seth didn't, I worried. More accurately, I compared. And I began to question my abilities as a parent: Am I spending enough time with him? Am I waiting too long to introduce him to new concepts? Am I doing it all wrong?

Self-doubt plagued me for months as I watched Seth's peers pass him in skill after skill. Then I read Philippians 4:11 . . . gulp! I suddenly realized what I had been doing to my poor little toddler! I had been operating totally out of want. Never content in his current stage, I constantly pushed him to the next level.

By comparing him to other children, I was teaching Seth a dangerous habit. I was leading him into the trap of discontent. Thankfully, God graciously revealed my error while Seth was too young to learn it.

Now, when I catch myself comparing his performance, I recite Philippians 4:11 and find joy in his stage. I have learned to encourage my boys, but not to push them. The difference lies in wanting the best for our children, but not wanting more than they can give.

Gracious Lord, teach me to be content in all circumstances. Help me to always want the best for my children, but not more than they can give. Grant me wisdom to know the difference.

Set your mind on the things above, not on the things that are on earth. (Colossians 3:2)

I awoke to a sick baby, a sink full of dirty dishes, a broken dishwasher and a pile of laundry. Could I start over, I wondered, feeling my head begin to pound. By noon, the baby's crying had shattered my nerves, his fever had increased, and I couldn't get him into the doctor until late afternoon. The dishwasher part wouldn't arrive for a week, and the piles of dishes and laundry were growing.

On days like that, working outside the home seems especially appealing! Let's face it, when your kids have a bad day, so do you. And those are the days you don't feel qualified for the job. All stay-at-home moms have those stormy days, so how do we cope in the midst of them?

I've found it helps to change my mind-set. I try to focus on more pleasant things. In the midst of such trials, I need to look to God. To help me do this, I set up a rainy day box. This simple box contains encouraging cards from friends and family, favorite Scripture verses on index cards, uplifting notes from my husband and friends, even lyrics to a cheery song or poem clipped from a magazine. When I'm feeling discouraged or anxious, my rainy day box helps me focus on the "things above," as well as the positive words of others. When I gird myself with strength this way, the challenges of the day diminish.

Having a tough day, week, month? Write down a few favorite Scriptures and start a rainy day box. Every time you receive an uplifting card or read an inspirational thought, add it to your collection. It will help you get through those rainy days.

> *Lord, when I'm having a bad day, help me run to Your shelter instead of getting drenched in a downpour of negativity. Show me how to set my mind on the things above, so that I can cope with the here and now.*

February 8

For this reason I say to you, her sins, which are many, have been forgiven, for she loved much; but he who is forgiven little, loves little. (Luke 7:47)

This verse is one of great beauty and meaning. To grasp the full meaning of today's Scripture, you may want to read the entire story in Luke 7:36-50.

Jesus' declaration of forgiveness speaks volumes for the woman at His feet, a community outcast because of her sinful lifestyle. Those who tend to be unforgiving and judgmental, like the Pharisees, are those who haven't felt the need for much forgiveness. Therefore, they don't know how to love deeply.

When we fully grasp the concept of God's love, we understand that we are not worthy of His love, because we are sinners. Yet, He loves and forgives us anyway. He tells us to hate the sin, not the sinner. When I came to grips fully with this passage for the first time, it was like a veil was lifted from my eyes, and my heart. I became more inclined to love, and less inclined to judge. More inclined to forgive, and less inclined to hold a grudge.

Maybe this realization of "he who has been forgiven much, loves much" came easier for me than it will for you because I have a stormy past. I have felt the unconditional love and forgiveness of the Savior. Have you? If you've been forgiven, then you have felt it too. But have you really experienced His forgiveness? Have you really received it? When you do, you will be able to look at others differently.

Spend some time today meditating on God's love and forgiveness. The next time you are tempted to look at someone judgmentally, remind yourself of God's view. No one sin is worse than another. In God's eyes, sin is sin. Learn to love and forgive. They are qualities you will need as a mother. If your children have been forgiven much, they too, will learn to love much.

Lord, thank You for Your love and forgiveness. Teach me to model those qualities to my children, my husband, my friends, my neighbors, to all I come in contact with. Help me to see others through Your eyes and to love with Your unconditional love, reserving judgment for You.

But the fruit of the spirit is . . . self-control. (Galatians 5:22-23)

I am convinced that the largest reason children get into trouble these days is a lack of self-control. Sadly, most kids lack training in it and grow into adulthood lacking it. The absence of self-control also gets adults into trouble. Without self-control, people fall into all kinds of sin: obesity, gossip, fornication, pornography, drunkenness, adulterous relationships, even murder. A classic biblical example of a man who failed in the area of self-control is David. He acted upon his lust for another man's wife—Bathsheba—and then plotted the man's murder to try and cover up his sin! (See 2 Samuel 11:1-17.) Now that's lack of self-control! David found himself in quite a mess, and it took him some time to repent and start anew, all because he could not control his desires.

If we begin to teach our children self-control, we will see it manifested throughout their lives. Everything from the temper tantrums of toddlers to a teenager's experimentation with drugs is a result of a lack of self-control.

Like any living thing, the seed must first be planted, then watered, fertilized and exposed to sunlight regularly to grow into a healthy product. So it is with the fruit of the Spirit. We have to plant the concept, spend time modeling it, talking about it and validating it with God's Word. I saw a marquee that read, "Don't be afraid to go out on a limb, that's where the fruit is."

The fruit of the Spirit is out on a limb too—it takes time and effort to reach. Self-control is not produced overnight. Start working with your children to teach them this valuable and godly characteristic now. It will serve them for the rest of their lives. And with self-control intact, they will better serve God.

Lord, thank You for showing me the importance of self-control, in my child's life as well as my own. Show me how to teach it to my children. I pray the rewards of exercising self-control in all of our lives will be great.

———— ❦❀❦ ————

*Older women likewise are to be reverent in their behavior . . . that
they may encourage the young women to love their husbands, to love
their children, to be sensible, pure, workers at home, kind, being
subject to their own husbands, that the word of God may not be
dishonored. (Titus 2:3-5)*

*Y*oung stay-at-home moms tend to get discouraged more easily than
those with years of experience. They tend to think they will blunder
through parenthood, figuring it out as they go along. But it doesn't have to be
that way. God has a much better plan.

Scripture admonishes younger women in the faith to learn from older
women. We can learn a great deal from those who have walked before us.
In biblical times, the younger women counted on the older women to teach
them so that God's Word would not be dishonored.

I have developed a wonderful friendship with a woman who has three
teenage boys. She has led women's Bible studies on family-related topics. I
learned so much from her marriage Bible study that I began to seek her
counsel on personal issues. A seed was planted, and a friendship began to
blossom. I have grown in every area of my life as a result.

Finding an older woman to teach and encourage you is part of God's
plan. If you are a young mother, seek out an older woman in your church
body from whom you can learn and grow. Consider asking her to disciple
you, and spend time together weekly. If you are an older mother with expe-
rience and wisdom, don't keep it all to yourself. There's a young mom out
there who needs you. Ask God to show you whom He wants you to influ-
ence for Him. If you know who it might be, invite her to lunch and begin a
friendship. God will do the rest.

*Help me Lord, to be an encouragement to other women. Bless those
who have strengthened me.*

There is no fear in love; but perfect love casts out fear. . . .
(1 John 4:18)

For many years after my husband and I married, I did not want to have children. I was afraid of the responsibility. I felt more qualified in my corporate career, where I was steadily climbing the ladder. I couldn't see kids climbing up the rungs with me, and I definitely couldn't see myself staying home all day changing diapers and doing laundry. But God changed my heart.

Jimmy and I received a visit from friends we hadn't seen in a long time. They had a two-year-old, and I was nervous about them visiting. When the doorbell rang, I glanced nervously at our crystal candy dishes and ceramic figurines, all within a toddler's reach. But to my delight and surprise, we spent the next two hours laughing, talking and catching up while this supposed tornado sat on his dad's lap doing puzzles and reading books.

My girlfriend had given up a full-time career as a registered nurse to stay home with their little boy. She talked about how rewarding it was. She seems genuinely happy, I thought. But there must be a catch. This was not the motherhood I'd heard about.

"What is your secret?" I asked suspiciously. Her answer surprised me: "Doing it God's way." She explained that living according to God's commands, including raising children with biblical principles, was the secret of their success as parents. She also pointed out that it wasn't popular in today's culture. Popular or not, I could see that it worked.

Jimmy and I talked for a long time that night. We realized that our fear of parenting had distorted our view. When we love the Lord, we have nothing to fear. He can guide us through anything, including parenting.

Lord, in Your love, there is no fear. Thank You for taking away my fear of parenthood. Help me to be a shining example of a stay-at-home mom.

Delight yourself in the Lord;
And He will give you the desires of your heart. (Psalm 37:4)

This has long been one of my favorite verses. I have seen it lived out in my life over and over. When I first committed my life to Christ, I didn't understand the difference between loving Him and delighting in Him. Lots of people love God, but do they delight in Him? The dictionary defines delight as "to give great joy or pleasure" and "to rejoice." Do you give great joy or pleasure to God? Or are you consistently breaking His heart? Do you delight in serving Him? Or do you begrudge it, only serving out of some sense of duty? Do you rejoice in Him, giving Him thanks for all He has given you? Or do you constantly whine and complain about what you don't have?

Delighting yourself in the Lord takes a willing heart and produces a renewed spirit. Attitudes change when we learn to rejoice in the Lord, despite our circumstances. Sometimes it's difficult in the midst of whiny children, a dirty house and piles of bills. But something happens when I give myself over to joy. I begin to sense that God takes great joy in me. I then can rejoice even more in the Lord, for all that He is, for all that I have, and He begins to give me the desires of my heart.

Ever since I was a little girl, I wanted to be a writer. I wrote for years, but I wasn't published until I wrote an article that gave glory to God. In delighting Him, He gave me the desire of my heart. Even now as I write, I only do so when my children are napping or have gone to bed. They deserve my full attention during their waking hours because God called me to be a wife and mother first. In so doing, I delight God because my priorities are in order with His commandments. Being a stay-at-home mom is serving Him. It doesn't take any experience to serve God, just a willing heart. Won't you delight yourself in the Lord today?

Lord, I delight in You. I rejoice that I am a child of God. Help me to find joy in serving You and my children. Thank You for giving me the desires of my heart.

For by grace you have been saved through faith; and that not of yourselves, it is the gift of God; not as a result of works, that no one should boast. (Ephesians 2:8-9)

Grace is the cornerstone of the Christian faith, and the stepping-stone for everything else in life—including parenting. Once I grasped God's grace, I looked at life differently. It has to do with mercy: grace is receiving what we don't deserve, and mercy is not receiving what we do deserve.

We can't do anything to earn salvation, and we certainly don't deserve it based on our merits. Who of us is the perfect servant of Christ? And yet, God hands us this gift of eternal life because He is gracious. How often do we act unbecoming or sinful? Such acts truly deserve punishment instead of the graciousness and love that God bestows upon us. But because He is merciful, we don't get what we deserve: separation from God. His love, grace and mercy are always available to us.

God's Word says we can't save ourselves; we merely need to accept His gift of grace. It's a simple principle that we make complicated. God knew that we, in our finite humanity, could never measure up. When I fall, there will be forgiveness—not because I deserve it, but because God is gracious and merciful.

I do the job of stay-at-home mom by grace. I don't have great prior knowledge or experience, but I don't need it. I have God's grace. In difficult days, I rely on God's grace to help me be patient, loving, sensitive, wise, creative and energetic. He is everything that I am not, and by His grace I become what I need to be.

> *Oh gracious Lord, thank You for the gift of eternal life through Your Son Jesus. I acknowledge that I can do nothing to deserve Your grace and mercy, and I thank You that You give it to me despite my shortcomings. Help me to apply Your grace in all I do.*

———————— ✽❀✽ ————————

Therefore be imitators of God, as beloved children; and walk in love, just as Christ also loved you and gave Himself up for us. . . . (Ephesians 5:1-2)

The tradition of expressing love to those we hold dear precedes the legend of Saint Valentine sending violets in the mouth of a dove from his prison cell. The greatest act of love in history is the gift of God's Son—the gift of eternal life. He made the ultimate sacrifice to demonstrate His love for us. We should never again feel unloved!

God tells us in Ephesians 5:1-2 that children are the best "imitators of God." They know how to love more purely than adults. They haven't yet learned to put conditions on love. Unfortunately, we teach kids how to do that. They see us modeling "if" love: I will love you if . . . and I will love you because. Children don't put limits on their love. We can learn a lot from them.

They can learn from us if we teach them the way God intended. He commands us to "be imitators of God" and to "walk in love." That means loving unconditionally, as God does. Because we are human and perfectly imperfect, achieving this kind of love will be tough. But that's where "walk in love" comes in. It is a process. It takes time to learn to love.

We can learn to make unconditional loving a way of life. God gave us an example when He sent His Son to earth. If we study Jesus' life and how He treated people, we can learn to be "imitators of [Christ] . . . and walk in love." Teaching our children the same is one of the greatest gifts we can give to them.

Lord of love, thank You for sending Your Son as a gift of Your love. Just as I have experienced Your unconditional love, may my children experience it in me. Help me to walk in love and show me how I can teach them the same.

Above all, keep fervent in your love for one another, because love covers a multitude of sins. (1 Peter 4:8)

This verse came alive for me when I became a parent. As my sweet, helpless baby who could do no wrong began to grow, so did his sin nature. As he began to crawl and walk, I noticed a pattern. He wanted to do anything and everything I told him not to do. And yet, no matter how many times he disobeyed me, I always seemed to have plenty of love and forgiveness to give him.

My love for my children covers up their sins. That love, growing deeper with the passing years, wipes away all their mistakes and wrong choices. One day as I watched my firstborn attempt to open a kitchen cabinet I had instructed him to stay out of umpteen times, I realized that he could never destroy my love for him. I won't always love what he does, but I will always love him.

So it is with our heavenly Father. We constantly do things that His Word instructs us not to do, and He continues to love and forgive us. That cycle is transferred from God to us, as parents, and then to our children. What better way to instruct them about God's love and forgiveness than to model it?

A child who experiences genuine love learns to love others. Think about your relationship with your children. Do you communicate your love freely, even fervently, to them?

Thank You Lord for the never-ending love and forgiveness that You have shown me. Help me to extend it as graciously to my children. Just as Your love, may my love for them be deep enough to cover all of their sins.

For His lovingkindness is great toward us. (Psalm 117:2)

God demonstrates His love for us in so many ways. One is through the encouragement of a friend. One day I was feeling particularly overwhelmed and under-experienced on the motherhood front. I was feeling that nothing I did yielded the results I was looking for—an obedient child. I wanted to throw in the towel when something wonderful happened. I received a note from a friend who praised my skill and godly manner in handling my son. She said that Seth was a beautiful and obedient little boy—a true joy to be around. What an encouragement and what timing. God knew that I needed it that day. He used someone else, who acted in obedience, to encourage me.

I like a saying that punctuates such kind acts, "The smallest act of kindness is better than the greatest of kind intentions." The friend who sent the note may have thought it a small act, but it was a big encouragement to me. If she had only thought about writing it, it never would have impacted me and lightened my heart the way it did. I may have continued to storm through the day, sulking and feeling fruitless.

Is there someone you know who could use a word of encouragement? Stop thinking about it, and do it! It only takes a few moments to jot down your thoughts on a card, and yet it can have a lasting impact on someone's life. Won't you help to demonstrate God's lovingkindness today?

> *Dear God, thank You for all the ways that You show Your lovingkindness to me. Thank You for the friends in my life who are tangible reminders of Your love. Show me how I can demonstrate Your lovingkindness to those who need a fresh view of You.*

Greater love has no one than this, that one lay down his life for his friends. (John 15:13)

*L*ove is an action, not a feeling. When you say you love someone, you are using the word as a verb. Jesus clearly defined just how active love is by dying on the cross for us. He made the ultimate sacrifice, out of love. Although this act was part of the Father's plan, it wasn't easy for Jesus. He prays in the garden of Gethsemane for this cup to pass (Luke 22:42). Yet, He was willing to succumb to His Father's will, death on a cross. It would mean hours of pain and suffering. But for Jesus it was the only option because it was His Father's will. Some days you may feel as though choosing to be a stay-at-home mom was not the best option. You may feel that you have no time to yourself, no one appreciates you, your life lacks purpose, you're bored, you're tired of the financial sacrifices, or you're just plain tired. Motherhood is a sacrifice.

Staying home with your children is one of the greatest gifts of love you can give them. Some days it will be painful, but make no mistake, there is blessing through obedience. Although you may not see it or feel it now, you will be blessed for the time that you nurture your children when they are young. By choosing the role of a stay-at-home mom, you are choosing God's best. You are acting out your love for your kids, just as Jesus did by His death on the cross. Being a stay-at-home mom requires no experience, just lots of sacrifice. And in the end, even more blessings.

> *Lord, thank You for giving me the courage to choose what's right—what's best according to Your standard. I know that staying at home with my kids is Your will and I pray that You will remind me of that fact when I'm feeling discouraged. Remind me of the ultimate sacrifice that you made for me, and that in light of Your death, my sacrifices pale in comparison.*

February 18

God sees not as man sees, for man looks at the outward appearance, but the LORD looks at the heart. (1 Samuel 16:7)

How many times have you driven down the road and seen a destitute person holding a sign that says, "Will work for food"? Do you think, *I'd never hire someone looking like that*, and drive past without another thought? I confess that I have.

Now, think back to the last time you had a really bad day at home. One of the kids was sick, maybe you were coming down with something, the house was a mess, and you were behind on the laundry. Your sick child was putting more demands on your time than you could handle. Between changing sheets, changing diapers and changing channels, you barely had time to change clothes, much less take a shower. Yet, you were doing your best to nurse your sick child and give him all the love and extra attention he required while on bed rest. Now, suppose a friend were to drop by unannounced for afternoon tea. Would you want her to judge what kind of mother you are based on your appearance and your disarrayed home?

We need to be careful not to judge people by their appearance—not the man in the torn clothes on the street corner, or the neighbor struggling to get control of her life and her kids. What about the woman at church who is always nicely dressed and polite to everyone? She's got it all together, right? Maybe not. How do you look at people? Do you look only at their outward condition, or do you look at the condition of their heart? Do you know what's really going on inside? We need to learn to look at people with Jesus' eyes, not our own. Only then can we really see them. All it takes is a heart for God.

Dear Lord, forgive me when I judge others based on outward appearances. Help me to look at people through Your eyes. Show me their hearts that I might reach out and show Your love.

Iron sharpens iron,
  So one man sharpens another. (Proverbs 27:17)

Some of the best experience we can get comes from the experiences of other stay-at-home moms. If you could save yourself from pain by learning from another mother's mistake, wouldn't you? I have.

When Seth was twenty-two months old, we had the opportunity to fly to Orlando on business with my husband. We were thrilled at the chance to take a family vacation. We planned to enjoy all of the surrounding attractions, including Disney World. Our plans were thwarted, however, when Seth became ill after only the third day. He developed a high fever and congestion. A rasping cough made it difficult for any of us to get much sleep. With each passing day, his condition worsened and so did my husband's mood. We saw more of the room service attendant than Mickey Mouse.

When we returned home, Seth's fever was at an all-time high. We rushed to his pediatrician who said that Seth had developed a serious sinus infection—the result sinus pressure on the flight to Orlando. "Didn't I tell you to put a few drops of decongestant in his nose before you got on the plane?" the pediatrician inquired. "No," I said through clenched teeth. "You mean this could have been prevented?" He shot back, "Absolutely. Sorry." He handed me a prescription and left the room. Less than forty-eight hours later, Seth was back to his usual toddler rowdiness.

I have since told this story to many friends who are planning to fly with young children. The results have been healthy kids and successful trips. "Iron sharpens iron."

> *Dear Lord, thank You for giving me wisdom through the experiences of others. Give me opportunities to help other moms with what You have taught me. May I always glorify You in what I do and say.*

For whatever is born of God overcomes the world; and this is the victory that has overcome the world—our faith. (1 John 5:4)

Are you an overcomer? According to the above verse, once you have invited God into your life or "been born of God," you have the power to overcome the world. This means that you are no longer deceived by the enemy or his standards. Over the past fifteen years, I have watched the decay of our world's moral conscience. There are no longer absolute wrongs or rights. Everyone just says, "If it feels good to you, it's right," and "What's wrong for one person may be right for another." This line of thinking is completely against the standard of God's Word. Issues such as homosexuality and abortion, which are clearly defined as sin according to God, have become the hot political topics of our day. The basic premise of right or wrong has turned into a moral war zone in the attempt to make these acts neutral.

Once you become an overcomer of the world, no moral neutrality will fool you. Sin is seen as sin, no matter how beautiful its wrappings. The enticements of the world—riches, alcohol, promiscuity, gossip—turn you off.

You can be a Christian five minutes or five years and have the power to overcome. If you believe God can make you an overcomer, then you will be one. And you need to be one for your children's sake, as well as your own. If they see you as an overcomer able to identify sin as sin and right from wrong, then so shall they.

> *Dear Lord, thank You for dying for me. Thank You that because I am born of You, I can be an overcomer of the sin in this world. May I keep my eyes always focused on You so that I will recognize sin, no matter how appealing. Help me to teach my children to be overcomers too.*

The heart is more deceitful than all else
And is desperately sick;
Who can understand it? (Jeremiah 17:9)

Have you watched the first ten minutes of the evening news lately? Murder, rape, abuse, kidnaping, molestation, theft—the crimes go on and on. I sometimes go for weeks without listening to a single minute of news intentionally. It's too depressing. Our media vividly illustrates the horrible condition of the heart of man.

There is no question that the natural condition of man is sinful. It leads to the ultimate destruction: spiritual death. I am appalled at the number of news stories about parents abandoning, neglecting and abusing their children. One story was of a young mother who left her two young sons in a car and pushed it into a river, drowning them. Her reason: She was separated from her husband and dating a man who was not interested in having children. So, out of desperation to be loved, I suppose, she got rid of the one obstacle: her boys. My tears flowed as I listened to the details unfold on the evening news. "The heart is more deceitful than all else and is desperately sick; Who can understand it?"

Left to our own volition, we will do many wrongs, some more horrifying than others. We so desperately need God's guidance. Qualified or not, ready or not, saved by the grace of God or not, any woman can become a mother. So when you are feeling unqualified or inexperienced, don't rely on your heart to give you guidance. It "is more deceitful than all else" and may steer you in the wrong direction. Trust in God, and pray for His guidance. He will never steer you wrong.

> *Oh Lord, sometimes I look around at the world I live in, and it*
> *scares me to be a mother. I feel so unsure of myself. When I look to*
> *my heart for guidance, I come up empty. Fill it with Your wisdom.*

Create in me a clean heart, O God,
  And renew a steadfast spirit within me. (Psalm 51:10)

Although the heart is indeed "desperately wicked," hope lies within this verse. The one who loves the Lord can have a clean heart before God. He can bring restoration, forgiveness and healing. He can purify your heart. If you have dealt wrongly with your children, whether it be in speaking too harshly, disciplining out of anger rather than love, or even abuse, there is forgiveness for you. (See 1 John 1:9.) I urge you to seek Him now. Ask Him to break the destructive pattern in you, however slight. Left unchecked, it can get out of control quickly. Today's Scripture verse also happens to be part of one of my favorite choruses. Perhaps you know the words:

> *Create in me a clean heart, O God,*
>   *And renew a steadfast spirit within me.*
> *Do not cast me away from Thy presence,*
>   *And do not take Thy holy spirit from me.*
> *Restore to me the joy of Thy salvation . . . (Psalm 51:10-12)*

Meditate on these words. Sing them to God and ask Him to search your heart and show you any sinful behavior you need to confess. Commit yourself as a stay-at-home mom to God. Ask Him to give you a steadfast spirit for this role. Are you easily moved or swayed according to your emotions or the circumstances surrounding you? Or do you remain steadfast in God, no matter what the situation? Make Psalm 51:10 your prayer today.

> *Create in me a clean heart, O God,*
>   *And renew a steadfast spirit within me.*

Trust in the LORD with all your heart, And do not lean on your own understanding. In all your ways acknowledge Him, And He will make your paths straight. (Proverbs 3:5-6)

Shortly before Seth turned two, his doctors recommended that we have tubes surgically implanted in his ears. To reject the surgery meant a possibility of permanent hearing loss.

As we waited for Seth's surgery, we also discovered that he was far-sighted and needed to wear glasses. "How am I supposed to keep glasses on a two-year-old?" I shrieked as the ophthalmologist handed me Seth's prescription. He merely smiled in reply. I went home and cried. "Lord," I whimpered, "how can You put Seth through all this? He's so young; it doesn't seem fair. First surgery and now glasses. What if the other kids make fun of him?"

Sprawled across my bed, face wet with tears, I sensed His gentle touch drying my eyes and His Word came flowing from my memory: "Trust in the LORD with all your heart, and do not lean on your own understanding." His Word reminded me that though I did not understand, I needed to trust God anyway. He knew what was best for Seth, and He loved my son even more than I did. That's hard for a mother to imagine, but true.

We went through with the surgery and the glasses. Within a week, we discovered he was a different child. His speech improved because he could hear better. And I still remember the first time he wore his glasses. Staring at my husband sitting on the floor next to him, he reached out and touched his face. "Hi, Daddy," he whispered softly, as if meeting him for the first time. Teary-eyed, I realized what a blur the world must have been to him. I thanked God that His ways are best, even when I don't understand.

Thank You, Lord, that You know what is best for my family. I acknowledge Your wisdom and invite You to direct my path. Keep me on the road, Lord, that leads to You.

*And without faith it is impossible to please Him, for he who comes
to God must believe that He is, and that He is a rewarder of those
who seek Him. (Hebrews 11:6)*

The entire eleventh chapter of Hebrews supports verse six, citing
story after story about the incredible circumstances of many godly
men and women and the faith that sustained them. There's the example of
Noah. He had faith to take God at His word and build an ark, even though
there wasn't a cloud in the sky. The story of Abraham illustrates his un-
shakable faith. He believed that God would bring him to the Promised
Land and give him many descendants, although he had no children.

The Bible is full of stories of men and women who had complete assur-
ance that God would keep His promises. That is part of the reason God in-
spired man to write His Word. They recorded the stories of old and words
of truth to encourage us to live by faith. As recorded, the rewards are great!

The living examples of faith we read should inspire us to believe the
promises God makes to us as mothers—that He will equip us to do our job
properly. So, if you've been feeling like you just can't hack it—have faith!
Look at such passages as Philippians 4:13, "I can do all things through
Him who strengthens me." Claim Christ's strength in your life, especially
in your role as a mother.

Search the Scriptures for other promises that will encourage you. Recite
them when you have a difficult day. Standing on God's promises will help
your faith to grow. Having steadfast faith will get you through many
rough spots as a parent. That firm foundation of faith is all the experience
you need to be a good mother.

*Almighty God, I thank You that You demonstrated Your faithful-
ness to Your people again and again, and then documented it in
Your Word. Help me to draw strength from the stories of my ances-
tors.*

And not only this, but we also exult in our tribulations, knowing that tribulation brings about perseverance. (Romans 5:3)

How do you gain experience as a mother? It would be much less painful if we just knew how to rear our children the instant they were born. Unfortunately, the only way we become seasoned mothers is by experiencing all the ups and downs, trials and tribulations of parenting.

Since the beginning of time, parents have endured testing with their children. Adam and Eve suffered a tremendous loss when Cain killed his brother Abel. Still, Adam and Eve kept going—they persevered. And so must we when trials befall us.

The key word in today's verse may surprise you—*knowing.* When we know that the trial we're experiencing will bring about perseverance, we focus on the outcome, not the trial at hand. When I hit a rough spot in life, I have learned that if I can focus on where I'm going, rather than where I'm standing, I can get through turbulent circumstances with a minimum of bumps and bruises.

God is using the trials in our lives to shape us into His image. The testing that we endure is building experience, which is the foundation of maturity. As we mature both as a mother and a follower of Christ, we learn to persevere. And perseverance is the key to getting through the good, the bad and the inevitable times of testing in between.

Lord, I want to know that the trials I experience will bring me closer to You. Give me eyes to see not what I am, but what I am becoming. Just as Your Word proclaims, may I exalt in all the trials and tribulations that help to get me there.

For we are powerless before this great multitude who are coming against us; nor do we know what to do, but our eyes are on Thee. (2 Chronicles 20:12)

When Jehoshaphat was the king of Judah, times were turbulent. But Jehoshaphat was a godly man and he sought God's guidance in every decision. We find him in another critical situation in Second Chronicles 20. The Jews had finally settled into the land of Judah, which God had promised to Abraham in His covenant years before. So Jehoshaphat knew they were supposed to be on this land. Yet, he received word that two groups of people planned to fight him for the land. His immediate reaction is found in today's verse.

Jehoshaphat knows that God has brought them into Judah for a purpose, and he is willing to defend it. However, the key to his reign and success is in his petition to God—he admits that they are powerless against their adversary. The armies coming against him would be bigger and stronger. Still, he did not panic. He took it to God and said simply, "We are powerless," but You are not. When we admit that we are powerless, God can exercise His power. Until we are willing to do so, He cannot work. He will not intervene in the tribulations of our lives unless we invite Him. Jehoshaphat knew God's power would bring them victory. And it did. They didn't even have to fight. (Read 2 Chronicles 20:13-25.)

You may feel that your inexperience as a stay-at-home mom leaves you at a disadvantage, but it doesn't. In your weakness, you can find strength from God.

God of power and might, help me to trust You the way Jehoshaphat did. In my inexperience with raising children, I pray You will take over. My efforts without You are futile. Bring me victory as You rule and reign in me.

But seeing the wind, he became afraid, and beginning to sink, he cried out, saying, "Lord, save me!" (Matthew 14:30)

Do you ever feel that being a mother, particularly a stay-at-home mom, is a sink-or-swim experience? I know I do. When your children are young, it can be downright scary. Remember the first time you had a sick child? Or the first day of school—who was really more frightened, your child or you? I have found that if I keep my focus on God and His Word, and not on the circumstances, I am less likely to panic and drown myself.

I can picture the disciples fishing and enjoying the day at the sea. They don't notice the wind increasing and night coming. The waves begin to swell, and suddenly, they find themselves far from shore and in the middle of a full-blown storm. They are frightened. They look out to sea and rub their eyes in disbelief. Is that Jesus walking toward them on the water? Jesus speaks to them gently, trying to calm their fears. Peter takes a step of faith when he says, "Lord, if it is You, command me to come to You on the water" (14:28). So Jesus does. And so Peter does. The moment that determines if Peter sinks or swims as a man of rock-solid faith is now. Will he keep his eyes on Jesus, or will he divert them to the storm raging about him? All of the disciples hold their breaths—there he goes. One step. Two steps. Then, catastrophe. Peter's eyes shift from Jesus to the huge waves. He begins to sink. Of course, the Savior saves him once again.

How do you react when you find yourself in the midst of a storm? Do you focus on the circumstances and drown in the seemingly hopeless situation? Or do you look to Jesus, Commander of the storms of life?

Help me to keep my eyes on You at all times, Lord, especially in the midst of a trial. Build in me a faith in You that will overcome the most horrendous storms. May I keep my head above water as I learn to be the kind of mother You want me to be.

Indeed, there is not a righteous man on earth who continually does good and who never sins. (Ecclesiastes 7:20)

Do you sometimes feel that no matter how hard you try to teach your children to do right, they continually do wrong? They are part of the human race, and when Adam and Eve ate the forbidden fruit in the Garden of Eden, we all became part of a sinful race. With that act of disobedience came the depravity of man's condition. We will continually make mistakes and bad choices. That's why we need Jesus. And that's why we need to teach our kids that they need Jesus.

Still, it can be discouraging when your children make bad life choices. I have a sibling who has made choices that have nearly broken my parents' hearts. Now that I am a parent, I understand their grief. Parents are tempted to blame themselves for a child's wrong behavior or to take credit for his good behavior. But that is not healthy. We have to realize there is a time when our responsibility to train our children is over, and they must take responsibility for the choices they make.

When you are discouraged by your child's behavior and tempted to blame their choices on your parenting, remember this: God was the perfect parent to Adam and Eve, and they still disobeyed Him. They chose sin.

Are you struggling with choices your children have made? Stop right now and pour out your heart to God. Give up the responsibility for their behavior and ask God to release you from your guilt.

Lord, I sometimes feel so inadequate and inexperienced. I need Your help. Help me to understand where my responsibility for my children's choices begins and ends. Show me how to do the best I can and to leave the rest in Your hands.

February 29

"For the eyes of the LORD move to and fro throughout the earth that He may strongly support those whose heart is completely His. . . ."
(II Chronicles 16:9)

I remember agonizing over my firstborn's kindergarten year. My husband and I had ruled out public school which left private Christian school or home school. We set appointments at the three Christian schools in our town. In the interim, I began to research home schooling. The more I learned, the more frightened I became. What if God called me to home school? I wanted to be obedient, but the prospect overwhelmed me.

I put a lot of pressure on myself to make the "right" choice and one night, I broke down in tears. I cried out to God, "What am I supposed to do, Lord? I want to make the right choice. I love You and my son with all my heart. But I don't feel qualified to be Seth's teacher."

In the darkness, I heard God's still small voice saying, "I have seen your heart. I will support your decision."

An amazing peace flooded me, and I felt refreshed and no longer afraid. I knew I could do whatever God called me to do. And because I had surrendered my heart to His, I somehow knew that either decision was okay with Him.

During an appointment at one of the private Christian schools, my husband and I knew immediately that it was the perfect place for Seth. Everything fit. Again, I felt peace.

A few months into the school year, I was observing in Seth's kindergarten class. I felt that same peace as I watched him interact with his teacher and classmates. I knew that we had made the right choice, or that God had chosen to support the one we made.

As mothers, we often struggle with decisions—especially those in areas where we don't feel well-qualified. I have learned that when we give our hearts completely to God, He will guide and support us. He is just waiting for us to surrender to a more qualified person—Him.

Lord, as I seek your support in all that I do, I give you my heart—completely.

March:
Working Hours

What about vacation and sick leave?
Do I get time off for good behavior?

Exhaustion—the word is synonymous with mom. There are times in every mother's life when the pressures of raising a family nearly collapse her into a heap. Being a stay-at-home mom is more exhausting in some seasons than in others. One is the infant stage. The needs of a baby are never-ending: 2:00 a.m. feedings, constant diaper changing, bottle-washing and answering that cry. The work is maximal and the sleep is minimal.

Then there's the toddler stage. I'm convinced God designed a child's development with a sense of humor. As soon as mom starts getting a full night's sleep, the baby begins to explore. Everything has to be touched, turned over, opened up or poured out. God knew we'd need our rest to keep up with the pace of our own Energizer® bunny. Once the kids reach school, we think we'll have some time to ourselves. Not so. They get involved in activities—all occurring at different times and places. We race around at breakneck speed trying to keep up with our children's schedules. So the cycle goes. It is a twenty-four-hour-a-day job!

I informally polled stay-at-home moms in my community on the frustrations of mothering. Exhaustion was at the top of the list. Overwhelmingly, it is the number one struggle. So where does a stay-at-home mom go to rest? The Scriptures are full of words of encouragement and instruction for tired moms who make a living out of caring for their families. God's Word also holds many promises of blessing for the mom who endures and continues to make her family a priority.

Whoever . . . serves, let him do so as by the strength which God sup-
plies; so that in all things God may be glorified through Jesus
Christ, to whom belongs the glory and dominion forever and ever.
Amen. (1 Peter 4:11)

The speaker at a women's church retreat shared some things that re-
ally hit me. Addressing the subject of burnout, she challenged us to
think about the number of activities we are involved with outside the
home. Are they excessive? Does the church family get more of our time and
energy than our family at home? Then she said that for many of us who are
tired and burnt out, it's not the amount of activity that causes our exhaus-
tion; it's our approach to the activities. Are we approaching the task on our
own power or drawing from God's power? If we're relying on our own
strength, we will undoubtedly burn out quickly. We have limits but God's
power is limitless!

I discovered that it's easy for me to get swept away with something that
I'm naturally gifted in. Sometimes I don't stop to ask for God's help and
strength when I think I can handle it. Yet, I run to Him when I'm chal-
lenged in an area that doesn't come naturally to me. Those are the times
I'm most concerned about my performance, and yet, they are the times I do
best—when God is my sustenance. I need to bring all of my involvement
before God. When everything I do is in His power, only then will I not run
out of steam.

Think about your commitments. Are you feeling weighed down because
you are trying to do too much, or is it because you are doing it all in your
own power?

Stop right now and ask God to enable you with His strength.

Oh Lord, You are mighty and powerful. I thank You that you can
supply the strength I need for all of my tasks. Help me to rely on
Your power when I serve. I pray that I may serve You in a way
that would bring glory and honor to Your name.

A gentle answer turns away wrath,
but a harsh word stirs up anger. (Proverbs 15:1)

Have you ever noticed when you're really tired you are short with your kids? I know that's the case in my household. If I'm tired and irritable, my family usually pays. That's good enough reason for me to be sure I'm well rested. During one particular month, I was heavily involved in outside activities and consequently, I was not getting adequate sleep. I noticed an unwelcome pattern. I was snapping at my two-year-old instead of speaking gently to him. My patience was short-lived, as well. When I raised my voice at him, he would raise his voice with me. I would shout my protests more loudly, resulting in his full-blown scream. One day, I realized to my shame that I was the one creating the negative cycle of emotions. He was simply reacting to my anger and impatience. I decided to try an experiment.

When Seth was doing something he shouldn't, I would approach him and kneel at his level. I looked him in the eye and in a soft voice, quietly reproved him. The results were wonderful—Seth began responding to my correction without protests and screaming. When I spoke gently, so did he. Even when he didn't understand "why" he couldn't do something, he did not whine and complain. He just pouted quietly! "A gentle answer turns away wrath." Gentleness has power. Try modeling "a gentle answer" in your home. See if it cuts down on the whining and shouting. When you are tired, speaking gently will take effort. But I can assure you that the peace it brings to your home is well worth it.

Lord, forgive me when I speak harshly to my children. Help me to
control the tone of my voice, especially when I'm tired, and to speak
kindly and gently.

Come to Me, all who are weary and heavy-laden, and I will give you rest. (Matthew 11:28)

I have found that when I am burdened physically or emotionally the best place to rest and recoup is in the arms of my Savior. My personality bends toward doing. I make "To Do" lists and work to check off the next item on the list. However, I expect to accomplish more in one day than any reasonable person would. It has taken me years of working to exhaustion, as well as a husband pleading with me to slow down, to come to this realization.

The reality is that there is always more to do when you're a stay-at-home mom. The list never ends! That could be a wearisome thought if not for the promise in Matthew 11:28. Jesus never intended for us to carry our burdens alone. He says that if we come to Him, He will give us rest. All we have to do is lay our burdens at His feet.

When I begin feeling weary in my role as a mom, I find a quiet place and rest for a moment. I close my eyes and recite this verse, picturing myself walking to the very throne of Jesus. I lay all of my responsibilities, worries and burdens down before Him. I visualize myself crawling onto His lap. As He wraps His arms around me, I nestle into His shoulder and fall fast asleep. Occasionally I have awakened a short time later to find that I actually did fall asleep!

The visualization of laying my cares and concerns before the Lord works wonderfully. A fresh energy and attitude that can only come from God always replaces my weariness. The next time you are feeling weighed down and weary, give this mental exercise a try. See if your load doesn't become lighter.

Lord, thank You for Your promise to bring me rest when I bring my burdens to You.

━━━━━ ✣❀✣ ━━━━━

Consider it all joy, my brethren, when you encounter various trials, knowing that the testing of your faith produces endurance. And let endurance have its perfect result, that you may be perfect and complete, lacking in nothing. (James 1:2-4)

*D*o you know the difference between happiness and joy? Most people think of them as synonymous, but they aren't. Happiness is rooted in circumstances—joy is not. Only God can give true joy. It depends on a right relationship with Him. When we know the Lord and trust Him, He teaches us to live in joy regardless of our circumstances. Joy rises above dismal circumstances and even finds the benefits within them. James talks about this when he says, "Consider it all joy, my brethren, when you encounter various trials."

He says that trials inevitably test our faith. Facing difficulty makes us stronger. Top athletes build up their endurance by training hard. They spend hours getting their bodies in shape for top condition. We spend hours every day taking care of our families; we should consider ourselves in training for their hearts and souls. The enemy will bring about hard times as he attempts to tear apart our families. But if we have grounded our children in the faith, they will overcome.

As we commit our trials to God, He gets us through. That process matures our faith. We even learn to experience joy in spite of what surrounds us. James says that when we endure, we will be "perfect and complete, lacking in nothing." Of course, this means perfected only in Christ, not on our own accord.

Being a mother requires enormous time, energy and commitment. But if we pace ourselves, as a marathon runner does, we will endure.

Lord, use my trials to make me stronger. Give me joy to live victoriously despite my circumstances.

Cease striving and know that I am God. (Psalm 46:10)

Some translations say, "Be still and know that I am God." Either way, the message is the same. When we are weary, we need to be still and quiet ourselves before the Lord. We need to take a few moments for some time alone with Him. That is what knowing God is all about. When we spend a few reflective moments reading God's Word and talking to Him, we are building a relationship with Him. When we take the time to think about God, we can go on despite the hectic pace of life. Knowing Him brings assurance that He is able when we're so tired we just don't believe we can do any more.

When I am feeling worn out and facing a full day, I need to "be still" the most. What? With all I have to do, I should be moving and going, not sitting still. But if I take a few moments at the beginning of a busy day and acknowledge that I need God's help, then I am better equipped to handle the day's events. I am actually more productive and less exhausted. When I tap into my true source of strength, the supply is limitless. All I need to do is ask.

Are you tired? Do you strive in your own power or God's? Take a few moments right now to be still and reflect on who He is and what He can do for you. Tell Him your need and thank Him for His strength and power working in you.

> *Thank You, Lord, for sustaining me when I have grown weary in my daily responsibilities. Empower me that I might accomplish what You have given me to do as a wife and mother.*

March 6

For consider Him who has endured such hostility by sinners against Himself, so that you may not grow weary and lose heart. (Hebrews 12:3)

The Pharisees were among the many people who opposed Jesus. They were aginst Him because Jesus contradicted their teachings about the Old Testament law. He spoke of a law that fulfilled the Old and offered the gift of eternal life, the forgiveness of sins and grace. While the old law dealt with sin by symbolically covering it with the blood of animals, Jesus preached forgiveness and the removal of sin as far as the east is from the west. Jesus knew that He was right and continued His ministry despite His critics.

There will be times in your parenting when people will disagree with how you handle your children. They many openly criticize you. But as long as you do what is right, according to God's Word, ignore the criticism and press on. Don't let others dishearten you. Think of Jesus teaching the multitudes in spite of His opposition.

One thing I have learned is this: Biblical ethics will always challenge the status quo. Many people will not like that we raise our children according to the standards of God's Word, because parenting in our society is full of humanistic philosophy. They will challenge our biblical ethics, criticize us, even oppose us. But do not lose heart. Rather, regard the opposition as a reminder that you are doing something right. Just look to the Author of the standard; He will steady you if you begin to grow weary.

Lord, help me to raise my kids according to Your standard. Give me courage when I come against opposition to my parenting style. Help me to stand up for You.

Love . . . endures all things. (1 Corinthians 13:7)

What does it mean to endure? One mother said, "to keep up with life even when I'm too tired to." Life doesn't stop when we get weary, does it? A dictionary definition of "endure" says, "to put up with or tolerate." There are many days as a stay-at-home mom that I put up with things I don't much like, such as messes left on the kitchen counter or clothes thrown on the floor. I tolerate some of it because I love my family. If I didn't, I'd be screaming at them constantly to pick up and clean up after themselves. (I do remind them however, and I try not to nag.) I haven't walked out because I am tired of picking up after them. I tolerate misbehavior from my children because I love them. I seek to correct it and train them properly, hoping they will make the right decision the next time. But I haven't left them behind just because they embarrassed me in public. I did fantasize about it once when Seth threw a tantrum in aisle eight of the grocery store.

We endure messes, misbehavior, inconveniences, insensitivity and even mistreatment as mothers every day. Why? Because we love our children. Love is not always neat or proper or convenient. Love makes mistakes. Our love is imperfect because we are imperfect. That is why we need God's help. When we love them with His love, we are able to endure anything.

The kind of love I want to have for my family is the kind Jesus demonstrated on the cross—completely sacrificial, unconditional love. I am not able to love that way on my own. But with God's help I can learn an enduring love that surpasses my own weariness. And so can you.

Lord Jesus, thank You for modeling perfect love when You died on the cross. Help me to love my family with an unconditional love.

March 8

You will surely wear out, both yourself and these people who are with you, for the task is too heavy for you; you cannot do it alone. (Exodus 18:18)

These words, spoken to Moses by his father-in-law, came at a crucial point. As the leader, Moses did everything himself. Rather than teaching the Israelites skills so they could settle some things for themselves, he was at their disposal day and night. He told them what to do and how to do it at every turn. Little did Moses realize that this dependency would soon wear them all out. Thankfully, a very wise father-in-law appeared in time to see the destructive pattern Moses was weaving. Moses decided to heed Jethro's counsel and soon, according to Exodus 18:19-26, everyone was taking on some responsibility.

This early scenario in Moses' leadership career depicts many of our households. Mom is often bogged down with all the household responsibilities. The rest of the family depends on her for everything from making a bed to making a sandwich. This unhealthy dependency leaves all members of the family frustrated and exhausted. Your family will tire of relying on you for everything, and you will be exhausted for obvious reasons!

We can avoid such exhaustion by sharing the load. Children can be taught age-appropriate tasks to help out. It would be unrealistic to expect a three-year-old to clean the bathroom, but he can help set the table. If we spread out the workload, we bring balance to our homes. In addition, learning responsibility builds self-confidence and maturity in our children.

God did not intend for you to run your household single-handedly. Enlist your spouse's help in dispersing the workload and update responsibilities as your children get older.

Lord, give me wisdom as I seek to balance my home by teaching my children to share household duties. Give me strength for my own responsibilities.

March 9

Let your foot rarely be in your neighbor's house,
lest he become weary of you and hate you. (Proverbs 25:17)

We have all experienced visitors who have overstayed their welcome:
the neighbor who stops by for a "minute" and leaves three hours
later; the brother, sister or other relative who comes for a weekend and is
still camping in your living room a month later. Situations like these add
tremendous stress to your home life. You feel responsible to see that guests
are happy, well-fed and entertained. The stress mounts when you try to
tend to your household responsibilities with someone hanging around all
day.

It is difficult to discern when guests have overstayed their welcome.
Scripture tells us to serve one another, so where is the line? Only you and
your family can determine that, with help from the Lord. It's different for
every family. But when a guest's stay begins to wear you down or rob you
of private family time, it is time to assess the situation. Go before the Lord
in prayer and ask Him for wisdom and guidance in handling the circum-
stances. On the flip side, be sensitive when you are the guest in someone
else's home; whether you are visiting for a "minute" or a weekend, be sure
you don't stay longer than you said you would. If you are considerate, you
will be the neighbor, friend or relative who is always welcome!

Lord, give me a servant's heart when it is time to open my home to
others. Show me how not to neglect my family, and give me love and
discernment when I need to handle the friend who has stretched the
limits.

Yet those who wait for the LORD
    Will gain new strength;
They will mount up with wings like eagles,
    They will run and not get tired,
They will walk and not become weary. (Isaiah 40:31)

My husband and I had the pleasure of taking a boat trip up the Rogue River in Oregon one summer. We saw beautiful wildlife: deer, beaver and many rare birds. Most enchanting of all was the bald eagle.

We watched the eagle soar above us tirelessly, without ever flapping his wings. It was as if he hung suspended from the sky on invisible strings. He displayed a certain majesty as he circled endlessly, head held high, always surveying his surroundings. We learned that eagles make their homes high on mountaintops and treetops so that when they fly for the first time, they just push off and start to soar. Beginning at such a vantage point requires almost no effort. All they have to do is soar; it requires no tiring wing-flapping. When hunting for food, they circle their prey until the time is right, then swoop down and grab it. The momentum often carries them right back up where they started, with barely the flap of a wing. They also ride air currents for miles.

If we would position ourselves on the mountaintops of God's power every day, we too could accomplish much with little effort. When we begin at the highest heights and search for God's hand to carry us, we have boundless strength. I have experienced this mountaintop majesty by beginning my day with Bible reading and prayer. If you begin your day this way, you will find yourself on the mountaintop, looking at your tasks below. At the right time, God will empower you to swoop down and conquer them without exhausting yourself.

Lord, thank You for the beautiful reminder in the eagle's strength.
As I begin each day climbing to the mountaintop to meet with You,
empower me to soar as tirelessly as that majestic bird.

*Jesus therefore, being wearied from His journey, was sitting thus by
the well. (John 4:6)*

The road was hot and dusty, His journey long. He had traveled many miles preaching and sharing the gospel, and now He was tired. Rest was crucial. He still had much to do and many miles to cover. As Jesus rested by the well, a Samaritan woman came to draw water. Jesus spoke with her. He shared who He was and the good news of the kingdom. His insights fascinated her, and she ran to tell the people that she had met the Savior (John 4:7-29).

If Jesus had not taken time to rest, He would have missed a divine appointment to share the truth with this woman. How many times do we rush through life, passing by opportunities to rest and share time, maybe even truth, with another? Resting can take place by yourself, of course, such as an afternoon nap. But sometimes sitting and talking with a friend or our children can be restful—and needed.

This Scripture inspires me to take a breather when I need one. Jesus did. Even short breaks, such as Jesus took at the well, can provide more than just rest. They can be a chance to share our faith. Such moments can't happen if we don't stop long enough to enjoy the company of others. After all, it's hard to speak when you're out of breath.

*Help me to slow down, Lord. Let me learn from Your example that
it's OK to take a break. Help me not to miss the opportunities You
put in my path to share with others, including my children.*

What is my strength, that I should wait?
And what is my end, that I should endure? (Job 6:11)

Of all the biblical men and women who endured hardship, Job was definitely one of the hardest hit. He endured everything from head-to-toe boils to the destruction of his entire empire. God allowed Job to lose everything—except his own life. At times, Job wished God would take his life. He just wanted out of his pain and misery. In Job 6:11, Job wonders why he should endure his agony. Yet, he remained faithful to God. He trusted that God's way was best, even if it hurt.

There are times when I am so tired as a wife and mother that I just want out. There are times when I wonder, *How can it get any worse than this?* In those moments I need to step back from my feelings and trust that God will sustain me. Just as God remained near to Job, so will He be near to me. When I am worn out, I realize that my supply of strength is finite, but God's is infinite. He will supply me with the courage to persevere. Perhaps He allows me to wear down so that I'll depend more on Him. God wants our ultimate dependence. If He has to take us through the fire to get us there, He will.

All that he went through strengthened Job spiritually. He depended on God completely. When you are singed from the flames of a trial, fall at the feet of Almighty God. He who brought Job through the fire will certainly bring you out as well.

Lord, help me to endure when I am weary from my day-to-day responsibilities. When calamity strikes my household, may I trust You with every detail. Give me faith that, like Job's, can weather any storm life blows my way. Help me to instill that kind of faith in my children.

And let us not lose heart in doing good, for in due time we shall reap if we do not grow weary. (Galatians 6:9)

Staying home with our children is a good thing. My mom stayed home with my two brothers and me as we grew up. When we were all in school, she went back to work part-time so that she could still be home when the school day ended. What a difference her presence made! I can remember coming home from school after I had done poorly on a test or been teased by a classmate. Her warm hugs and loving words always made me feel better. I have fond memories of baking chocolate chip cookies, playing games or going for walks after school with her. I never zoned out on television or got into trouble with other kids after school.

Many of my friends whose moms worked outside the home wanted to come to my house after school and "hang out." They quickly took to the nurturing environment my mother provided. When we were in high school, many of them would come home with me just to talk to my mom about a problem. We jokingly called her "Dr. Mom." After I left for college, a few of my friends who stayed near home continued to call my mom or stop by just to chat.

My mom always made time for me, no matter how much laundry or housecleaning she had to do. I knew that she cared about me because she made herself available. And so I trusted her. We have built a close relationship and she is one of my best friends.

We have the opportunity as stay-at-home moms to plant seeds of love, trust, understanding and godly wisdom in our children's hearts. If we are available, they will come to us when they need us. The result will be a bountiful harvest of right relationships.

Oh Lord, may I never lose heart in doing what is good for my children.

But the Lord answered and said to her, "Martha, Martha, you are worried and bothered about so many things; but only a few things are necessary, really only one, for Mary has chosen the good part, which shall not be taken away from her." (Luke 10:41-42)

I remember the first time this verse hit me between the eyes. My husband and I had just moved for the seventh time in four years of marriage. This was before our parenting days, and he was working long hours at his new job. That left me spending most of my time alone in our apartment in a new and strange city. After six weeks of searching, I had not yet found a job. I was growing more depressed by the day. I thrived on activity; this break was not setting well with me. Every evening when Jimmy came home from work, I would burst into tears and complain that I was bored.

Then one morning I read the story about Mary and Martha; tears spilled from my eyes. I felt God's gentle nudge of correction. "I'm an out-of-control Martha," I whispered to myself. "I don't know how to relax." For twenty-seven years I had done nothing but strive and organize and plan and achieve—sometimes to the point of exhaustion. I didn't know how to be a Mary; I didn't know how to sit at Jesus' feet. God had been trying to give me peace and rest, and I had been begging for busyness!

God changed my heart that day; I have learned to take those periods of rest when He provides them.

God has blessed me with a special friend who is a "Mary" in personality. I have learned from her about the serenity and peace that a more relaxed lifestyle brings. If God gave you the temperament of Martha, great! Just learn to balance your fervor for accomplishment with relaxation. If God gave you the temperament of Mary, then God bless you—you are special. At the Savior's feet is the best seat in the house!

Thank You, Lord, for the wisdom that You provide by the example of these two sisters. Show me the balance of work and rest. Thank You for the chances to rest that You often provide; help me not to overlook them in my busyness. Use those times of repose to bring me closer to You.

March 15

Like cold water to a weary soul,
So is good news from a distant land. (Proverbs 25:25)

I remember a time when I was heavy with weariness. I was in my eighth month of pregnancy, and the days seemed to stretch into eternity. The physical load of carrying a baby and the emotional drain of caring for my almost three-year-old were like lead weights. In addition, I was on the women's retreat committee at our church. With the retreat date nearing, preparations and meetings were becoming more frequent.

Like a drink of cool water, a friend leaned over to me in Bible study and said she'd like to take my son for a day so I could rest. I protested at first, so she left the invitation open. A few days later, stumbling from the burdens of exhaustion, I decided to accept. Her offer was a God-given opportunity to rest. It took me a few days to realize He was providing a drink of cold water to my weary soul.

The next time someone offers to take the kids for a day, or even a few hours, don't politely decline! We don't like to admit we could use a break, thinking we have to appear strong and independent. But God brings us into the body of Christ so that we can help each other. I have had friends offer to take my children for a day when I had been praying for God to provide me with extra rest! If you know someone who is really struggling under a heavy load and you can take her kids for a day, do it. God will bless you for bringing a drink of cold water to her. When you are thirsty for rest, you may look up to see a glass of your own.

Thank You, Lord, for providing rest to me when I most need it. I pray that You will bless the special friends in my life who have so generously provided for that rest. Help me to be a drink of cool water to someone in return.

". . .{T}hus says the LORD to you, 'Do not fear or be dismayed because of this great multitude, for the battle is not yours but God's.' " (2 Chronicles 20:15)

Since we are home full-time, we can often become consumed with the affairs of our household, forgetting that it is God who governs our homes, our families and our problems. We are soldiers in His army, so the battles we wage are His. We are merely His instruments.

When a soldier becomes distracted, he becomes easy prey for the enemy. Likewise, when we take our focus off Christ, we become an easy target for Satan. He will try to steal our peace and trust in God.

King Jehoshaphat was afraid for himself and his people when the Moabites and Ammonites united with the Meunites to make war against Judah. The enemy's numbers were much greater than his meager army, and the odds didn't look good. But the king was wise; he turned his concern over to the Lord and admitted his fear. The Lord responded. Despite the ominous outlook, the king trusted God and took Him at His word. He ended up victorious in battle.

When we feel defeated and discouraged, we must turn our attention to God. He will gently remind us that the battles we face are not ours. If we trust Him, He will bring us victory.

Lord, help me to remember that the battles I face are not mine. Make me a strong soldier in Your army. Bring me victory in the problems my family encounters.

The LORD will sustain him upon his sickbed;
In his illness, Thou dost restore him to health. (Psalm 41:3)

One benefit that the job of stay-at-home mom lacks is sick leave. I remember one afternoon when the flu suddenly hit me. Seth was not quite two years old. He had just awakened from a nap. I had been resting on the couch myself, because I was feeling kind of "off." When I arose to answer Seth's cry, I made my way down the hall. But when everything started spinning, I didn't quite make it. Thank goodness the bathroom was closer. Somehow I managed to get him up, change him and settle him at the table with a snack.

Glancing at the clock, I realized my husband wouldn't be home for another three hours. *I can make it*, I reasoned. Another run for the bathroom changed my mind. I dialed his number at work. When Jimmy answered, I mumbled something about being sick and needing to lie down. Since I am not the sickly type and I hadn't even had as much as a cold for over three years, Jimmy knew I was in trouble. Yet, so was he. "I'm right in the middle of a big project, honey, and I can't leave right now." Hearing me moan, he added, "But I promise someone will be there to help you right away."

Having no idea who Jimmy planned to send to my rescue, I prayed for strength as I hung up the phone. Thirty minutes and two more trips to the bathroom later, help arrived. I answered the door and looked into the loving faces of our dear friends. I had never been happier to see them in my life.

"Mike came by the school to get me," Brenda said as she draped an arm around me. "And thank goodness he did. You look terrible."

I breathed a sigh of relief and thanked God for the help of friends.

We all have friends we can call on in a time of need. That's what the body of Christ is all about. God never intended for you to handle everything alone, especially when you can't stand up!

Lord, thank You for the times You sustain me through the loving care of another. Keep me healthy and strong, so that I may better care for my children.

These things I have spoken to you, that in Me you may have peace. In the world you have tribulation, but take courage; I have overcome the world. (John 16:33)

With young children, there are many times I don't get a good night's sleep. When they don't sleep well, I don't sleep well. After a restless night's rest, the first thing I do when I awake is ask God to give me energy to get through the day. And He always does. Even in the absence of physical rest, an inner rest comes only from knowing God and trusting Him to sustain me.

Sometimes other things drain my energy, such as the tribulations of daily living that John speaks of in today's verse. I have a friend with three teenage boys—and believe me, she has plenty of tribulations! Although her boys are basically good kids and all believers, they are still teenagers, so some discord is bound to occur. Yet, in the midst of the everyday crises that hit her household, she remains inexplicably peaceful. It only makes sense when you understand the peace that God can give.

If your life seems out of control, and you are often restless, you too can have peace. Just ask Jesus to come into your heart and life and give you His perfect peace. It is the kind that the world cannot give; it only comes from knowing the Prince of Peace. Once you invite Him into your life, you will have peace. No longer will the world with all its trials and tribulations overcome you, but you will overcome the world.

Lord Jesus, Prince of Peace—thank You for overcoming the world for me. All I have to do is believe in You and trust You as my Lord and Savior. Take my heart and my life; give me peace and fill me up with Your all-sustaining rest.

March 19

When I am afraid, I will put my trust in Thee. (Psalm 56:3)

I had taken my three-year-old to his favorite fast-food place for lunch. He loved the large indoor playground, and he was anxious to climb on the stairs, run through the mazes and jump in the balls. On this day, however, I looked around nervously at the crowded play area. There must have been fifteen children, all several years older than Seth.

After lunch, Seth pleaded to play. I reluctantly complied. I watched him disappear into the first maze. My eyes nervously shifted back to the mazes just in time to see a child run past Seth and knock him down without looking back. I jumped up and yelled some instruction about watching out for smaller kids. The child ignored me, but Seth caught my eye, smiled and waved, picked himself up and continued undaunted. I had now convinced myself that Seth was going to get knocked over in part of the maze I could not see. I thought about taking him home when these words flashed through my mind: "When I am afraid, I will put my trust in Thee."

I finally whispered, "OK, Lord, I am afraid for Seth's safety. I'm afraid a bigger kid will knock him down and hurt him where I cannot see. But You can see him, Lord. Put a shield about him and keep him safe. Help him to find his way out of the maze into the safety of my arms. Until then, You keep him in the safety of Your arms." A peace came over me as I finished my prayer. Then I saw Seth going round in circles. He could not find his way out, but he did not look panicked, just determined.

Finally, Seth appeared at the bottom of the big slide. Running full speed, he threw his arms around me, yelling with delight, "I did it, Mommy!" Then he ran off to do it again and again.

Driving home, I thanked God that he had stopped me from cutting Seth's playtime short. Sitting in the seat next to me, he beamed over his new accomplishment. I had almost stolen a moment he needed to conquer his own fear. We had both conquered fear that day, thanks to the Lord.

Lord, thank You for reminding me that when I am afraid, I need to put my trust in You. As a mother, when I become afraid for my children's safety, help me to put them in the safety of Your arms and to trust You completely.

*But I am full of the wrath of the L*ORD*: I am weary with holding it in. (Jeremiah 6:11)*

I was fuming. Seth is strong-willed and can sometimes frustrate me to the point of anger. We were having one of "those days" when he didn't want to listen. *Why can't he just listen and obey?* I thought wearily. As his defiance persisted, so did my anger.

I fought to keep my emotions in check. *Don't lash out at your son; discipline him in love*, I reminded myself. But by the end of the day, I prayed desperately for self-control. When my husband arrived home from work, I was about to boil over. Jimmy took over, and I went for a walk.

That evening after we put Seth to bed, I told Jimmy about all of Seth's challenges. He patiently listened as I talked and cried.

Our children receive the wrong message if we discipline in anger. They think they are being punished because we are angry, not because they have done something that needs correction. If you have a problem with anger, talk about it with your spouse or a trusted friend. Holding it in will only cause it to build, and soon, erupt like a volcano. In that moment of eruption, you will likely spew out all kinds of hurtful things. I didn't realize I had a temper until I had children. I surrender it to God, and only by His power I can control it. Don't become weary from holding it in; instead, talk it out.

> *Lord, I know that You are a God of love, and yet Lord, You too have felt anger toward your disobedient people. I know I can come to You when I am angry, and You will understand. Help me to deal with anger by talking it out; not taking it out on my kids.*

March 21

———— ❧❀❧ ————

He gives strength to the weary,
*And to him who lacks might He increases power. (Isaiah
40:29)*

*I*was in the last trimester of my second pregnancy and feeling very
heavy, literally! Everything was more cumbersome: bending over
to pick things up, getting down on all fours to scrub tubs and floors, even
pushing a vacuum. My husband and I agreed that for a short time we could
indulge in hiring someone to clean the house once a week. It would be a
stretch financially, but we decided it would be worth it.

I set up a date with a cleaning lady recommended by a friend. The
morning she was to arrive, I reveled in feeling a little spoiled. *I can go run er-*
rands and when I come back, my house will be shiny and bright, I thought. It was
a wonderful feeling.

An hour and a half later, I wondered what had happened to our appoint-
ment. I left a note on the door and a key with the neighbor—just in case.

However, when I arrived home the house remained untouched. I sunk
into a chair, hot, tired and wanting to cry. I looked around at the film of
dust on the furniture, the sticky floors and the spotted bathroom mirrors.
"I don't have the energy to clean this house, Lord," I cried out. "And now I
have to try to find another cleaning lady. How long will that take?" I
shouted up to the heavens. From somewhere inside I heard a voice telling
me to be patient.

The next day, I set up an appointment with another cleaning lady for
the following week. I hung up the phone, looked around at my still-dirty
house and decided it could wait. What was more important—a clean house
or a happy child? I took Seth's hand and we headed for the backyard.

Help me, Lord, to balance my responsibility to keep a neat house
with my responsibility to my own health, and that of my children.
Thank You for providing help for me in a time of need.

March 22

It is for discipline that you endure; God deals with you as with sons; for what son is there whom his father does not discipline? (Hebrews 12:7)

We live in a very child-centered age. Many philosophies on rearing children make children the center of the home. Psychological "experts" claim that this kind of parenting brings about emotionally healthy children. Bringing discipline or correction into the parent-child relationship destroys the bonds of love and trust, they say. God's Word, on the other hand, says, "He who spares his rod hates his son, but he who loves him disciplines him diligently" (Proverbs 13:24). Maybe these worldly philosophies explain why we have such a selfish and unruly generation sprouting up. Kids today are generally spoiled and do what they want regardless of the cost or consequences. The onslaught of teenage violence, pregnancy, abortions, drug abuse, murders and suicides in the last decade is alarming. This trend should awaken us to look hard at how we raise our children and who they are growing up to be.

The biblical mind-set for raising children is the only method that is "other" centered; the rest of today's methods are "me" centered. Which kind of child do you want to raise—one who thinks of only himself, or one who thinks of others first? To raise our children according to God's standards not only brings about emotionally healthy children, but it also brings about morally healthy children, which is even more important. If our children are morally healthy, it naturally follows that they will be emotionally healthy.

Raising children the right way takes discipline and endurance. I need to remind myself when I am weary that my job counts for the long run—eternity. God promises to reward those who diligently serve Him. I want to be able to stand before my Father in heaven and hear Him say, "Well done, good and faithful servant." Don't you?

Lord, help me to endure. Some days I get tired, letting my children's undesirable behavior slide. Help me to remember that correction helps them and lack of it hurts them. May I raise up children today that will make a difference for You tomorrow.

Truly, truly, I say to you, unless one is born again, he cannot see the kingdom of God. (John 3:3)

Happy Birthday to me! I love birthdays. They hold so many promises. They are a time for reflecting on the blessings and challenges of the past year. They are a time for measuring our own personal growth, emotional, intellectual and spiritual, and setting goals for the next year. It is a time for celebrating the very special day that God brought you into the world!

My mom and dad always made birthdays exciting when I was growing up. Not because they showered me with expensive gifts or a big party every year, but they sprinkled little acts of love and kindness on me throughout the day. I was dubbed "queen for the day" and didn't have to do any chores. I found a card at my place at the breakfast table and maybe a small gift. Dad cooked and served me breakfast in bed if my birthday fell on a weekend—that was always a special treat! I would find encouraging notes around the house or in my lunch. Mom always let me choose my birthday dinner. The whole family ate dinner together, complete with a cake with candles and the birthday song. My parents did a great job of "building me up," like the Scripture says to do.

Birthdays are a good time for celebrating eternal life, as well as life here on earth. As we celebrate their births, we can talk about the "spiritual birth" our children will someday experience when they give their hearts and lives to Jesus. Of course, you don't have to wait to talk about this until your child's birthday!

Lord, thank You for setting aside a day just for me to be born! May I always celebrate life in You.

And the peace of God, which surpasses all comprehension, shall guard your hearts and your minds in Christ Jesus. (Philippians 4:7)

It's amazing how one bad day can rob our peace. For me, a bad day is one where I don't get anything accomplished from my "to do" list. Being a stay-at-home mom with small children means many interruptions. I used to view my children as "interruptions" until I heard a pastor address the issue of life's frustrations. He broke them into three categories: interruptions, inconveniences and irritations.

Interruptions may be anything from unexpected visitors or phone calls to children who need something. Or maybe they just need you for a while! While interruptions are usually people, inconveniences are usually "thing" situations: the washer breaks down, your car gets a flat tire, you can't find something you need. Then there are the irritations of life. Some of mine are waiting in the doctor's office or at the grocery store, bad customer service and whiny children. Unfortunately, we cannot eliminate the frustrations of life. But we can learn to live in peace in spite of them. The secret is to stop and pray.

If we take the time to stop when we experience an interruption, inconvenience or irritation and give it to God, even thanking Him for it, He will help us to remain peaceful. Most of the frustrations that cause us so much grief are small things that seem big at the time. We can see them as small by viewing them from God's perspective. I know that those little people I often call "interruptions" are far more important to God than my "to do" list. Caring for my children and training them up in godly character may not feel like much, but it is a task that counts for all eternity.

Lord, turn the frustrations of life into opportunities to trust You and experience Your peace.

Is it not indeed from the LORD of hosts
That peoples toil for fire,
And nations grow weary for nothing? (Habakkuk 2:13)

Do you ever feel as if you work, work, work and yet get nothing accomplished? I do! Part of the frustration from spinning my wheels comes from the way I spend my time. Or waste it. Television is a big time waster. Another is procrastination. Do you stay with one project or task until it's completed, or do you begin several things simultaneously, never finishing any of them? We definitely have plenty to do as stay-at-home moms. We have to be good organizers of our time in order to be productive.

Americans have more time-saving devices yet seem to have less time than any other people in the world. We have computers, e-mail, faxes, copiers, cellular phones, personal planners and shoppers, home delivery service and drive-thru's galore—all designed to save time.

Given the responsibilities of the woman who chooses to stay home with her children, it is humorous to me that society often views her choice as a "waste of time." She is usually the one who does all the cleaning, cooking, sewing, ironing, laundry and shopping—not to mention caring for her children on a daily basis. This includes feeding, dressing, changing, bathing, teaching and playing with them. Does that sound like the schedule of a lazy woman?

My neighbor shared with me that her brother-in-law does not agree with her choice to stay home with her two children. He constantly asks, "What could you possibly have to do all day? Aren't you bored?" Another friend says family members and working moms who think she has plenty of free time constantly ask her to do various things.

The schedule of a stay-at-home mom is full, which is why we need to pay heed to God's Word when planning our days. Be sure to begin each day asking God to show you His plan for what you are to accomplish. When we walk in His will, our work will be blessed.

Lord, help me to make the best use of my time each day. Help me to
trust You and walk in Your will so that I will not grow weary.

March 26

And his resting place will be glorious. (Isaiah 11:10)

Most people go on vacation to rest and get away from the daily grind. They look forward to the break from work and their responsibilities. For some, a restful vacation might be a week at the beach, lying in the sunshine and swimming in the surf. For others, it may be a ski trip where they play all day in the snow and unwind by a cozy fire at night. It is my experience, however, that there is no such thing as a vacation from being a mother—even when you go without the kids.

My husband and I had an opportunity to turn one of his business trips into a vacation for just the two of us. The demands of motherhood had taken their toll, and I looked forward to a week of R&R. The morning we were to leave, however, our two-year-old had a terrible asthma attack. After much deliberation, we decided to make an appointment with the doctor and allow our friend who was caring for him to take Seth to it. We got on our plane as scheduled. "Kellie is a skilled mother of two," my husband assured me. "She can handle it."

It was difficult to relax on the flight, and I called Kellie as soon as the plane touched down. She had the necessary medicine from the doctor and assured me Seth would be fine. But I heard him coughing in the background and I worried anyway.

After two days of his medicine and several phone calls, I felt that Seth's asthma was under control. I began to relax. That lasted for a day—until we got a phone call from Kellie saying that Seth had developed a nasty ear infection. By now I wondered if it was worse to take my kids on vacation and have them get sick or leave them at home sick. Either way I was miserable. I can't relax when my kids don't feel well, no matter what beach I'm lying on.

I'm convinced that the "resting place" that God has for moms in heaven will be glorious, just as His Word promises. He knows that we will need a very special place because we worked so hard on earth. Until then, we'll just have to find rest in the promise that we'll get a real vacation when we get to heaven!

Help me, Lord, to cherish every moment of vacations I take with my family, however imperfect they may be. Thank You for Your promise of a glorious resting place in heaven.

The generous man will be prosperous, and he who waters will himself be watered. (Proverbs 11:25)

believe God calls all Christians to open our homes sometimes and to be warm witnesses to the outside world. I love having guests, but I am a much better hostess if I have time to prepare. However, God doesn't always bring people into our lives with advance warning. I remember one such time.

I was just winding down from a hectic day. The house was in disarray, but I was in no mood to clean it. I was poking my head into the freezer to see what I could throw together for dinner when the phone rang. It was Jimmy, who was on his way home with an out-of-town dinner guest. They'd arrive in ten minutes.

I looked around the house. How could I straighten up and start dinner in ten minutes? *This is the worst possible night for company!* I fumed as I threw Seth's toys in his closet.

Twenty minutes later my husband and Ramaj arrived—with a pizza. Ramaj didn't seem to mind the makeshift dinner or the clutter. We laughed and talked late into the evening over coffee and cookies. The conversation turned to spiritual things, and Ramaj asked questions that reflected his search for God. I cringed at the thought that I had almost turned him away because it wasn't "a good night."

Sometimes God sends us people in His timing, not ours. I learned that night that if I make my home open to those who need warmth, love and hospitality, God will bring them. Even when I'm not "properly prepared," God will take care of the details. When I concentrate on refreshing others, God will in turn refresh me!

Lord, forgive me for my self-centered attitude. Help me to open my doors to those who need a place to be refreshed, both in flesh and in spirit.

For how can I endure to see the calamity which shall befall my people, and how can I endure to see the destruction of my kindred?
(Esther 8:6)

Queen Esther was an incredibly strong woman, spiritually and emotionally. Then she caught wind of Haman's plan to destroy her people, the Jews. His determination to succeed at his wicked plot put her in a vulnerable position. Yet she held steady, sought God, made a plan according to her available resources and relationships and carried it out. (To fully understand her situation and its outcome, read Esther 2-9:19.) To paraphrase: Esther's ability to keep a cool head saved her people.

Esther's story is a wonderful example of enduring a life-and-death situation. Still, she held steadfast to her God and approached the one person who could help her people: the king. It wasn't by accident that God had previously granted her great favor with the king.

God sometimes allows people into our lives for the sole purpose of helping us. They may hold a position of influence, such as the king in Esther's day. Don't be fooled into thinking you're taking advantage of that person if you ask for his help—provided you didn't get into the situation because of your own foolishness! Esther did nothing wrong or foolish; she was simply helping her people.

As mothers, we will be called upon to help our children out of a bad, or even dangerous, situation. In those times we will do well to remember the strength, faith and resourcefulness of Esther. If we emulate these traits, we will come out victorious as well.

Lord, give me the strength, faith and resourcefulness of Esther to overcome bad circumstances. Thank You for the people You have already brought into my life that will someday help my family.

Moreover, man does not know his time? (Ecclesiastes 9:12)

I lost three of my four grandparents in less than six months. It was a difficult time for our family. The loss of a loved one is never easy, even when we know he or she is spending eternity in heaven with Jesus. For us, it seemed we were just getting over the death of one we held dear when another passed on. My father lost both his parents within ten days. In his grief, my father gained strength and courage from the Lord. If we look only to ourselves, we will come up empty and weary.

I was fortunate enough to spend some time with all of my grandparents in their last days. We had advance warning of each one's failing health and knew we didn't have much time left with him or her here on earth. In spite of the busyness of daily life, I made time to spend with each one. And I'm so glad I did. Some of my sweetest memories of each grandparent are from those last moments. We don't always have that luxury. Often the death of someone we love is untimely and unexpected. That is why it is so important to consistently spend time with the ones we love.

God's Word clearly states that we do not know how much time we have to live, love and serve on this earth. So you have made a wise choice to stay home with your children. Make the most of every moment with the ones you love most. You have probably heard the saying, "You've never seen a hearse pulling a U-haul®." We can't take possessions with us when we go, so why work so hard at acquiring things instead of relationships? The memories we build from time spent with people we love will last through this life and, perhaps, even into eternity.

Father in heaven, show me every day how I can demonstrate love to those who mean the most to me. Give me the wisdom to spend my time building relationships instead of empires.

March 30

Be devoted to one another in brotherly love; give preference to one another in honor. (Romans 12:10)

Being a mother is a round-the-clock job, there is no question about it. We are on call twenty-four hours a day. Mary, too, the mother of Jesus, was strongly devoted to the upbringing of her child. God knew Jesus needed an earthly mother to provide the nurturing, comfort and love that only she could. He could have brought the Son of God into the world any way He wanted, and He chose Mary to give birth to Jesus and raise Him. That choice emphasizes the importance of a mother's role.

In Scripture we find Mary by her Son's side all the way to Golgotha. He is bruised and beaten and, finally, no longer able to carry His cross. She knows this is part of God's plan, but still she weeps for her Son. She stays at the foot of the cross and watches Him take his last breath. As a mother, I think that must have been torture. But she was devoted to her Son. She didn't leave His side until after Jesus was laid in the tomb.

"Devoted" means to give up one's time and energy for the good of another. Your choice to be a stay-at-home mom shows that you are devoted to your children, because it is not an easy job. In some cases "devote" literally means to give up oneself. Isn't that what Jesus did for us on the cross? He died to His own desire to live so that we could have eternal life. That was and always will be the ultimate sacrifice. But with sacrifice comes great reward. What could be greater than eternal life? Your willingness to give up your desires to put your children's well-being first is also a sacrifice. And so also, in the end, will be great reward.

Lord, thank You for being so devoted that You sent Your Son to die. Help me to be devoted to my children. Give me the strength and wisdom to raise them to love and serve You first, no matter how much time it takes.

"And these words, which I am commanding you today, shall be on your heart; and you shall teach them diligently to your sons and shall talk of them when you sit in your house and when you walk by the way and when you lie down and when you rise up." (Deuteronomy 6:6-7)

His blonde hair glistened in the sunshine as he marched forward. His boots left small, deep tracks. "Look, Mom," Seth said as he pointed at the ground. "There's my footprint! It means I've been there."

I smiled as my thoughts drifted along Seth's words. I had been discouraged about leaving proof on Seth's heart that I had "been there." Training Seth in godly character seemed to grow increasingly difficult with his age. Bible stories and craft projects didn't keep his attention anymore. He was five, on the move and into "fun."

Seth's sudden fire of questions broke my reverie. "Did you know that when you sin, you have to kill an animal? And that no one really knows where the Garden of Eden is today? And Satan is a fallen angel—did you know that?"

Seth's spontaneous interest in spiritual matters stunned and delighted me, and I recalled a bit of Scripture from Deuteronomy. I realized there were lots of different ways to teach my son God's ways. One of those is when we are on the move: "when you walk by the way."

I breathed in the crisp mountain air as we continued along the trail. I understood that if I wanted to be successful at leaving my footprints on the heart of my active little boy, then I had to watch for and seize the teachable moments as they appeared. Those moments when Seth was most interested in learning about God—like right now!

I quickened my pace to catch up with my son, leaving deep imprints in the dirt beneath my feet.

Thank You, Lord, for reminding me that there are so many ways to teach my children about You. Help me not to get stuck in a rut, but to grow with them and teach them diligently all the way.

April:
Job Benefits

The job pays how much?

For a stay-at-home mom, one of the most frustrating things about the job is the low pay and the long hours. She sees her neighbor working full-time outside the home and bringing in money. She looks down at her juice-stained T-shirt and flops into her well-worn sofa feeling exasperated and a bit envious too. She would like to have all of those nice things, but her husband's paycheck has little room for extras.

Maybe I should get a part-time job she thinks, *just to bring in some extra spending money*. She looks over at her little boy playing happily with his blocks, who runs over and flings himself in her lap. "Uv ooo," he declares in baby lingo. His "I love you" may not have made sense to anyone else, but she understands every word. Wiping away a tear, she decides staying at home is worth the sacrifice.

I struggled a great deal some days with staying at home full-time. I would like to have many things we cannot afford. The sacrifice has taught me about what is really important: the little people sleeping in the next room. Their character and heart condition are at the mercy of whoever is around to shape and train them. The benefits of staying home with my kids come in hugs, kisses and strong moral character—things of eternal, not temporal, value.

Changing our mind-set is a daily struggle because we live in a world that measures success by how much you own, not who you are. But the time we put into relationships can never be taken away. When you give time to your child, you invest in something of eternal value: a human life.

April 1

Jesus said to her, "I am the resurrection and the life; he who believes in Me shall live even if he dies." (John 11:25)

This time of year is a season of hope and promise. The freshness of spring breathes new life, and the warm sunshine brings a radiance that dissipates the winter chill in the air as the leaves on the trees sprout new green buds. Nature everywhere paints a vibrant portrait of new life, as does a glimpse into the Easter story. Spring brings with it the significance of our Savior's resurrection.

The death and resurrection of Jesus is the greatest illustration of new life there is. Through His experience, Jesus has been able to promise new life to those who choose to believe in Him as Savior and Lord. Jesus died on a cross for you and me—the most painful kind of death there is. He sacrificed everything to bring us new life, a life that never ends. Death is nothing to fear when Jesus reigns in our hearts, because we will live again for all eternity in heaven with Him. There are no cold, chilly winters in heaven—only streets of gold and warm sunshine.

When we make the decision to stay home with our children, we die to some of our selfish desires like the desire to have more money and more possessions. Those are things that we sacrifice when we make the choice to be at home. But the eternal benefits of the time we have with our kids far outweigh the temporal pleasure of material things.

As you consider the changing of seasons and the approach of Easter, consider any changes you need to make. Just as we have a choice to stay home to raise our children, we have a choice to invite Jesus into our hearts. Have you given your life over to Jesus? When you die to wanting things your way and give up control to let God have things His way, you will really be living life to its fullest!

Precious Jesus, thank You for dying on a cross for my sins and bridging the gap between me and God. Forgive me for my own failures and bad choices and come to live in my heart. I give You total control of my life and ask that You would be my Savior and Lord. I thank You for the promise of eternal life that comes with this commitment to You.

And He said to them, "Beware, and be on your guard against every form of greed; for not even when one has an abundance does his life consist of his possessions." (Luke 12:15)

One young stay-at-home mom I know shared with me that she constantly struggles with the feeling that because she no longer brings in an income, she feels that she's not "contributing" to the family. She realizes of course that raising a child is a very big contribution, but the lack of financial reward makes it difficult for her to put a value on what she is doing. Since she grew up in a family where her mother had to return to work just to help with the monthly living expenses, she gets caught in the trap of thinking that because she's not helping pay the bills, she's not doing anything of real significance. The intangible rather than the tangible benefits of staying home with her daughter cause a daily struggle for her. That whole thought process plays on her self-worth, and that is where many stay-at-home moms begin the downward spiral of inadequacy, which can at times even turn into a mid-life crisis with mom running off to "find herself."

In God's eyes, what this mom is doing is invaluable. Still, she struggles to put a "value" on her time. If moms would look to the Word of God for their definition of who they are, they would begin to see the value in what they are doing. My friend says that's the only way she wins the mind-control battle against the enemy. She stores God's truth in her heart and mind and pulls it out when she needs to check herself—she always checks her thinking against God's Word. In it she discovers, as in the above verse, that even when a woman has much in the way of material wealth, it does not make her valuable. Our worth will never be measured according to our possessions, no matter what the world says.

Lord, remind me daily that my self-worth is obtained from who I am in You, not what I have. Thank You for loving me and for showing me that my job as a stay-at-home mom is of the greatest worth.

April 3

> *House and wealth are an inheritance from fathers,*
> *But a prudent wife is from the LORD. (Proverbs 19:14)*

The dictionary defines "prudent" as "capable of exercising sound judgment in practical matters; cautious or discreet in conduct; sensible; not rash." "Rash" is the opposite of prudent and is defined as "too hasty in acting or speaking; reckless." That's quite a contrast, isn't it? Do you find yourself speaking hastily, saying things you wish you hadn't? Or acting recklessly in your behavior—causing damaging consequences that are irreversible? Ouch! I know I've certainly caught myself in such behavior!

I would make the assertion that a prudent wife is worth much more to her husband and children than any amount of money or possessions. That is the way God presents it in His Word. I have had to learn to be more prudent in my spending habits. When we went from being a two-income family, to a one-income family, it necessitated exercising prudence in sticking to the budget—something I had never had to do before. It took a lot of self-control to shop sales, clip coupons and stretch dollars every way I could. It was difficult for me, but as with any habit-forming behavior, the prudence I now exercise in spending simply took time and discipline to develop. My husband voices his appreciation often for my "learned" prudence in this area.

Today's devotion is a real thought-provoker. Take some time right now to reflect on your behavior as a stay-at-home mother and wife. Prudence is a godly character. It is obvious from the above verse that God takes it seriously. Its evidence in your life is a real gift you can give your husband and children. How do you measure up—would you be defined as prudent or rash? Do you make hasty decisions, or do you think things through and act on what is best for your family? In what areas do you need to become more prudent? Search your heart.

> *Oh Father, there are many times in my life that I am ashamed to admit I would be defined as rash rather than prudent. I recognize that prudence comes from You. Teach me how to be more prudent, Lord. Help me to think before I speak and assess before I make decisions.*

He who loves money will not be satisfied with money, nor he who loves abundance with its income. This too is vanity. (Ecclesiastes 5:10)

Have you ever known someone who has more money than he knows what to do with but never seems satisfied? I do. Someone very close to our family is what I would classify as wealthy—he's in the top ten percent of earners in the United States—yet he is one of the saddest individuals I've ever known. He has lived his entire life working, pushing, striving for more, more, more. His workaholic tendencies have alienated his family and friends. He has tried to patch up relationships that he has neglected by buying expensive gifts. Unfortunately, the emotional wounds he has inflicted by his neglect of relationship-building have been there so long that no dollar amount can make up for them. The gifts go unappreciated and unwanted. All anyone ever wanted of him was time. But he was too busy working, accumulating, strategizing on how he could have more. And for what?

The real tragedy is not in what has been done, but in what can never be undone. This man now looks back on his life and realizes that he made a terrible mistake, that his priorities were all wrong. I have heard him admit it. The people he now longs to spend time with—his children—are no longer there; they have moved on to the next chapter in their lives. They are now grown and have families of their own. Now they are busy. It is too late.

Don't get caught in the web of worldly success. I urge you to remain at home with your children because of sad outcomes like the one above if you choose otherwise. Top-of-the-line bicycles and expensive tennis shoes will soon be forgotten, but time with your children will remain in their hearts and minds forever.

> *Lord, help me to train my children up according to Your Word, and above all, help me never to choose money and possessions over time with them.*

This is the day which the LORD has made;
Let us rejoice and be glad in it. (Psalm 118:24)

One of the aspects of being a stay-at-home mom which I find to be of great benefit is the fact that I am in charge of what I will do with each new day. Now of course I do not have complete and total freedom with every waking moment because there are certain responsibilities that cannot be ignored—such as feeding my children and changing my toddler. And yes, most days there is laundry to be done, dishes to be washed and meals to be cooked; so I haven't totally lost perspective here. But think about it—you don't have to report to a boss every day and account for your every task. There is tremendous freedom in your day. You can choose when you want to do the laundry; mid-morning or maybe not until after dinner—or perhaps you'll choose to just forget about it until tomorrow. It's your decision.

I often revel in the freedom and flexibility that being at home brings. I remember one day when there was a lot that needed to be done around the house—dishes for one, vacuuming for another—but it was a beautiful day and so I decided to pack a picnic lunch and take my kids to the park for a few hours. Later that day, during nap time, with the dishes still staring me in the face, I made myself comfortable on the couch and caught up on some reading I'd been wanting to do but could never seem to find the time for. That day, I made time. I have that freedom. You have that freedom. You don't punch a time clock. You don't have a boss breathing down your neck for an overdue proposal. There is much to be thankful for in the flexibility of a stay-at-home life. Of course, we can't live every day in this fashion, shrugging off our household responsibilities until tomorrow, but knowing that we can, is quite liberating. Give thanks to the Lord for each new day. Be glad for the opportunities you have to shape your schedule and manage your time as you see fit. It's one of the benefits of being a stay-at-home mom, so enjoy it—the dishes will still be there tomorrow!

Thank You, Lord, for the benefit of being my own time manager.
Help me to use each day wisely and view it as an opportunity to
give praise back to You. May I honor You with the use of both my
time and resources.

For a day in Thy courts is better than a thousand outside.
I would rather stand at the threshold of the house of my God,
Than dwell in the tents of wickedness. (Psalm 84:10)

eing a follower of Jesus Christ may mean living a less glamorous lifestyle than if you were serving the god of money or power. But those things will soon die away while the time invested in serving the Lord of lords will count for all eternity. Once we commit our lives to God, we are all His servants. That may mean giving up some things. But the psalmist has the correct perspective when he states the above verse. He goes on in verse 11 to say, "For the LORD God is a sun and shield; the LORD gives grace and glory; no good thing does He withhold from those who walk uprightly." This verse promises riches of a different kind to those who walk "uprightly." The kind that will not perish. God does not withhold good from us to punish us. He withholds things sometimes that we may think are good, but in His wisdom, He often knows better. God never disappoints us; we just think He does when we don't get our way. Often our way is not the best way.

Being a servant of God will bring much more reward than being a holder of power. The reward may not be an immediate tangible item, such as a new sofa; however, that is all that serving the wrong god will bring. Don't desire what money can buy; desire what it can't. It will last much longer and bring you much more joy. Consider where you spend your time and efforts. Is it in trying to "stand at the threshold of the house of God" and serve Him, or is it in trying to get in good with those who "dwell in the tents of wickedness" and experience some of those earthly pleasures? Think about where you are headed now and where you want to end up, and make sure they are one and the same.

Lord, show me how to make every day count for You. I don't want
to waste my time on earthly pleasures. Give me a seat in Your house
of service in which to dwell.

Behold, I am the LORD, the God of all flesh; is anything too difficult for Me? (Jeremiah 32:27)

The money had run out. We were going through a tight time and were living on a strict budget. My husband instructed me not to write any checks until the end of the week. Yet I had an appointment scheduled for Seth with the eye doctor at the beginning of the week. I couldn't put it off because he was undergoing therapy that was necessary for a certain time period every month. We didn't know what to do, so we did the only thing that made sense: we asked God to take care of the situation.

I parked outside the doctor's office that morning. "OK, Lord, You say that nothing is too difficult for You, and I believe You," I prayed. "Please provide for us in order that we may honor You with our finances and not write any bad checks." Upon completion of Seth's eye exam, I asked the receptionist how much I owed. "There's no charge today," she said. I almost fell over. I know my jaw dropped. We had been taking our son for regular appointments for over a year, and none had been "no charge." I left the office surprised and delighted.

I learned a big lesson that day about trusting God. If I trust in Him then nothing is impossible. I thanked Him for placing me in a situation where I could experience His provision. I felt His love for our family that day. I knew we could get through any financial difficulty as long as we put our trust in God.

Lord, thank You for meeting our financial needs time and time again. May I always put my trust in You.

Honor the LORD from your wealth,
And from the first of all your produce;
So your barns will be filled with plenty,
And your vats will overflow with new wine. (Proverbs 3:9-10)

In the early years of our marriage, my husband and I weren't tithing faithfully. We continually had financial problems and often couldn't meet our monthly bills. We began tithing faithfully when we learned that it was a direct instruction from God's Word, even when it meant we wouldn't have enough money for bills that month. And you know what? When we were faithful to God, He was faithful to us—somehow, we had always had enough to pay the bills. We continue to practice the principle of tithing, and God continues to meet our financial needs. I have heard story after story from friends who have also experienced God's provision this way.

Susan, a friend who is also a stay-at-home mom, had an infant who required an expensive formula. One month Susan had enough money only to tithe or buy her baby the formula he needed for the rest of the month. She tithed the money, asking God to provide for her baby. The next day she got a phone call from her aunt who had received three free cases of this special formula from her doctor. She had called to see if Susan wanted it!

The Bible is very clear that we are to honor God from our wealth, and some passages even give clear direction on just how much we are to give. (See Genesis 14:20, Leviticus 27:32, Deuteronomy 14:22 and Hebrews 7:4.) Aside from the fact that tithing is an act of obedience to God's Word, it also inevitably brings blessings into our lives. God is faithful—always. Will you be faithful and tithe even when it seems there is not enough money to do so?

Lord, thank You for faithfully supplying all of my financial needs.
Build my faith through tithing so that I will trust You to provide
for my family no matter what the circumstance.

Do not be deceived, God is not mocked; for whatever a man sows, this he will also reap. (Galatians 6:7)

This passage definitely applies to child rearing. The benefits of staying home with your children are both immediate and future. If you sow lots of time with your children, then you shall reap a good relationship with them—and you will have godly children. It takes time and tenderness to harvest a healthy crop. The same is true of our children. When left without enough attention and proper care, our relationship with our children will wilt just like a poorly tended field of corn.

God has given us our own little crop to raise for Him. If we want to reap the fruit of the Spirit—love, joy, peace, patience, goodness, kindness, faithfulness, gentleness and self-control—in our children, then we need to sow those seeds and carefully tend to their growth. Those qualities won't magically appear, just like a field of barley doesn't mysteriously spring up. Sowing the seeds of time with our children will produce close relationships now and godly character to come.

> *Lord, help me to sow now in my children what I want to reap later. May I properly tend to them so that they will grow into ripe, rich fruit for Your pleasure and service.*

April 10

For the love of money is a root of all sorts of evil, and some by long-ing for it have wandered away from the faith, and pierced them-selves with many a pang. (1 Timothy 6:10)

*D*id you know that God gives more instruction in the Bible on the subject of money than any other, except love? Seems to me He wanted to get a point across. Perhaps we should consider that when look-ing at the benefits of being a stay-at-home mom.

Notice the verse says the "love of money is a root of all sorts of evil." The key word here is love. It is when we "love" money that we get into trouble. It is not wrong to have money. I know many Christian families who have been blessed with great wealth and have all the right priorities. God simply chose to bless them with money—probably because He knew they would handle it correctly!

I remember when my husband and I were first married and struggling to make it. He was still a full-time college student; I had graduated and was working to support us. We lived in campus housing and didn't have much, but we made our studio apartment warm and comfortable.

Even though my husband and I had little money then, we had some of the greatest fun. None of the other couples had much money either, so we did things that didn't require it. We'd make homemade pizza and stay up half the night playing cards and board games. We had snowball fights and built snowmen and laughed over cookies and hot chocolate. We took long bike rides and all-day mountain picnics. And none of it required busting the budget!

Sometimes having less brings us more.

Lord, give me a heart that longs for You, not money. Help me to be content with what You have given me—may I be rich with a grateful spirit.

Let your character be free from the love of money, being content with what you have; for He Himself has said, "I will never desert you, nor will I ever forsake you." (Hebrews 13:5)

Here is another Scripture that urges us not to get caught in the "love of money" trap. This one specifically talks about our character. Stay-at-home moms often experience discontent and forget the benefits of being home with our kids because we get caught up in the "love of money" that Scripture talks about. We see all the things our neighbor has from that extra paycheck, and we begin to think that if we had those things too, we'd be content.

That is a dangerous mind game, and it is simply not true. I know because I've played it.

During my first year as a stay-at-home mom, I became so obsessed with wanting more "stuff" that I didn't spend quality time with my son. I spent entire days trying to figure out how the budget could produce more. My mind was not where it should have been—with my child. Thank God, He convicted me one day as I read this passage in my Bible. I knew He was speaking to me.

"He Himself has said, 'I will never desert you, nor will I ever forsake you.'" Shouldn't that be enough? Life is complete knowing that my God is always with me. Having a new washer and dryer does not complete my life!

Lord, thank You for rescuing me from the "love of money" trap. Help me to focus on my relationship with You and my family so that I won't be easily diverted. May my desire be for You, not the material things of this world.

But you shall remember the L<small>ORD</small> your God, for it is He who is giving you power to make wealth. . . . (Deuteronomy 8:18)

Many successful Christian businessmen and women get caught up in the whirlwind of money and power. They begin to lose sight of where they came from and where they are going. They begin to empower themselves, believing that they are responsible for their achievements. Granted, it generally takes hard work to make money. But God gives us even that ability. In and of ourselves, we are powerless. Just as quickly as He allowed us to possess great wealth, He can take it away.

I am reminded of the story of Charles Keating. He was one of the wealthiest men in the world and highly respected in the business community. He could buy virtually anything he wanted—except integrity. The empire he built was based on fraud and deception. He had been scamming elderly people out of their life savings. He was convicted and imprisoned, and his empire crumbled. God, in His righteous judgment, took away that which was wrongfully gained.

If we lose sight of the One who gives us all we have, we will not have it for long. God in His fair and just manner will eventually bring those temporary pleasures to an end. And we will be left with nothing.

Lord, help us always to remember that You have given us the power to attain what we have, and it is only by Your grace and mercy that we are privileged to have all that we do. May we honor You with our money at all times, ever mindful that You could choose to take it all away tomorrow. Help us to keep our focus and perspective where it should be—on You.

The earth is the LORD's and all it contains, The world, and those who dwell in it. (Psalm 24:1)

Trying to teach children to share can be difficult, particularly when they are preschoolers. I have gone through many times when my children play happily one moment, and the next they are screaming and fighting over a toy. It's usually the toy that sat in the corner for hours unnoticed. Suddenly one child discovers it, and then the others want it too! In trying to help my children understand the principle of sharing, I've found today's Scripture helpful. All other methods of explanation seemed to go unheard until I implemented God's explanation.

I began to read this verse to my children when they were not sharing. I explained that their toys and possessions really weren't theirs—they all belonged to God. God loaned them those toys for a while. Since they were rightfully God's, they had no right to not let others play with them. Amazingly, they seemed to grasp that, and sharing was no longer a battleground in our house. My boys have their moments of selfishness (Don't we all?), but grabbing and greediness no longer characterize them.

Rather than "sharing," some child care centers teach "ownership," feeling it adds to a child's sense of confidence and self-worth. I think "ownership" breeds selfishness and is contrary to God's Word. Sharing is a basic life skill and a characteristic of godliness. That is another benefit of staying home with my kids: I am their teacher. While they are young and impressionable, I can control what they are taught. When they are in another's care, I lose that control. At home with them, I can open their eyes and hearts to God's world.

All that I have is Yours, God, and comes from Your goodness. May I model this belief to my children in attitude and action. Help me to creatively teach them that all they have ultimately belongs to You.

The rod and reproof give wisdom,
But a child who gets his own way brings shame to his mother.
(Proverbs 29:15)

One day as I nursed my baby, I decided to switch on the TV. A talk show on "out-of-control" teenagers held my interest. Mother after mother complained of her child's defiance and disrespect. Some children were actually battering their mothers. One mother said that her daughter had slapped her in the face, punched her in the stomach and kicked her. Another mother said her son continuously beat up a younger sibling and had once thrown her down the stairs. I sat in shock as the children proudly admitted their unruly behavior and boasted of further violence. One even said she would kill her mother if she could get away with it!

One mother scolded her teenage daughter. "How can you treat me this way after I've given you everything you've wanted?" she asked. "You wear $80 sneakers and designer clothes."

I wanted to scream into the television: "She doesn't want all that stuff. She wants you!" All these mothers had provided material things, but they didn't provide the love, discipline and boundaries that their children so desperately needed. When the show's host asked an eleven-year-old how his mom could get him to behave, he replied, "That's for her to figure out; she's supposed to be in control." How much clearer could the message be?

Our children will give us exactly what we expect of them. If we expect respect, obedience and honor, we will get them. But those expectations will be met only through active training. Staying home with our children gives us time to train and correct them to meet the standards we place in their hearts. A child who loves and respects us is the greatest benefit we can derive.

> *Lord, thank You for showing me how important it is to be home with my children. Give me the tools I need to train them in righteousness. I pray I would instill love, respect, obedience and honor in their hearts.*

April 15

Pray without ceasing. (I Thessalonians 5:17)

One of the single most important things that we can do for our children is to pray for them. The enemy is after them. We see and hear his influence in the media, arts, entertainment, and it is entering public schools as well.

Satan works overtime on kids who come from Christian homes. He can disrupt the entire home if he gets to the hearts of our kids. That's why our early influence on their values is crucial. We all want to protect our children, but we cannot isolate them from the world. The only way we can truly protect them from the schemes of the devil is to pray for them. He is sly, subtle and devious, and if he can trick our kids, he will certainly try. If we are praying for things such as wisdom and discernment and for the Lord to guard their hearts and minds against the attacks of the enemy, then God will protect them.

Sometimes stay-at-home moms become discouraged when our children want material things that we cannot provide. But out of our sacrifice can come an offering far greater and eternal: prayer. Pray without ceasing for your children.

> *Lord, protect my children from the schemes of the devil. Give them discerning hearts and wise minds to steer clear of the enemy's traps. I pray that You would provide a hedge of protection about them all the days of their lives.*

*Holding fast the word of life, so that in the day of Christ I may
have cause to glory because I did not run in vain nor toil in vain.
(Philippians 2:16)*

One day as I fixed my hair and make-up before leaving for a meeting,
four-year-old Seth asked if he could go with me to a "grown-up
meeting" sometime. I responded gently, "Only grown-ups will be there,
Seth. I think you'd be really bored." His eyes brightened and he said, "Oh
no, Mommy, I wouldn't be bored. You'd be there, and I love to be with
you!"

Those words were a breath of life to me. Staying at home with young
children can be so draining. I am left feeling lifeless at times, wondering if
my efforts are in vain. But moments like those with my sons bring life back
into me. It is words such as "I love to be with you, Mommy" that reassure
us. The benefits of staying home with our kids are found in treasured state-
ments like this. In moments of discouragement, we can recall a memory to
renew us.

One way to recall those precious moments is to write them down. Get a
journal and record when your children do or say something that blesses
you. Write down everything that will encourage you later, no matter how
small. It's often the little things that bring big reward!

*Lord, thank You for sending me encouragement through the words
of my children. Help me to remember that being home with them is
priceless and life-giving.*

———— ✿ ————

Then the LORD said to Moses, "Behold, I will rain bread from heaven for you; and the people shall go out and gather a day's portion every day, that I may test them, whether or not they will walk in My instruction." (Exodus 16:4)

When the Israelites were stuck in the wilderness for forty years they had plenty to worry about. What would they eat? Where would they sleep? How would they survive? These were legitimate questions. But the Israelites forgot one important thing: The God of the universe was with them. They focused so intensely on their circumstances that they forgot the power of the Almighty God. I'm sure many of us, had we lived in that day, would have been grumbling with them. God proved His grace and provision to them repeatedly, however.

The Israelites had the same problem as many of us today; we wonder if we are going to have enough until tomorrow. Many households today live paycheck to paycheck. The Israelites too lived day to day, collecting the manna that God rained down on them. There was always enough. Still, some Israelites disregarded the instructions and collected more than a day's worth of manna at a time. Their disobedience led to rotten food filled with worms (Exodus 16:20).

When the Israelites finally decided to trust God and obey His instructions precisely, they had nothing to worry about. God met their needs, one at a time. They never had extra, but they didn't need extra. They only needed enough, and that is what God gave them.

As a one-income family, we have learned to survive on "just enough." God instructed the Israelites to gather extra manna on the sixth day to last for the Sabbath day of rest. In the same way, God will provide extra when we need it. He knows what lies ahead, and He will carry us through.

Lord, thank You for Your provision. You have always provided us with enough. Forgive me when I only want more. Teach me to be content with what I have and to be a good steward of all that You have provided.

*He said to them, "It is not for you to know times or epochs which the
Father has fixed by His own authority." (Acts 1:7)*

This day of the year is special to me; it was the day my second son
was born at 3:10 a.m.! Levi's arrival was unexpected; I had gone
into labor seventeen days before his due date. I would like to say I was
ready for him to join us, but I wasn't. I was planning to attend a women's
retreat one week before he was due, and his early arrival put a kink in my
plans. Sometimes God brings about events in a different way than we
would prefer. Being a parent can be inconvenient. In the eyes of my hus-
band, it wasn't exactly convenient to be awake and alert at 3:00 a.m. But
that's what being a daddy required.

There are times when being a mother means inconvenience, interrup-
tions or changed plans. But I have learned that God's timing is not always
the same as ours. We enjoyed one of our biggest blessings at an unexpected
moment.

The circumstances surrounding Levi's birth remind me that all we do is un-
der God's authority. Being a stay-at-home mom means trusting in God's tim-
ing. You never know when a teachable moment or memory-building
opportunity will surface. I will only be able to enjoy those moments if I am
around. I don't understand how we will make ends meet as a one-income fam-
ily, but I don't have to understand it. I just need to rely on God's timing, be-
lieving that He knows best—even at 3:10 a.m.! The best often comes at the
most unexpected times.

*Lord, I acknowledge that You are in authority over my life. I put
my trust in You. May I rest in the assurance that Your timing is
perfect.*

And let the favor of the Lord our God be upon us;
And do confirm for us the work of our hands;
Yes, confirm the work of our hands. (Psalm 90:17)

Our older son is gifted in any game that involves a ball. As a toddler, that's all he ever wanted to play. When he neared preschool age, however, I realized I needed to help him develop other skills.

We worked diligently on learning colors, shapes, numbers and the alphabet. But he had a difficult time coloring in the lines. He could not sit still long enough to focus on coloring neatly in the lines of a picture. This frustrated me because I felt he needed to learn patience and self-control in this area. At first my frustration led to comments such as, "You're not finished" and "You can do better than that." Slowly I realized that my negative remarks were de-motivating him.

I decided to take a different approach. "Today, Seth, you get to pick the picture and color as much or as little as you like. But I'd like you to try as hard as you can to color in the lines. It helps you learn how to focus, and focusing is an important skill that you will use often, even in playing ball. So just try, and I promise I'll be excited about your picture, no matter what."

That day for the first time Seth colored in the lines—for the most part. I praised his work, and he kept on coloring. That day marked the beginning of Seth's love for drawing. Now his artwork won't all fit on the refrigerator. I tape them on the inside of my kitchen cabinets. Every time I open one, I remember to "confirm the work of [his] hands."

We need to affirm our children in areas in which they struggle. Their performance will improve at the rate of our encouraging words. Try an experiment. For the next week, praise them for their efforts in their difficult areas. Do not utter one negative remark. Speak only positive words and see if it improves their efficiency. New self-confidence will result. Nothing improves a child's hearing more than praise!

Lord, thank You for showing me the benefits of encouraging words.
Help me to affirm my children in everything they do.

April 20

I was very glad to find some of your children walking in truth, just as we have received commandment to do from the Father. (2 John 4)

We were enjoying the company of friends at a backyard barbecue at our home. Several kids played in the backyard and adults had congregated in the kitchen. We were talking about the new carpet I wanted but couldn't afford. Then a scream shattered the quiet. Outside, my four-year-old stood staring at the little boy who had screamed. He was holding his face and crying. Then he began pointing at Seth. When I asked Seth what had happened, he silently hung his head. I sent him to his room, following close behind.

"I'm sorry, Mom," Seth said. "I just got frustrated because he wouldn't do what I wanted him to do, so I hit him!" His honesty shocked me. I was expecting him to defend his actions, not take responsibility for them. Now sitting on the edge of the bed, I slipped an arm around Seth's sagging shoulders.

"Well, Seth," I began. "It was wrong of you to hit that boy, but it was right of you to tell me the truth. We need to talk about some constructive ways for you to handle your frustration."

Seth broke in, "Well, Mom, the Bible says to always tell the truth, so I had to!"

Wouldn't it be great if we all looked at the truth that way? I was proud of Seth because he chose to walk in truth despite the negative consequences. It is a lesson in truth I have never forgotten, and a benefit I reap from staying home with my kids to teach them the truth of God's Word. I'd rather carpet my home in truth than a new shade of shag any day.

Lord, thank You for children who walk in the truth of Your Word. Help me to be diligent in teaching this virtue. I pray they would always see the benefit of speaking the truth in every circumstance.

A good name is to be more desired than great riches. (Proverbs 22:1)

My husband glared at me. With calculator in hand, bank statements spread out before him, he reprimanded, "Laura, you bounced more checks! When are you going to stay within the budget?" he demanded.

"When you give me a budget I can stay in!" I retorted defensively, and I retreated to the den to read—sulk, actually—in peace.

That conversation was a monthly event at our house for years. Jimmy set up a budget for the month, and I exceeded it. We exchanged a few heated words when the bank statements came. He generally ended up mad, and I, hurt. I tried to stay within the budget, but unexpected expenses always seemed to pop up and, checkbook in hand, I would take care of them. Inevitably, I bounced a check or two . . . or three or four . . . every month.

Our "system" simply wasn't working. Jimmy often reminded me that an overdrawn checking account was not a good Christian witness. He was concerned that our name would soon be tarnished, and I was concerned that he wouldn't give me the checkbook anymore. One month we implemented a new idea that broke the dangerous cycle of overspending.

We heard an idea that a Christian financial advisor was promoting on the radio. He suggested cashing your paycheck each week and putting it in envelopes marked groceries, gifts, baby-sitting, clothing, etc. The amount in each envelope depends on what remains after fixed expenses are paid. The idea is to use the cash instead of the checkbook. Once the money is gone, it's gone!

The envelope method has worked well for us. Budgeting is no longer a stressful experience. Our kitchen table is no longer strewn with bank statements; instead it is covered with envelopes!

> *Lord, thank You for showing us how to budget our money and spend it wisely. May we always be responsible with our finances and, as a result, possess a name that brings honor to You.*

"Whoever then humbles himself as this child, he is the greatest in the kingdom of heaven." (Matthew 18:4)

Children have incredible faith. They take God at His Word. They take us at our word. A friend who is also a stay-at-home mom told me about an incident that illustrates this.

With only one car in the family, Kellie was constantly chauffeur to her husband or her daughter, Hannah. Kellie kept paper and markers in the car to help entertain Hannah during their frequent car rides. One time, Hannah talked about drawing a picture for Jesus, and she drew one filled with colorful balloons. When they arrived home, Hannah ran down the sidewalk holding the picture high above her. "Mom, where is the wind? I want to send my picture to Jesus in heaven!"

In her childlike faith, Hannah was determined to get her picture to Him—with a little help from the wind. We adults fret, worry and lack faith that God will take care of our needs. A child doesn't doubt. It is this kind of loyalty that God desires of us. Usually, our maturity stunts our faith. Ironic, isn't it?

Listen to comments your children make about God; watch what they do. They believe, they trust, they are humble. "Humble" means to become like a little child, exhibiting trust, openness and an eagerness to learn. We should seek these qualities. Ask God to once again give you childlike faith.

Lord, I know You are able to take care of my every need. But at times I allow worry and fear to cloud my faith. Give me the faith of a little child, faith that sees only You, not all the circumstances that try to crowd You out.

"It is easier for a camel to go through the eye of a needle than for a rich man to enter the kingdom of God." (Mark 10:25)

These words, spoken by Jesus, settle any discrepancy about the benefits of money versus mothering. He was telling the story of a rich young ruler who had come to Him. (See Mark 10:17-25) This ruler had all the material possessions that money could buy. Still, he lacked something. He implored of Jesus, "What shall I do to inherit eternal life?" The ruler felt relieved when Jesus listed a few commandments, because he had a clean track record. But when Jesus touched on the issue closest to this man's heart, the ruler sadly retreated. He was not willing to give up his possessions to gain the most valuable treasure of all: eternal life.

This passage exposes a problem with the human heart. This man's love of material wealth outweighed his devotion to Christ. A friend of mine says that this is the problem of the heart. Many of us would rather have more "stuff" than more of God. We pursue selfish dreams and desires rather than what God would have us to do.

Many new mothers return to a full-time job, leaving the care of their small children to someone else. Some truly have no alternative. Others, though, want money's earthly pleasures more than they want children who are firmly rooted in God's Word. If you are not the main influence in your kids' life, then someone else is. I don't want to leave my children's understanding of salvation up to someone else's teaching. More than a new wardrobe is at stake; we're talking eternity!

Grace, not performance, is the pathway to salvation. God's grace comes when we recognize that our need for a Savior is greater than our need for money.

Where is your heart?

Lord, guide my heart to complete devotion to You. I pray that my family will always be more important to me than money and possessions. Help me to keep an eternal perspective.

"And do not seek what you shall eat, and what you shall drink, and do not keep worrying." (Luke 12:29)

During the first few years after I stopped working, it was difficult for me not to worry about money. It seemed that no matter how carefully we budgeted, unexpected expenses always came up. When we were told that Seth needed to have tubes surgically implanted in his ears, we had just changed insurance companies. Our new insurance carrier would not commit to cover the expenses. My first response was to worry: How are we going to pay for this? Seth had to have the surgery. I had a choice: I could either trust God, or I could worry. Luke 12:29 seemed like the logical choice: "Do not keep worrying." Worrying would not change the situation, but I knew that God could. I chose to trust Him. The next week we received an unexpected check in the mail. It was enough to cover our cost for Seth's surgery!

You may have a financial need right now that has caused you to worry instead of trusting God. He will provide for you if you will trust Him. It may not be an unexpected check, but His means for provision are limitless. Over time I have learned to trust God with every financial need. It is a conscious choice to trust instead of worry. I have learned that I cannot live in a state of anxiety and trust God at the same time; fear and faith cannot coexist.

Lord, thank You for faithfully taking care of my family's financial needs. When the unforeseen happens, Lord, I want my first instinct to be faith, not fear. Teach me to trust You.

His radiance is like the sunlight. (Habakkuk 3:4)

When home with our children, we are often blessed by special moments that we would otherwise miss if they were in someone else's care. The mom who is rushing to leave the house in the morning cannot step through "windows of opportunity" that our children open. One such moment occurred for my friend Melinda.

As Melinda dressed three-year-old Emily one morning, the sky was overcast and a hazy film floated through the air. Suddenly, the sun popped out from behind a cloud and filled Emily's room with its brilliance and warmth. Emily stood transfixed, squinting into the bright window. "Look Mommy, God is coming in to say good morning to us," she said. Her daughter's words warmed Melinda's heart. "Yes, Emily, you're right," she said. "It does seem that God is popping in to say hello."

Children have an extraordinary way of seeing God in the ordinary. Emily's perception of the sunshine refreshed her mother's view of God and how He communicates with us. This preschooler's observation was a window of opportunity for mother and daughter to talk about God. We need to recognize the opportunities our children present to us. As stay-at-home moms we more often can do that because our time is our own. That benefit is bigger than we sometimes appreciate.

> *Lord, I pray that You would bring about moments of sharing and teaching with my children. Help me not be too rushed or distracted to miss those opportunities to teach them about You.*

And everything you ask in prayer, believing, you shall receive.
(Matthew 21:22)

As my friend Missy shared bedtime prayers with her two young sons, she prayed for the children's great grandmother, who had been hospitalized that week. "My great grandma is in the hospital?" four-year-old Zachary asked, and he immediately began sobbing. Missy held her son close, trying to soothe him. "You know, Zachary, you could help Great Grandma by praying for her. That is the very best thing you can do." He nodded and lay his head on the pillow.

After the children were asleep, Missy and her husband got a sad report. His grandmother's condition was worsening and unstable. Missy thought of Zachary's sensitive heart and decided to keep this new information to herself.

The next morning, Zachary bounded from bed. He reported that he had prayed for his great grandma, and he knew she would be fine. In fact, he wanted to go see her! As she loaded her sons into the car, Missy prayed that her son would not be disappointed. At the hospital, Missy was surprised to see her grandma sitting up and eating breakfast. They were thrilled to discover that, after a week on it, she no longer needed oxygen! Grandma announced, "God touched me last night." Zachary smiled knowingly.

Our children teach us to pray with a believing heart. God's Word tells us to walk by faith, not by sight. As Zachary demonstrated, children see with their hearts, not their eyes. Ask God right now to give you a heart of faith.

Lord, fill my heart with faith that does not waver in the midst of circumstances. Teach me to pray, believing with all of my heart that You will hear and answer.

But godliness actually is a means of great gain, when accompanied by contentment. (1 Timothy 6:6)

In this Scripture, the author contrasts godliness to material gain. He continues in the next verse, "We have brought nothing into this world, so we cannot take anything out of it either." These two verses paint a clear picture of where our priorities should lie with money and possessions. I once heard someone say, "If you can't take it with you when you go, then it's not important." The time and love we put into our children will always be with us and them. Relationships will last into eternity.

This verse has a condition within it. Godliness alone does not necessarily define great gain. Only "when accompanied by contentment" is it considered great. Godliness is a gain by any definition—isn't that what we strive for? The secret lies in contentment. The author wants to be sure Timothy knows that godliness without contentment will not bring true satisfaction. If we constantly strive for more than what we have, we are not content. If we are not content with the circumstances God has given us, then we will never know true godliness. Part of godliness is doing the best with what we have been given.

Are you content with what you have, or are you constantly saying, "I'll be happy when I have this or that"? Decide today to be satisfied with what you have. Choosing contentment will give an inner peace that money cannot buy.

Lord, thank You for all You have given to me. Forgive me for never being satisfied with what I have. Help me to be content in my circumstances and, as a result, bring me closer to godliness—and to You.

"For this boy I prayed, and the LORD has given me my petition which I asked of Him. So I have dedicated him to the LORD; as long as he lives he is dedicated to the LORD." (1 Samuel 1:27-28)

Many women can relate to Hannah's longing to be a mother. (See 1 Samuel 1.) Hannah loved God and her husband, but she felt a void that only a child could fill. She poured out her heart to God, not just to her friends. He chose to make Hannah wait because He wanted her to lean on Him alone for her security. When she entered into deeper commitment to the Lord, He gave her a son.

A dear friend and her husband wanted a child desperately. They eventually turned to medical experts. Tests revealed that fibroid tumors on her uterus were preventing pregnancy. She underwent surgery to remove the tumors and, after a time of healing, tried to conceive again. After six more months, God blessed her, and today she enjoys her newborn son.

Waiting for two years for God's perfect timing was difficult. As my friend poured out her heart to Him, she learned to be grateful even without children. She struggled and fought feelings of anger. When she finally surrendered it all and told God she would be happy even if He never gave her children, He gave her a son!

Perhaps you feel the same pain that my friend and Hannah experienced. I want to encourage you to trust the Lord and surrender your desires to Him. Pour out your heart to Him and believe that He will answer your prayer in His perfect timing. Will you still trust Him if the answer is "no"? He will give you the strength to get through whatever lies ahead, as long as you lean on Him.

Lord, thank You for blessing me with two beautiful sons. I confess that I do not express my gratitude enough. Instead I complain about the work of caring for two busy boys! Teach me to cherish them. I dedicate them to You.

April 29

In all labor there is profit,
But mere talk leads only to poverty. (Proverbs 14:23)

We all have bills to pay. We all need the basic necessities of food, shelter and clothing to live comfortably. We all need a certain amount of money to afford these "necessities." The Bible clearly states that if we want to eat, we need to work. Most of us will not dispute these needs. But what one classifies as a "need" another classifies as a "want." The choice to stay home boils down to one thing: How much do you really need?

Jim Elliot, the young missionary who was martyred serving God in Ecuador, knew the value of labor. He labored all of his days for the Lord. He owned little of material value. Rather, his treasures were eternal. He said, "He is no fool who gives up what he cannot keep to gain what he cannot lose."

Our children need us more than we need new furniture. We cannot keep material possessions, but we can keep relationships we build with our children. When we give up working outside the home, we gain time with them—a necessity in building relationships. When we gain the trust of our children, we can guide them into a relationship with the Lord. That is something they will never lose. You may be laboring away outside the home to provide for many "wants." But what about your children's wants? All children want to spend more time with Mom!

I'd rather be financially bankrupt than spiritually bankrupt. The biggest bank account means nothing in eternity, but our spiritual bank account means everything!

> *Lord, I pray that You will help me to focus on the eternal benefits of laboring for You while raising my children. Give me Your perspective as I define the needs and wants in my life. May I be willing to sacrifice what I cannot keep to gain what I cannot lose.*

Therefore if any man is in Christ, he is a new creature; the old things have passed away; behold, new things have come. (2 Corinthians 5:17)

Before I became a Christian, I wanted to have children—someday. But I did not want them to get in the way of my career. I planned to be an executive at the top of the corporate ladder. Somewhere along that climb, God got hold of me and changed my perspective. As I read my Bible, I discovered that God had a plan for mothers too.

Some days, seeing the benefits of staying home with my two young sons is a struggle. They demand so much time and energy, and with other duties of running a household, I often feel overwhelmed. The enemy uses stress and anxiety to get us off course. Satan wants us to run with our plan, instead of God's. The beauty of being a Christian is that I can run to God anytime I need His help. When I get stuck in my old frame of mind, I ask Him to renew it. And He does! Faithfully!

In renewing my mind, I choose to change my thinking to the truth of God's Word rather than basing it on fluctuating feelings. I feel the temptation to work outside my home full-time and put my children in someone else's care. But the truth of God's Word is that I am to be "a worker at home" (Titus 2:5), and that includes investing my life in my husband and children. When I dwell on the truth instead of my feelings, it is easy to see the benefits of being a stay-at-home mom.

> *Lord, thank You for making me a "new creature" in You. I pray that You will help me to live by the truth of Your Word every day rather than by my feelings. Transform my mind into a reflection of Your Word.*

May:
Coffee Breaks

I need a break!

If you are not taking a couple of hours weekly just for you, then you are headed for trouble in the sanity department—especially if you care for toddlers all day. "Sounds great," you say. But who will take care of the kids? I have a simple answer: "Mom's Morning Out" (MMO).

Three other mothers of toddlers and I formed a MMO. Every Tuesday morning one of us watched all of our kids while the other three moms did whatever they wanted for three hours. We rotated and cared for the children at our homes. I looked forward to that time every week. All you need to form your own **MMO** is at least three willing friends with preschoolers.

In addition to time for ourselves, we also need friendships with other women. Most women don't feel they have the time to develop such crucial relationships. Yet, the rewards are worth the effort. Whether it's lunch out with a friend or coffee and conversation while the kids play together, women encourage and energize each other.

Women can comfort each other in time of crisis in ways men cannot. But to do that, trust has to be established, a friendship built—and that takes time. I urge you to carve out that time. This month we will discover the imperative function of refueling for stay-at-home moms. It is part of God's perfect plan.

May 1

We who had sweet fellowship together,
Walked in the house of God in the throng. (Psalm 55:14)

From infancy to adulthood, all of us have a God-given need to feel loved and accepted. Many people try to deny that desire and listen to society say we are to be self-sufficient. Women who stay at home fall into the trap of the "super-mom" image: They must keep a perfect house, have perfect children and always look perfectly attractive. We set ourselves up for sure failure when the goal is perfection. It leads to feelings of inadequacy, a negative self-image—and more isolation.

God did not create us to be alone. That's why he created Eve for Adam (Genesis 2:18). We were created for fellowship with God and with one another. Women's friendships supply nurturing that we all crave. Now is your chance to climb out of the "super-mom" trap and begin to develop friendships with other women. If it is hard for you to reach out to others, ask God to bring a special friend to you. He will provide fellowship for you. It is part of His plan for your good.

> *Lord, thank You for creating fellowship. Help me to make the time to enjoy fellowship and friendship with other women. Protect my mind from the lie that I have to be self-sufficient and independent. Help me to strive not for perfection, but for Your perfect plan for my life.*

But if we walk in the light as He Himself is in the light, we have fellowship with one another. (1 John 1:7)

God ordained fellowship, and when we walk in obedience to Him, fellowship naturally follows. Relationships with family and friends are affected by our relationship with God. When we are out of sync with God, we are out of sync with the people surrounding us, as well.

When I am short on patience with my children, or don't have time to spend with them, it is a day that I have neglected to spend time with God. I lack understanding for a friend who needs to talk when I have not begun my day with God. I am irritable with my husband when I cut out my daily Bible reading and prayer in order to clean the house. Yet, when I take a few minutes each day for fellowship with God, I enter a sacred place that allows sweet fellowship with all others in my life.

"Fellowship" is defined as "a mutual sharing." One of its synonyms is "companionship." This week, share time with God first *and* with a friend. Fellowship in the proper order will satisfy more than your social needs; it will satisfy your soul.

Thank you, Lord, for showing me the proper order to fellowship. May I begin each day in fellowship with You so that my fellowship with others will be as You intended.

That I may be encouraged together with you while among you, each of us by the other's faith, both yours and mine. (Romans 1:12)

We sat at Kelly's kitchen table in tears. The mothers of strong-willed toddlers, we were discouraged, disheartened and just plain exhausted. More than two years ago, we had begun meeting at her table over coffee and complaints. The first time we shared what burdened us, we did so cautiously: I had wondered if she would think I'm a terrible mother if I told her of my frustration. But she had been wondering the same thing. Within minutes, we were pouring out our hearts to each other.

Kelly and I instantly became friends. We confided in each other often; we laughed and cried over the ups and downs of motherhood. We were never afraid to be completely honest with each other. The best part was that we shared a relationship with God. From that foundation, we encouraged each other. God never allowed us to be really down at the same time. When one of us was struggling, the other had an encouraging word

I'll never forget the day Kelly told me she was moving to the East Coast. "Florida! That's as far away from Arizona as you can get!" I gasped. "I know," she replied with tears in her eyes. My heart felt heavy, as if a part was being ripped away. We had shared so much together in our three years of friendship. I realized that our friendship would survive the distance because it was built on faith. God brought Kelly into my life when He knew I needed her the most. His love would build a bridge between our hearts all the way from Arizona to Florida. But my life wouldn't quite be the same without our regular talks at Kelly's kitchen table.

Thank You, Lord, for the very special friends you have put into my life. Help me to be the kind of friend I want to have. Show me how to encourage and build up others.

To the woman He said, "I will greatly multiply your pain in childbirth, In pain you shall bring forth children." (Genesis 3:16)

No doubt about it: Giving birth is painful! I have several friends who suffered those nightmarish forty-eight-hour labors. My labors were relatively short, but not pain-free! The pain of childbirth is a reminder of the severity of Eve's transgression in the garden. It is proof that we often suffer the consequences of sin long after.

Unfortunately, the physical discomfort of giving birth does not disappear immediately. A time of healing and rest is necessary after the exhausting experience of labor and delivery. Although a husband can be a great help during this time, there is a certain comfort that only another woman can provide. A man does not have the capability to give birth, so he will never completely understand how it feels. My friend Debbie had given birth to her second child four days earlier when she called me. The baby had been up all night crying, depriving the entire household of sleep. She was still swollen and sore from giving birth, and she was now in pain from the engorgement that first accompanies milk production. I could hear the edge in her voice and knew she had been crying. I had given birth to Levi two weeks earlier, and she was calling for encouragement. I assured her that I had experienced those problems. Talking with me gave her hope that she, too, would get through them.

Women need other women. God uses us to sometimes comfort and encourage when a man simply cannot.

Lord, thank You for the miracle of giving birth.

But I say, walk by the Spirit, and you will not carry out the desire of the flesh. (Galatians 5:16)

When you become a mother, you are suddenly responsible for others' lives. Sometimes that means sacrificing what you *want* to do for what you *need* to do—when that is best for your children. When your desires conflict with God's will, you have an important decision to make.

I had an important decision to make. Our church had a women's retreat scheduled, and I was looking forward to the weekend away. The retreats had proven to be a wonderful time of fellowship with other women and with God. I had pioneered this ministry at our church, so it had a special place in my heart.

To my surprise, eight days before the retreat, I went into labor and gave birth to our second beautiful son. Some would consider that a clear sign that I should not attend the retreat. Not me! I still felt I was to go to the retreat and take the baby with me. My husband and mother both voiced concern over taking a newborn into a crowd of women, risking the possibility of germs and illness. I prayed for God to give me an answer through Levi's pediatrician. When he advised against it, I had my answer. Later that afternoon, Levi ended up in the hospital where he spent forty-eight hours because of severe jaundice.

As much as I wanted to go to that retreat, I knew it was not what God wanted. It was in my son's best interest for me to stay home. It was not an easy decision, and yet I knew it was right. I also knew it would not be the last time that God would call me to put the needs of my children above my own desires.

Lord, help me to always look out for my children's best interests, even when it means sacrificing my desires. Help me to listen to Your voice instead of my own. Give me a selfless attitude as I serve my children and You.

May 6

Therefore encourage one another, and build up one another, just as you also are doing. (1 Thessalonians 5:11)

As part of our women's ministries at church, we have a "Secret Sister" program. The goal is to secretly do small acts of kindness and encouragement for the woman whose name you have drawn. It is a wonderful way to practice anonymous giving and serving, which Jesus encourages in His Word. In turn, you have a secret sister making you feel special. It is a beneficial and uplifting program; I encourage you to start one. I was feeling really down one day about my abilities as a mother. Seth was a challenging two-year-old. Some days felt like one long power struggle, and I was exhausted. I had begun to wonder if my efforts to train him with biblical standards were making any kind of impact on his little heart. Then my secret sister sent a note to say that she had been observing the practices with which I raised my son. She said she was impressed with my mothering skills and the results they produced in Seth! She called him an obedient and delightful little boy.

She had no idea of the power of those words; they were like water for a thirsty soul. The most amazing thing was that somehow she knew what I was going through. God had communicated to her for me.

A few years have past, but my secret sister's words still encourage me today. Words are powerful. Use them to build up someone today.

Lord, show me how to encourage the other women around me in their efforts as stay-at-home moms. Make me sensitive to the individual needs and situations of my sisters in Christ.

Let no unwholesome word proceed from your mouth, but only such a word as is good for edification according to the need of the moment, that it may give grace to those who hear. (Ephesians 4:29)

Just as encouraging words can build up others, discouraging words can tear them down. My family has adopted today's Scripture verse. We use this verse to remind each other when we are not speaking kindly. Words are powerful because, once spoken, they cannot be erased. They have the power to either fashion or destroy. Certain actions can be undone, but once something is said, it cannot be altered. Whether it is a family member, a friend or even a stranger I am speaking to, I try to live by Ephesians 4:29. I make many mistakes, and that is why I ask my family to gently remind me if I do not reflect this Scripture's truth.

Another verse our family uses is Ephesians 5:4: "And there must be no filthiness and silly talk, or coarse jesting, which are not fitting, but rather giving of thanks." A simple hand signal to the speech offender is a quiet and gentle way of holding someone accountable. Sometimes you won't like the correction, especially if it comes from your child. You must be ready to live by the standard by which you train your children.

If you have difficulty with a certain temptation or an ungodly habit, consider confiding in a friend. Give her permission to hold you accountable if she sees you in error. Do not become offended—remember, you asked for help. If you will yield yourself to God in the areas of your life that you know do not please Him, and bring a trusted friend into your quest for godliness, you will be strengthened.

Lord, may every word I speak glorify You and edify others. Help me to say only things that are true, wholesome, kind, necessary and honorable.

He makes me lie down in green pastures;
  He leads me beside quiet waters. He restores my soul. (Psalm 23:2-3)

This story comes from Kay Arthur's book, *Lord, I Want to Know You.*

The muffled, distant sound had broken the quiet reverie of his walk across the meadow. The sharp barking of a dog almost irritated him. It was abrasive in that tranquil setting. As the barking grew louder his eyes scanned the meadow, looking for the culprit. Suddenly, a small doe broke through the edge of the woods. Now he understood. Leaning against the fence post, the man watched with compassion as the doe cut across the broad expanse of meadow. She was running straight toward him. He stood motionless, not wanting to add the fear of man to the animal's frustration. As the frightened fawn leaped the fence, she staggered. The chase had taken its toll. Her wet coat gleaming in the sun, the doe stopped, took a few steps in one direction, then, ears held high, looked back toward the sound of the barking. The dog had broken through the woods. Eyes wide with fright, seemingly confused and worn out, the doe surveyed her surroundings until she discovered the man standing beside the fence. Looking back again at the dog in hot pursuit, then at the expanse of open field before her, she turned weakly and walked straight toward the man and buried her head in his tummy. Compassion filled his eyes. She had found a protector.

What a beautiful picture! This story illustrates the need for rest and protection. As stay-at-home moms, our levels of frustration and exhaustion can tip the scales when our energy is spent. When we reach such valleys, we want nothing more than to run and hide. To rest. To be alone. Where do you run when you are all used up? Do you run to the Great Shepherd to protect you? Run to Him now.

> *Lord, when I am weary of the demands of being a mother, give me the strength to take my last steps into Your arms. May I find peace.*

May 9

And to whom did He swear that they should not enter His rest, but to those who were disobedient? (Hebrews 3:18)

You have heard that the Sabbath is supposed to be a day of rest. Families used to take this seriously, enjoying time together at church in the morning and then having a family day for the rest of the day. No one was allowed to work; the day was reserved for rest and relaxation. I remember when I was growing up, my parents took this command seriously. Although my father worked many hours Monday through Saturday, I don't ever remember him working on a Sunday. We went to church for worship services and then we spent the rest of the day together. Whether it was a special trip to the zoo, the beach or the park, or just a day spent playing croquet or badminton in the backyard, the whole family knew Sunday was our day together. We looked forward to it. (Even as teenagers, my brothers and I might not have admitted it to our parents, but we liked the idea of doing something together.) It provided a certain sense of security. We knew that my mom and dad cared about us and wanted to spend time with us. Unfortunately, our society has gotten away from this holy day of rest. Many men go to work because they "have so much to do" and after church, if they go to church, mom goes her way and the kids go theirs. When we refuse to follow God's guidance on this issue, keeping the Sabbath holy, as a day of rest, then we will enter unrest in every area of our life. Even God rested on the seventh day after completing creation, and He commands us to do the same in His Word. Everyone needs a break. It's not healthy to work all the time—that includes mothers. Sundays should be the day you take a break from the washing, ironing and cleaning. Go out to eat if you can afford it, or have everyone pitch in to help at home with the family meal, so you don't get stuck in the kitchen all day.

Take some time to rest and play. Start by setting up a family meeting and discuss the importance of having a "family day." Make it positive! Be ready to present ideas of fun things you can do and ask the children for their ideas. Take turns each week letting family members pick the event for the upcoming Sunday. Then, relax and enjoy the rest God intended you to experience!

Lord, draw my family closer together through consistent designated "family time." Bless our home.

A friend loves at all times,
And a brother is born for adversity. (Proverbs 17:17)

My husband often says that at the end of his life, if he can count his closest friends on one hand, he will die a fortunate man. Five good friends may not sound like much, but think about it for just a minute. We're talking close friends—Proverbs 17:17 friends. The ones who laugh with you, cry with you, walk through the storms in your life with you, sometimes even carry you through those storms. The ones you can call in the middle of the night if you need to—and they won't hang up on you! The ones you can be "real" with and they'll still love you. The ones who aren't afraid to tell you when you're wrong, and rejoice with you when you're right. The ones who will stand by you at any time, no matter what. I have a dear friend who knows every horrid detail about my past, and she still loves me! She has trudged with me faithfully through all the muck and mire of my life. Do you have any friends like that?

To build a friendship like the one described above takes a lot of time and effort. Many people don't want to expend the energy necessary to build such a friendship but they want to reap the benefits. Unfortunately, it doesn't work that way. You can't reap what you don't sow. To invest the time and energy into a few select women in our lives is well worth the effort. Knowing that I have a few friends I can call in the middle of the night for anything, and they would respond to my need, is a very comforting feeling. I have not always had friends like that in my life though. It has only been since I have invested time into these friendships that such results have been produced.

Friends, the kind Proverbs 17:17 talks about, are there for us when it is inconvenient and uncomfortable. They love us when we are the most difficult to love; they carry us when we are too weary to take another step and they pull out the umbrella when life starts to rain on us. How about you? Do you have any Proverbs 17:17 friends? Are you being the kind of friend that you'd like to have?

Thank You, Lord, for blessing me with some wonderful friends; I am so thankful for the times You have used them to show Your love to me and to get me through yet another storm in my life.

*Bear one another's burdens, and thus fulfill the law of Christ.
(Galatians 6:2)*

his Scripture verse is love in action. Bearing someone's burden turns love into a verb—an action verb. We were taking a weekly parenting class with five other couples for a period of seventeen weeks. One of the men was struggling with an illness and had been in a great deal of pain for about a month. We had been praying for Clark and his family throughout the ordeal. One evening he was so ill he stayed home from class, but his wife came. We had just wrapped up our session when Clark called looking for his wife. He was in excruciating pain and needed Kimberly to take him to the emergency room. She had already left to pick up her kids from the baby-sitter. Instinctively, we moved into action.

I have never seen a group of people react so immediately and so unselfishly. We devised a quick plan and scattered in various directions. A few people went to Clark's house to get him to the hospital, someone went to the baby-sitter's house to intercept Kimberly and pick up the kids and a few of us stayed to pray, answer the phone and wait for the children to arrive. The situation continued into the next day until Clark was finally scheduled for emergency surgery and things were under control. During all those hours their two children were cared for and fed, and there was someone with Clark and Kimberly in the hospital at all times. Following his surgery, he would be required to stay several days in the hospital so we immediately set up enough help with child care and meals to get them through that period.

The point is this: Not once did I hear anyone complain that they didn't have time to sit in the emergency room until 2:30 a.m., or that they had too many other things to do besides baby-sit or cook an extra meal. There was no second thought or selfish reaction to the burden our friends were experiencing. There was only one reaction—help Clark and Kimberly carry this burden. I witnessed love and friendship in action when the telephone rang that evening, and I experienced what it means to "bear one another's burden."

*Lord, thank You for teaching me to bear another's burden. Help me
to act unselfishly anytime a friend needs me. Give me the extra
strength I need to help carry the burdens my friends will face.*

May 12

The Lord's lovingkindnesses indeed never cease, for His compassions never fail. They are new every morning; Great is Thy faithfulness. (Lamentations 3:22-23)

I cannot count the number of times I have had a bad day, the kind when everything goes awry, and I wanted nothing more than to crawl into my bed and pull the sheets over my head, hoping that things would somehow look better in the morning. A good night's rest has a way of clearing my mind and heart, as well as my perspective. It's a challenge to think positive in the middle of a bad situation when my emotions are running high. Rest and quiet time alone with God are the best way to clear my head and set me on the right path. It often means I don't get even a moment's rest until my little ones are tucked into bed for the night. The demands of taking care of preschool-age children can leave me feeling so void of energy that I think I may never get out of bed again! I am not a morning person. It takes me a while to get going in the morning. I hit the snooze button half a dozen times before I drag myself out of bed. Since I get a surge of energy late in the evening, I often stay up later than I should, catching up on household duties or other projects. Some of my most productive time is when the rest of my family is asleep and the house is blissfully quiet. And yet, I have gone to bed time and time again glancing helplessly at the late hour on the clock, and pleading with God to "multiply my sleep." I am always amazed, when I do that, how rested I feel the next morning, even on the few hours of sleep I had.

God is merciful to me and gives me the energy I need to take care of my family. God always gets me through the next day, even when I think I'm so tired I'll fall flat on my face. His lovingkindness is bountiful and never ending. He wants to see us succeed as stay-at-home moms, and He will assist us if we call upon Him. When you have a bad day, go to bed asking God to give you His freshness for the next morning. You will be restored by His compassion and mercy.

Lord, thank You for answering me as I cry out to You in my weariness. Have mercy on me, as I sometimes struggle to meet the demands of raising a family and still get enough rest. Your lovingkindness to me is truly undeserved and yet, so appreciated.

"And the rain descended, and the floods came, and the winds blew, and burst against that house; and yet it did not fall, for it had been founded upon the rock." (Matthew 7:25)

I had a busy day planned with my two young children, then four and one. Things were carefully scheduled so we would make it home for lunch and naps—mothers of young children live for nap time! We began with haircuts for both. It was Levi's first. My husband thought his short curls made him look like a girl and insisted they be trimmed. I guess it's a "guy thing." Levi, however, was not ready for this ritual of manliness, and he screamed through the entire ordeal.

From the barbershop, we moved on to the pediatrician. After close to a one-hour wait, the doctor discovered Levi was anemic. We drove to the pharmacy to find that prescriptions would take up to forty-five minutes. I pointed to the tired, hungry, cranky one-year-old on my hip and said, "I think we'll take a drive while we wait."

We were all hungry but home was too far away and I was short on cash. So, I turned on some praise music to drown my kids' whining and just drove. "Help me Lord," I silently prayed. We returned to the pharmacy precisely thirty minutes later to be told we could have gotten the pills off the shelf without waiting. I bit my tongue to avoid saying something unkind.

When we pulled into the driveway, Levi was asleep, but woke up screaming as soon as I put him to bed and did not stop for several hours. My husband phoned to say he would be late. A while later, Seth threw up on the kitchen floor. At least it hit the linoleum, and not the carpet, I mused. There is always something to be thankful for! I continued praying for God's strength.

Somewhere between cleaning up Seth's mess and sitting with him until he drifted off to sleep, I found myself praying silently again. I had the clear sense that I was standing on Him, the Rock, despite the events of the day. In the midst of the storm, God had kept me dry and given me strength.

Lord, help me keep standing on You, the solid rock. Thank You for upholding me in the storms. Keep me strong as I anchor my life in You and bring me through the days when trouble pours itself out on me.

May 14

And he will be like a tree firmly planted by streams of water,
Which yields its fruit in its season, and its leaf does not wither;
And in whatever he does, he prospers. (Psalm 1:3)

Have you ever taken the time to admire an oak tree? Oak trees have sturdy, thick trunks and strong branches. They stand tall and majestic and can easily withstand heavy winds and rain. In fact, a storm will actually force an oak tree to spread its roots deeper into the ground. For every storm an oak tree endures, it gains strength and depth. Oak trees can live a long time and resist destruction through incredible storms primarily due to their strong roots. A willow tree, on the other hand, has a shallow root system. Its trunk is thin and pliable, and its branches are weak. A willow is easily uprooted during a storm. A strong wind will rip the branches from the tree and fling them destructively through the air.

How do you weather the storms of life? Are you like an oak, planted firmly in a relationship with Christ, only to spread your roots deeper into that relationship when trouble hits? Or are you like the willow tree, easily uprooted and thrown from your foundation when a trial comes?

We can be like the oak tree, standing tall and proud though life rages around us. All we need to do is to plant ourselves firmly into a relationship with Him. That includes spending time reading His Word. The Bible is like the fertilizer that will make us grow strong and send our roots deep. As mothers, we will certainly undergo many troubles and trials with our children. But those storms will not uproot us or destroy our families if we are firmly planted in Christ. When we spend time in God's Word, we will yield the fruit of peace and joy even in the midst of struggle.

Take a daily break from the storms of life in God's Word and see how you grow!

Make me strong, like the oak tree, Lord, able to withstand the
storms of life. May my roots go deep in You and may my family
flourish as a result of our relationship. Cultivate the fruits of righ-
teousness in me as I sink deep into Your Word.

He will die for lack of instruction,
And in the greatness of his folly he will go astray. (Proverbs 5:23)

When I was young, my brothers and I always seemed to get into trouble when we were bored. This typically occurred during the long summer months, when we were on vacation from school and there was suddenly a lack of structure in our lives. For some reason, we seemed to better stay out of trouble when there was structure ordering our days. Too much room to roam and suddenly, we had wandered into trouble. My mother did the best she could to provide instruction and structure for us to keep us out of trouble, but by the end of the summer, we were all a bit weary of each other, and the reins went slack.

One wise mom I know, who has raised four boys, had the same problem when her children were growing up. They constantly complained about being bored and badgered her for "something to do." She knew she needed to spend time with her kids, but she couldn't entertain them all day long and maintain her household—or her sanity! Realizing the need for a "break" from her kids during these long days, she came up with a great idea. She made a list of all of their toys and activities and categorized them. There was a category for outside toys, inside toys, board games, water toys and countless others. She was amazed when she made the list how much they really had to do! When any of her boys came to her and complained about having "nothing to do," she referred them to the list and required that they choose something to do. Each time they returned with a new complaint of boredom, she gave them a new category to choose from, and they were delighted that they had the opportunity to choose the activity. No more boredom and no more "nothing to do"!

Lord, help me to find the balance between creative play and the necessary structure and instruction for my kids. Give me patience and wisdom so that I might guide my children away from folly and foolishness.

May 16

But the fruit of the Spirit is love, joy, peace, patience, kindness, goodness, faithfulness, gentleness, self-control; against such things there is no law. (Galatians 5:22-23)

Grocery shopping with two young children wears me out! First, it is a major juggling act to fit both children and all the groceries I need into one cart. Then, I have to keep my toddler's hands off the fruit; he thinks they are balls just waiting to be thrown. And no matter what time of day I go, it seems that one of my kids gets fussy before we make it back to the car. Pushing around a whining, whimpering child and seeing the same shoppers over and over as I wind my way down the aisles is too humiliating. All the "extra" items—mostly cereals and cookies—I find in the cart when I arrive at the checkout counter is another problem. To save my place in line, I end up buying them knowing they will send me over budget and my husband into orbit!

After one such excursion I came across a poem called "Heaven's Grocery Store" by an unknown poet. It told the story of someone who ended up in a heavenly supermarket. An angel handed her a basket and told her to shop with care. Up and down the aisles she went helping herself to a box of wisdom, a bag of faith and a generous portion of free salvation. By the time she finished, the basket was piled high, but when she tried to pay for it, the angel said, "Jesus paid your bill a long time ago."

That poem actually changed my attitude about grocery shopping. Now, when I am pushing my cart with whining children, I close my eyes, breathe deep and pretend I am in Heaven's Grocery Store. I picture myself reaching to a top shelf for some patience, a bit of love and a little wisdom. As I near the once dreaded produce department, I imagine filling my cart with the fruit of the Spirit, as well as apples and oranges. At the checkout counter, no matter how high the bill, I smile, knowing that Jesus paid a much greater debt for me.

Lord, thank You for reminding me that You provide all I need. On days when the kids are wearing me down and I need a break, fill me up with the fruit of the Spirit.

And if one member suffers, all the members suffer with it; if one member is honored, all the members rejoice with it. (1 Corinthians 12:26)

My friend had been hurting for a long time and at last she was ready to talk. Over lunch in a favorite restaurant, the pain from the past few months spilled out with her tears. Right then she needed support, not advice. I patted her hand reassuringly and let her talk. Her high-profile position within our church made her an easy target for gossip and she felt a lot of pressure to keep up appearances, even though she was falling apart on the inside. As a church leader, everyone looked up to her. She feared if her struggles were exposed, she would be judged. In her mind, there was no margin for error in her life. *Where does that kind of pressure come from?* I wondered as I squeezed her hand again. Our lunch ended and I dropped her off with a few words of encouragement and a big hug. I promised to be a friend, no matter what.

As I drove home, I pondered the situation. In many ways I was like her. So many times, I find myself shouldering my burdens alone, and that is not what Christ wants us to do. He wants us to run to Him when we are hurting. However, sometimes we need the warmth of a human embrace. Like my four-year-old, who was afraid of the dark, said to me one night, "I called out to Jesus, but I needed a hug from someone with skin on!" Christ designed the church to be a body of huggers with skin on! We are to support each other in love and leave the judging to Him.

I want to be a supportive, loving person, not judgmental. I cannot change the entire church body, but I can change myself. And that is how the greatest changes take place, one person at a time.

> *Lord, help me to be the kind of friend to others that I want to have. Give me Your compassion, so that I may respond to others through love, not judgment. Show me how to comfort those who are hurting and how to celebrate with those who are rejoicing.*

And Moses cried out to the LORD, saying, "O God, heal her, I pray!" (Numbers 12:13)

The idea of intercessory prayer is first introduced to us in the Old Testament by Moses. He was praying for the healing of Miriam, who had been struck with leprosy. His prayers were eventually answered and she was indeed healed. Intercessory prayer is vital for mothers. We need to be both the recipients and the makers of such prayers.

One of the most effective ways friends can help us is to pray for us. I have a very special friend who seems to call at the times when I most need prayer. One day when both of my boys were suddenly struck with the flu, she called and said, "Is everything OK? For some reason, God just laid you on my heart, and I had to call!" God knew I needed someone to intercede on my behalf because I was so weary from caring for two sick children.

We also need to ask our friends how we can pray for them. Sometimes I will be in the middle of doing something and I suddenly think of a friend who has shared a need with me. I take that as a sign that God is telling me that person needs prayer at that very moment, so I pause in my task and intercede for them. These little prayer breaks in my routine help me to feel God's closeness all day long too.

We need to intercede in prayer for our kids too. Prayer is one of the single most important ways we can help them. Try praying over your children while they are sleeping at night. Pray for their salvation, their health, for them to make wise choices, for their friends and even for their future spouses. Praying parents make a difference in their children's lives.

Begin a routine of taking prayer breaks throughout your day. Call a friend to exchange prayer requests on a consistent basis, and begin to see what a difference prayer makes!

> *Lord, may I be more diligent in praying for my children, as well as other family and friends. Make me sensitive to Your voice, that I might know when I need to take a break and pray.*

May 19

And I said, "Oh that I had wings like a dove!
I would fly away and be at rest." (Psalm 55:6)

Have you ever been so overwhelmed with the duties of being a mother that you just wanted to run away? Even just for a day? It's not that you don't love your family, it's just that you are so weary from all of the demands on you that you know that you desperately need a break to avoid cracking up. We all know our limits for breaking up quarrels and picking up toys. Each of us knows when we are just beneath that boiling point.

Pressure is what makes volcanoes erupt. Pressure that has been built up over a long period of time. Sooner or later, it has to find release because it can't hold it all in anymore. Then it runs wild, and there is nothing that can stop it. We each have our boiling points too. There is a tremendous amount of pressure on a mother to often accomplish more than she is able. The pressure builds up, and if we don't have frequent outlets to relieve it, sooner or later we are going to explode. Unfortunately, it is usually the ones we care about the most that happen to be in our paths when we erupt. Consistent and frequent little releases of pressure in our lives will prevent us from spewing our feelings of frustration all over those we love.

Think about what relaxes you. It may be a hobby you enjoy, shopping, reading or exercising, maybe it's just taking a long walk outdoors. Whatever it is that loosens you up or calms you down, take time to schedule some frequent breaks to rest and release some pressure. Exercise has always been a great stress release for me. Taking a few minutes to read from God's Word also helps to calm me down if I am too close to a boiling point. I can run to God and spew all over Him and He doesn't mind! He wants me to pour out everything to Him. I often do and it always makes me feel much better.

There are days when I still feel like running away but they occur less frequently if I have been making time to take a break from the daily grind and release some pressure.

Lord, help me to run to You when I feel like I just can't take any-
more. Bring me rest and release through the time I make for myself,
as well as the comforting and renewing words of the Scriptures.

Worship the LORD with reverence,
And rejoice with trembling. . . .
How blessed are all who take refuge in Him! (Psalm 2:11-12)

I tried to sing the words to the worship song that the praise band was leading. I moved my mouth but the only sound that came out was something like a croaking noise. Realizing I was on the edge of tears, I sank into the pew and closed my eyes. I was so weary. My body felt numb. It had been a long week. Both of my children had contracted a stomach virus and for days, I had taken on the role of nurse in addition to all of my other "mom duties." Unfortunately, life does not come to a halt when the kids are sick. Answering frequent cries at all hours of the night for several nights in a row had led to sleep deprivation and had now given way to exhaustion. I hung my head in defeat. The tears began to roll down my cheeks. I couldn't stop them—I was so worn out, I didn't have the energy.

As I sat there, head now in my hands, trying to hide the tears from the curious eyes of those surrounding me, I quit trying to sing and just listened to the words that resonated around me. They spoke of finding peace in God alone and of drawing on His strength. One song followed another and I continued to sit and just rest in the words that were being lifted to the heavens, now words of His grace and mercy. I let the words of worship to the Lord envelope me and soon, I felt I too, was being lifted up to the heavens on the smooth melody of praise. I began to relax and the tears stopped flowing. I felt the presence of God and His sweet Spirit ministering to me within the words being sung. A new surge of strength lifted me to my feet and I joined in the chorus being lifted to God, sheepishly at first, then more boldly as my energy returned. By the end of the praise and worship time that morning, I felt like a new woman. I no longer carried the heavy load I had shouldered all week. It had been lifted up to the heavens on a song.

When you have had a tough week, seek the strength and renewal of the Lord through worshiping Him. There is refuge in His name!

Thank You, Lord, for the privilege of worshiping You and the blessing it brings to my life. When I am weary and I need a break, may I find comfort and strength in praising Your mighty name.

"The one who listens to you listens to Me, and the one who rejects you rejects Me; and he who rejects Me rejects the One who sent Me."
(Luke 10:16)

When someone rejects my faith, I take it personally. I was trying to develop a friendship with a nearby stay-at-home mom who had children very close in age to mine. We had many things in common, except one—our faith. I am a Christian; she is agnostic; she believes in God, but doesn't have a personal relationship with Him. I prayed for a clear opportunity to share my faith with my new friend. Since she already believed in God, I figured it wouldn't be too difficult to explain His desire to have an intimate relationship with each of us. I figured wrong.

One day, while walking, she asked me a question about the church we were attending. A flashing light went off in my brain: "Open door. Enter now!" I quickly prayed for wisdom, answered her question and then launched into a full presentation of the gospel, how it affected my life and how it could affect hers too. Then I invited her to church. She was speechless! Finally, she stammered that she was busy on Sunday and couldn't come. "OK," I replied, feeling a bit rejected. "Maybe another time." She shook her head as she hurried for her front door. "Sure. Maybe. Bye!"

I had totally overwhelmed her with my "saving grace" speech. In my zeal, I had gone way beyond the boundaries of the question she had asked. She wasn't ready to hear the gospel, but I had dumped it on her anyway. Feeling really rejected, I continued to beat myself up until God spoke to me: "She isn't rejecting you, Laura. She is rejecting Me."

That truth hit me hard. If we are hurt by rejection, think how much more it must hurt God. He is the One who is really being rejected. This realization gave me courage. We kept walking and talking, but not about church or God so much anymore. And I will keep praying for her. One day, I hope that my love for her will eventually bring her to the source of that love, Jesus Christ.

I know it makes You sad when people reject You, Father. It makes me sad, too. Thank You for Your unconditional love and acceptance. Help me love others as You love me and to communicate Your love wisely.

He who gives an answer before he hears,
It is folly and shame to him. (Proverbs 18:13)

On a recent visit to my parent's home with my husband and two children, I made an important discovery about the origin of a not-so-lovely habit I have. I interrupt. Often. Way too often. It is a bad habit that I have struggled with for years. Now, I realize that interrupting people is rude. I don't mean to be rude. I just love to talk and when I get into a conversation with someone, I lose control of my tongue, bursting into the conversation with enthusiasm. The Bible says this kind of impatience is folly, and brings shame to us. Ouch!

My four-year-old was asking me a question when my Dad abruptly interrupted Seth and asked me a different question. I stood dumbfounded, trying to listen to both of them at once. As a result, I didn't clearly hear either of their questions. They both stood staring at me, waiting for an answer. "Well?" my Dad asked impatiently. "Mom, can I?" my son whined impatiently.

"Just a minute you two—give me a break!" I returned. "You were both talking to me at the same time." I turned to my father and respectfully asked, "Do you realize that Seth was talking to me and you interrupted him?" Dad looked at me quizzically, "Huh?" was his only reply.

I learned the habit of interrupting at home. Sorry Mom and Dad, but it's true! Once I listened for it, I heard numerous occasions throughout the weekend at my parent's where my folks interrupted conversation. They didn't even realize they were doing it! Unfortunately, children pick up both the good and bad habits that their parents display.

I am trying to take a break from talking so much and be a more attentive listener. My husband has noticed a difference, but my husband says I still have a ways to go! Old habits die hard, but the habit of interrupting is one that I would like to put to death in my life. How about you?

Lord, help me to be quick to listen and slow to speak. Show me how to listen attentively and give me self-control over my tongue. May I show others respect by not interrupting them and pass this consideration along to my own children.

And if one can overpower him who is alone, two can resist him. A cord of three strands is not quickly torn apart. (Ecclesiastes 4:12)

Have you ever noticed the way rope is woven together? Three strands braid together to form one; a three-strand cord is much stronger than one with just two. Similarly, a triangular friendship is much stronger than one that is two-way. If one is not there to hold you up, the other will be.

Promise Keepers®, the Christian men's organization, promotes an idea for accountability groups that I think can be duplicated for women. When my husband was part of an accountability group, I watched him grow spiritually by leaps and bounds. I was so impressed that when one of the wives asked if I was interested in meeting weekly with her and a third wife, I said, "Yes!" Following the principles of Promise Keepers®, we formed a women's accountability group. We met weekly for one hour to talk, share and pray for each other. At first the sharing was superficial as we discussed topics like motherhood and marriage. But as our friendship and trust grew, we began to share real struggles that tug at our faith. We laughed a lot and cried some, but mostly we lifted up and encouraged one another in our faith in God.

Consider forming an accountability group of your own. Pray about who God would have you to meet with; ask each woman separately. You may want to consider having one woman that is slightly older in spiritual maturity and one slightly younger. This blend of wisdom and experience provides a nice balance that is in line with the spiritual principle of mentoring in Titus 2:3-5. If one or both women says she is not interested, don't be discouraged. Remember, they are rejecting the idea, not you! Continue to pray and seek God. He will bring together the perfect blend.

Lord, thank You for the principles of accountability modeled in Your Word. I am grateful for the friendships I have with other women who help me to walk closer to You.

"For I know the plans I have for you," declares the LORD, *"plans for welfare and not for calamity to give you a future and a hope."*
(Jeremiah 29:11)

God broke me into parenting with a trial. Seth was born five weeks premature and was hospitalized for twelve long days.

As I stared at him through the nursery windows, I felt so helpless. He was tangled in a web of tubes and cords. At five pounds, he looked like a miniature doll. I could hold him for only a limited time. I spent hours outside his isolette, reading or talking to him. Carrying on a one-way conversation gave me hope that he would pull through.

The first few days I worried constantly: He wasn't gaining enough weight. The lights weren't curing the jaundice. He might get an infection. Hhe wouldn't know how much I loved him. Mostly I worried that he wouldn't wake up. In my anguish I fell to my knees and cried out to God. I knew I had to release Seth to God. I pledged my trust in His sovereignty and pleaded for grace to handle whatever outcome He decided. Miraculously, my heart lightened.

The next time I found myself at the hospital nursery, I had a different view. I no longer saw the tangle of tubes. Instead I saw my heavenly Father's hands wrapped around Seth's body, holding him close. Seth's condition no longer seemed hopeless. Rather, it seemed an opportunity to trust God.

Today is Seth's birthday. He is healthy and strong, and the memory of his rocky entry into this life fades with every passing year. I will never forget how my heavenly Father sustained him, even when his earthly father and I could not. God has plans for Seth, to give him a future and a hope. He does for all our children, if only we will trust in Him and His plan.

I know that You have plans for my children, Lord. Plans to give them a future and a hope. Forgive me when I worry instead of lifting them up to You. Break the spirit of anxiety in my life that too often controls my thoughts and actions. I trust You with their lives.

For this reason I also suffer these things, but I am not ashamed; for I know whom I have believed and I am convinced that He is able to guard what I have entrusted to Him until that day.
(2 Timothy 1:12)

God's peace changes our entire countenance. I must have looked different in the days following my decision to trust God with Seth's heart. People said that I looked "more rested" or asked if I had "come to terms" with Seth's critical condition. When I explained that I had surrendered the situation to God, and that He had given me His peace, I met a surprising attitude. Disbelief.

Most gave me a condescending oh-you-poor-thing look or a blank stare. I didn't get encouragement; I cannot tell you the number of people who tried to talk me out of my faith in God. And some professed to be Christians! A nurse told me "not to get my hopes up." Isn't God a God of Hope? Someone else said, "Your faith will be stronger because of this if God heals Seth." But I knew that my faith would be stronger even if He chose not to heal Seth. My faith was based on who God is, not on what He does.

Faith based on what God does for us will waver with circumstances. If we only have faith when God does something that we want, it isn't really faith at all. Faith's definition is "unquestioning belief." It means trusting in God at all times, no questions asked. Anything short of that is not true faith.

My faith may have suffered a bit from others' ignorance or misunderstanding. But I was not ashamed. I knew my God was capable of healing my son, whom I had entrusted to Him, if He so desired. I proudly proclaimed this to anyone who asked. This strengthened my faith, not the fact that He chose to heal Seth. When we know who we believe in, we stand cemented in a faith that will prevail. That is true faith.

Lord, give me a rock-solid faith based on who You are, not what You do. May I never be ashamed of my belief that You are a great and mighty God.

Now may the God who gives perseverance and encouragement grant you to be of the same mind with one another according to Christ Jesus. (Romans 15:5)

"Are you thinking what I am thinking?" my friend asked. "Definitely," I responded as we made a beeline for the ice cream shop. We emerged with huge ice cream cones.

"Isn't it funny how we so often think the same things and don't even have to say a word?" she quipped.

I agreed. "It's like you can read my mind!" She nodded and then looked to the store ahead. Its display windows bulged with bubble baths and other luxurious body products. Our eyes met. We smiled, nodded and entered the little shop. Sweet smells of vanilla, green apple and lavender tickled our noses, and we grinned as we headed for the sale table.

Do you have a friend who thinks like you? Perhaps you will think something, and she will speak it. Or she will be in mid-sentence, and you will finish it. Being of the same mind with a friend is a wonderful gift from God. Friends like that are rare and precious. I have one in my life—two, actually. One is a woman and the other is a man—my husband. He and I often communicate by simply looking at each other and giving a nod of understanding. We don't have to say a word. This comes in handy sometimes when speaking my thoughts may not be appropriate.

If you have a friend such as this, a sort of kindred spirit, hold her in high esteem—especially if she encourages and strengthens your walk with Christ. Friends are like a rainbow in our lives. Each one gives a new color to the rainbow.

Lord, thank You for the gift of friendship. Help me to treasure my friends and treat them with dignity and respect. Thank You for the brightest color in my rainbow: that kindred spirit who encourages me to walk with You.

And by the seventh day God completed His work which He had done; and He rested on the seventh day from all His work which He had done. (Genesis 2:2)

It was the end of a long week, and I was suffering from sleep deprivation but desperately trying to complete my last writing project. I had just tucked both boys in for naps and settled at the computer. Fifteen minutes later Seth called from his room, "Is nap time over?"

I patiently called back, "No. Lay your head down and go to sleep." Type. Type. Type.

A few minutes later: "Mom, is nap time over?"

My not-so-patient reply: "No! I'll let you know when it is. Night-night!" Type. Type. Type.

Again the exchange occurred, my voice escalating this time to a loud shout. Type. Type. Type.

"Mommmmm!" With that, I stomped into Seth's room. I screamed, "Nap time is not over, and you will go to sleep right this minute! Now lie down and keep quiet!"

Returning to my keyboard, I heard a whimper. Suddenly aware of my harshness and anger, I dragged myself to my son's room. I scooped him up and held him tightly. Exhaustion gave way to sorrow, and I began to weep quietly. He pulled away to eye me, then asked softly, "Mommy, what's wrong?" I stammered, "Oh Seth, please forgive me. I shouldn't have yelled at you. I am so sorry. Mommy is very tired and I have too much to do, but it's not your fault." Taking my face in his precious little hands, my four-year-old looked at me with compassion-filled eyes. "Cheer up, Mom," he said. "You'll get your work done. You always do."

My preschooler was much wiser than I that day. I lay down next to him and Winnie the Pooh, and we all had a glorious nap. That evening, rested and refreshed, I finished my project.

Lord, help me to bring balance to my life by putting a high priority on rest. And give me peace and assurance that only come from resting in You.

Look to the right and see;
For there is no one who regards me;
There is no escape for me;
No one cares for my soul. (Psalm 142:4)

Have you ever felt betrayed by a friend? I remember an instance where two of my closest friends hurt me tremendously. They went on a trip together without breathing a word to me. I felt left out, hurt and betrayed.

That night I broke down and wept. "They don't care about me," I whined to God. I tried to say it didn't matter, but the pain in my gut told me differently. As I cried at God's feet, the Holy Spirit showed me that my attitude was all wrong. I was focusing on what they had done, not who they were. They were precious sisters in the sight of God. Not perfect, just forgiven—like all the rest of us.

Then God reminded me of something else. Something beautiful—He is my best Friend. I thought about that for a minute. . . . The King of kings is my best Friend! I had given Him that place a long time ago, but I put a higher value on those surrounding me. How betrayed must He have felt?

I had believed that if I had close friends who valued me, then I was worth much more. But God treasures me regardless of anyone else. Jesus is one Friend who will never betray us or let us down. He promises to never leave us or forsake us. Now, that's a true friend!

Lord, thank You for being my very best Friend. Remind me, when
I get off track, that my value and worth as a person is based not on
my friendships, but on who I am in You.

And after you have suffered for a little while, the God of all grace, who called you to His eternal glory in Christ, will Himself perfect, confirm, strengthen and establish you. (1 Peter 5:10)

There is a heartwarming story about a little boy who wanted to buy his mother a birthday gift. He saved his money and went in search of the perfect gift. At a lingerie store, he said that he would like to buy a slip for his mother. When the clerk asked the size, he said he didn't know. "Is she short or tall? Thin or heavy?" she asked. "Can you give me a general idea of her size?" The little boy mulled this over and brightly replied, "I think she's just about perfect!" The little boy proudly left the store with a size 34 slip. His mother had to later return the slip for a size 52.

Many of us are our own worst critics. We strive to attain perfection in every area of life: a perfect size 10, a perfect house, the perfect parent and perfect children. That is not reality. It is good to strive for excellence, but it is not good to aim at perfection. As today's Scripture passage states, God is gracious in all things—even our shortcomings as parents. In the process, He is working to perfect us, as well as to confirm, strengthen and establish us in an intimate relationship with Him.

Don't beat yourself up for the mistakes you make as a parent. Accept God's forgiveness and move forward in His grace. Give yourself a break! God sees you through much different eyes than you see yourself—and so do your children. You see weaknesses, they see strengths; you see failures, they see victories; you see unattractiveness, they see beauty. When we see the ordinary, children see the extraordinary. Chances are, if your children wandered into a lingerie store to buy you a gift and the clerk asked your size, they, too, would respond, "Just about perfect!"

Lord, give me the grace to accept my shortcomings with dignity. Keep me reaching for high standards, but keep me from the trap of perfectionism.

And my God shall supply all your needs according to His riches in glory in Christ Jesus. (Philippians 4:19)

My husband and I were approaching our ten-year wedding anniversary. We desperately wanted—needed—to get away together. Our biggest hurdle was finding someone to watch our children for a few days, but no one came to mind that we felt comfortable asking. We had just about given up on the idea when I remembered Philippians 4:19. I realized I hadn't yet asked God to supply our need. I prayed about this matter, asking God to show us who we could ask to care for the boys.

A few days later God met our need through some faithful friends! My husband and I enjoyed a beautiful weekend on the beach. We were truly able to relax, knowing that our children were well cared for and loved. The time alone together gave our marriage the boost it needed.

Nothing makes children more secure than knowing that Mom and Dad love and are committed to each other. Our boys greeted us enthusiastically upon our return—it is a good sign when your kids miss you! Four-year-old Seth noticed that we seemed rested and happy. He told his daddy that he was "happy Mommy and Daddy loved each other." What a great testimony of the importance of husband and wife spending time alone together! It is good for everyone.

If you have not spent a romantic night or weekend away with your spouse in a while, you can probably feel the tension in your relationship. Don't let concerns about who will care for your children stop you. Give it to God and He will provide. Consider finding another couple you can swap with. Parents need to get away for regular "breaks" together to revitalize the crucial spark in their marital relationship. Your kids will feel the chill if your fire has gone out!

Lord, thank You for supplying my every need. Help me to keep time alone with my husband a priority. I pray that our commitment to each other would positively affect our children.

May 31

For our struggle is not against flesh and blood, but against the rulers, against the powers, against the world forces of this darkness, against the spiritual forces of wickedness in the heavenly places. (Ephesians 6:12)

I had been invited to speak at a local church. It would be my speaking debut. As I waited on God in prayer, His Spirit began to show me what to share. I had final preparations to do. Then stomach flu hit Levi and, less than twenty-four hours later, Seth. My husband was working late. I watched the clock tick, knowing I had limited time to prepare. I continued to soothe my children's cries, and pray. Soon I realized that I was not at war with the stomach flu though, but with the enemy.

I immediately changed my prayers. I still sought God's help, but I also forbade the enemy to interfere with my children or the women who would hear me speak the next evening. I realized that the enemy did not want me to speak to them.

I sat by Seth's bedside and read Scriptures aloud. God's Word says that when His name is spoken, the enemy must flee. He did! Seth and Levi stopped throwing up, and I completed my talk—at 2:30 a.m. As I fell into bed, I thanked God that He can go to battle for us with the enemy.

The next evening, all went well at the speaking engagement. It was obvious that God spoke to many women there. It was an honor and thrill to be His instrument.

As stay-at-home moms, we are involved in regular spiritual warfare. Satan wants to enlist our children for his army. He will try to discourage, deceive and disarm you. Call on God to strengthen you in raising godly children. Put on your spiritual armor everyday (See Ephesians 6:13-17.), and protect yourself and the ones you love!

Give me eyes to see all sides of my battles, Lord, spiritual and otherwise. Protect my children from the enemy's lies and traps. Make them mighty warriors for You.

June:
On-the-job Networking

Is it possible to be a stay-at-home mom who's never at home?

When one dear lady asked me this, I laughed until I thought my side would split. She was asking *me*, the queen of overcommitment.

This is one of the enemy's biggest traps to get stay-at-home moms off track. Too much activity often masquerades as fulfillment. The many available activities seem more appealing, and more fulfilling, than folding socks.

I have lived out this scenario plenty of times. I have to evaluate my schedule constantly: Have I left enough time to take care of my family and home? Isn't that supposed to be my first priority? This is tough because I thrive on busyness—I'm the kind of person Satan loves to try to manipulate. He disguises "work for the Lord" as a tool for fulfillment, purpose and a closer relationship with God. But too much of the Lord's work can set us back in our relationship with God. When we get busy, one of the first things we cut out is our time with Him.

Last month, I urged you to get involved with women and spend time on yourself. Now I'm telling you to do so with caution. There's a crucial element to motherhood called balance. There is a fine line between involvement and overinvolvement. Thankfully, God's Word contains guidelines on this very subject. At first, balance can be difficult to achieve, especially if you have a do-it-all personality like mine. But finding it will bring peace to your life.

June 1

> The mind of man plans his way,
>   But the Lord directs his steps. *(Proverbs 16:9)*

We live in a goal-driven society. The philosophy "you won't have it if you don't plan it" is growing, even among the Christian community. While planning is a godly principle, we can go overboard with it. If our plans are outside of His will, they will not come to pass. God does not disappoint us; we become disappointed when we don't get our way. The Lord is a perfect Gentleman. He will not grab the steering wheel of our lives. We must hand it over to Him.

I have had carefully scheduled days where nothing went as planned, leaving me feeling grumpy and unproductive. I hate feeling unproductive. I've asked God to help me define "productive." I have learned that not getting everything done on my list does not mean I was unproductive. I have also planned to become involved in certain activities, only to have God change my heart when I have spent time in prayer. God is faithful! If we give Him the chance, He will direct our plans.

Do you plan out every day, week, month? Do you write your to-do list in a daily time planner? Are you easily irritated when things don't go as planned? If so, you may need to change direction. Forego your plan and release control to God, letting Him direct your steps.

> *Dear Lord, forgive me when I forge ahead with my own plans and exclude You. Direct my every involvement. Help me to submit to Your will, especially when it is different than what I have planned.*

For the mind set on the flesh is death, but the mind set on the Spirit is life and peace. (Romans 8:6)

Many of us get so involved in helping others that we neglect our husbands and children. I'm guilty. The majority of my activity involves church business. Many worthwhile and important ministries need enthusiastic volunteers. I tend to volunteer for everything at once. Then, I cannot keep up, and I burn out. My family suffers most, though. Time lost with them cannot be regained.

Excess outside activity is especially dangerous when the wife is a Christian and the husband is not. Many women in this situation throw themselves into the life of the church, leaving little time for the husband who has no interest. He cannot separate church activity from a relationship with God. The feeling of competition causes resentment and drives him further from the church, his wife and any hope of a relationship with Jesus Christ. Unsaved husbands and children will be won through a wife and mother who shines with the love of Jesus, not one who is weary from doing.

Dr. James Dobson has also warned of overcommitment. He says that husbands and wives must constantly guard against it. Even though our pursuits may be valuable and beneficial, overcommitment can easily become harmful to a marriage and family. We must make sure that our husband and children are the priority for our energy and time.

If you are trying to decide on outside activities, ask yourself why you want to be involved. Remember, "the mind set on the flesh is death." If you believe an activity will bring you fulfillment or make you happy, think again. That is the wrong reason to get involved. Getting involved because you believe it's where God wants you is the right reason: "But the mind set on the Spirit is life and peace."

Lord, I don't want to fall into the trap of overcommitment. I want to honor You with my time and involvements. Give me wisdom as I seek You and Your will.

Therefore be careful how you walk, not as unwise men, but as wise, making the most of your time, because the days are evil. (Ephesians 5:15-16)

My husband flung the calendar on the table. "We are too busy!" he exclaimed, throwing up his hands. "Why does this always happen to us? We have this same conversation every three to four months. We have to slow down!" I knew he was right. We could not find one free weekend in the next three months for a getaway. And yet, I didn't know how we could get *unbusy.*

"Well, what do we cut out?" I sighed. "Everything we're doing is important."

"That's the problem," he shot back. "Everything is important, but we cannot do it all. We need to set some priorities."

That was the beginning of a new handle on commitment. That evening was the catalyst that helped us to keep our priorities in order: God, family, work, friends and church activities. We didn't list them in one evening though. Our priority-setting resulted from hours in prayer and God's Word.

Now, when someone asks us to serve, we ask ourselves, "What will be eliminated if this is added? Is this activity in line with my priorities?" Those questions answer the request. We have learned that it's OK to say "no."

Do your everyday life and outside involvements clearly reflect your priorities?

Give me direction, Lord, as I seek to line up my priorities with Your Word. May I find the courage to say "no." Help me to find balance so that I might serve You and my family better.

For we do not have a high priest who cannot sympathize with our weaknesses, but one who has been tempted in all things as we are, yet without sin. (Hebrews 4:15)

As I watched the drama presentation at church, I began to squirm in my seat. It was a comical sketch about a man who was so burnt out from doing for others that he locked himself in a hotel room to rest. However, a persistent woman located him. She banged on his door, insisting that he help with another project. As others chuckled, my face grew hot and tears spilled from my eyes. This humorous look at overcommitment was hitting too close to home. I was exhausted, physically and emotionally.

Following the drama, our pastor spoke on overcommitment and burn out. I discovered that God created us with limits, and it is His will that we know and exercise them. We are to rely on His power to serve within those limits. If we push past them, we are in sin.

The secret is in learning to say "no." Jesus did. When He took the form of man and ministered here on earth, He didn't always do everything everyone asked of him. He turned down dinner engagements and invitations to speak if it put Him on overload. He even went out on a boat once to get away from the demanding crowds and rest. (See Matthew 14:13 and 15:39.) He didn't allow others to manipulate and push Him past His limits. He simply and gracefully said, "No."

Do you know your limits? Do you know how to say no once you reach them?

Dearest Jesus, help me to learn from Your actions when you walked on this earth. Right now I ask that You show me my limits and teach me how to say "no."

June 5

"And you shall love the LORD your God with all your heart, and with all your soul, and with all your mind, and with all your strength." (Mark 12:30)

Today's verse, spoken by Jesus Himself, was cited as the "great commandment." One thought strikes me when I read this verse: What if God measured how much I love Him by how much time I spend with Him?

Think about that for a moment. Most likely, one of the reasons you elected to stay home with your kids is because spending time with them is a priority. Your kids know you love them because you spend time with them. If you told your kids you loved them with all your heart, mind, soul and strength, but then spent time with them for only a few hours on Sunday morning, do you think they'd believe you?

If you are so busy that the first thing to go is your daily time with God, then you are too busy. You have to *make* quiet time with Him. You can hear from Him by reading the Bible, talk to Him by praying, praise Him by singing, glorify Him by recording discoveries and answered prayers in a journal and learn about Him by attending Bible studies and church worship. The more time you spend with Him, the better you will know Him and the more you will love Him.

The more time you spend with God, the more you will become like Him. Have you ever noticed when you spend a lot of time with someone, such as your spouse, you begin to think or even act alike? Imagine what could happen when you spent countless hours with God! Do you desire to be more patient, kind, loving, generous, faithful, joyful, gracious or merciful with your children? Spend time with God, and His characteristics will begin to rub off on you.

I love You, Lord. As I commit to spending time daily with You, teach me how to love You even more, so that my life might reflect Your face.

For where your treasure is, there will your heart be also.
(Luke 12:34)

esus spoke these words to His disciples. He was winding down from a lengthy session of preaching and teaching to a multitude of thousands. Their ears were alert from the wisdom that had fallen from His lips unto the hungry crowd. Where is your treasure? Do you treasure your relationship with God? Family? Friends? Or do you treasure your possessions? Status? Reputation? Accomplishments? Whatever you treasure has your heart.

A wise woman, who taught a Bible study I attended, suggested that we could glean even more meaning from this verse by substituting "time" for "treasure." For where your *time* is, there will your heart be also.

Take some time today to reflect on how you spend your time. Make a list of your activities every day for a week. Include everything: making meals, playing with the children, washing the dishes, talking on the phone, watching television, exercising, running errands, car pooling, kids' activities, meetings, helping with homework, folding the laundry, Bible study, etc. At the end of the week evaluate your list and put each item into a major category: God, family, friends, home responsibilities (work), church service, community, self. Where are you spending the bulk of your time? If you spend the biggest percentage of your time in service to your community, and your most important priority is your family, then you need to rethink your commitments. Where are you overcommitted? Where do you need to spend more time? Remember, where your time is, there will your heart be also.

> *Dear Lord, thank You for giving me twenty-four hours in every day. As I evaluate how I spend those hours this week, I pray that You will help me to be honest about any changes I need to make. Help me to line up my commitments with what is really important. Give me insight to spend my time more wisely.*

June 7

There is an appointed time for everything. . . . (Ecclesiastes 3:1)

One parental season is being the mother of a toddler. Serving your children effectively in this season requires a great deal of time and energy, which translates into not doing much else—at least if you want to get enough rest! It takes great amounts of patience and tenderness to parent a toddler in a consistent, godly manner, and that's not easy to do while suffering sleep deprivation. Toddlers grow and change so quickly that we had better be ready to give them much of our attention.

I realized when Seth was just twenty-two months old that I had not been giving him the time he needed. One day we were playing when the telephone rang. I jumped up to answer it and he began protesting wildly. "No, ma! No, ma!" he shouted.

"OK," I responded. "I'm sure whoever it is will leave a message. I can call them back when we're done playing." He smiled softly up at me. All was right with the world again.

I had volunteered to coordinate a women's function at our church. I had been on the phone almost daily the past two weeks for an hour or two, usually during Seth's waking hours. I dropped whatever I was doing, including playing with him, the instant the phone rang. Now, with two children, I limit my time on the phone when we are together. They know I'll only be a few minutes and then turn my attention back to them, so they are not threatened when it rings.

What is your season of life? Are your outside commitments enabling—or hindering—your family to get through this season victoriously? When this season is over, will your family know they were and always will be the most important people in your life?

> *Oh, God, the seasons of my life as a parent are many and unique. Help me to sense when my children need me most. Help me to make them my first priority, no matter what my outside commitments.*

. . . {B}e ready in season and out of season; reprove, rebuke, exhort, with great patience and instruction. (2 Timothy 4:2)

I discovered the inflexibility of my schedule when a friend called. She said she really needed to talk; could she come over for lunch one day that week? Looking at my calendar, I admitted that I didn't have a free afternoon for a month! By the time we got together, her problem was too deep for my help; she needed professional counseling. I was embarrassed and ashamed that I had missed the window of opportunity to minister to her.

That incident taught me a valuable lesson: If I am viewing the needs of others as an inconvenience or interruption rather than an opportunity to minister, then I am too busy. That easily happens with our children, too. We can be so busy trying to accomplish that we come to view their needs as interruptions.

God's Word says I need to be ready to "reprove, rebuke [and] exhort" both "in season and out of season." That means to be ready at *all* times—not just when it's convenient or fits into my schedule. God cannot fully use me to minister to my children or others if I don't allow time for the unexpected.

Lord, You were available to be with those who needed You the most. Help me to view the opportunities You give me to reprove, rebuke, exhort and instruct as a privilege, not an inconvenience.

He will call upon Me, and I will answer him;
  I will be with him in trouble;
  I will rescue him, and honor him. (Psalm 91:15)

friend of mine had gotten involved in more outside commitments than she could comfortably handle. With two little girls and a husband to care for, she began feeling the pressure. She couldn't keep up with the new pace, and she was constantly weary. Usually meek and patient, she found herself becoming short-tempered. Still, she felt she needed to follow through on her commitments. Then, she must decide which ones to discontinue.

These issues particularly burdened her as she attended a women's retreat. As she took a walk one morning, she cried out to God for strength and discernment. A solitary gust of wind blew the pages of her Bible to Psalm 91. Slowly, she read the psalmist's words, and a peace began to envelope her: "He who dwells in the shelter of the Most High will abide in the shadow of the Almighty" (Psalm 91:1).

She realized that because she was dwelling in God and what He wanted for her life, she would find shelter, strength and rest. She discovered in verse 15 that if she called to Him, He would answer her. He would rescue her. She knew God had heard her cry. He was answering it right now.

Are you under the pile? Overcommitted? Stressed out? There is comfort in the words of the psalmist. I urge you to read Psalm 91 in its entirety. Let God rescue you.

Almighty God, thank You that in Your presence I can find refuge.
Forgive me when I seek it in other people and things. Hide me in
Your shadow, cover me with Your peace, rescue me from the trap of
overcommitment.

. . . {A}nd all the world may become accountable to God. (Romans 3:19)

$\mathcal{I}$am going to be accountable to God for the use of my time. This usually makes me stop and think. I ask myself if a particular activity is a good investment of my time. Will something or someone else in my life suffer if I add it?

Each of us only has twenty-four hours in a day. Believe me, many days I wish I could extend the day to accomplish more. Sometimes we get more accomplished than we realize, however. If I spend time with my boys for an entire day, I may not feel productive—in my earthly assessment. But God sees it differently. Time spent with our kids is the *most* productive; children are precious in God's sight. And we are responsible to instill godly character in them. We cannot do that if we constantly have our heads buried in a project or are attending a committee meeting.

We need to learn what is of value to God. His Word tells us what is important. Are we spending time in those areas? The fund-raising committee meeting is important; but is it as important as my son's swimming lesson or our family picnic in the park? No. Other people can raise funds, but no one else will raise my children.

I will be accountable to God for the time I use to raise my precious little ones. That time is limited and valuable. I want to use it wisely. Don't you?

> *Gracious Lord, thank You for the gifts of children and time. Help me not to waste one precious minute. Give me wisdom in priorities. When I stand before Your throne to give account for the gifts You have given me, may You say, "Well done, good and faithful servant."*

It is a snare for a man to say rashly, "It is holy!"
And after the vows to make inquiry. (Proverbs 20:25)

ow many times have you promised something to someone, only later to regret it? Perhaps the commitment you made involved more time than you anticipated, or was costlier than you thought it would be. Maybe you've accepted an invitation you wish you hadn't. Or promised to have a project completed by a specific date, only to realize you couldn't make the deadline. The point is this—it's always easier to get in than to get out.

As a Christian trying to live out my faith and put others before myself, I think that I have to say yes to every request. There are so many needs, I think. Who will do it if I don't? Even in the name of God, we shouldn't overcommit ourselves. Today's Scripture solidifies that making rash decisions, and then wondering what we have done, is a snare!

How many times have you, out of a feeling of obligation, agreed to do something against your better judgment? I have many times. As a mom, you must guard your time. Pick and choose your commitments carefully. When someone makes a request, don't be embarrassed to say, "Let me check my calendar and get back to you." Or, "Give me a few days to think about how that commitment would affect my family." Through careful consideration, you will make better decisions for you and your children, because our absence affects them. It is always better to under promise and over deliver in every area of life!

> *Gracious Lord, thank You for helping me follow through on my commitments, even when I have gotten in over my head. Help me to consider my promises carefully and to think before I speak. Give me wisdom to evaluate my involvements and the courage to say no when I need to.*

June 12

But now finish doing it also; that just as there was the readiness to desire it, so there may be also the completion of it by your ability. (2 Corinthians 8:11)

*I*f you are a real doer, then this month's readings may strike a chord with you. But let me stress that if God is convicting you of overcommitment, you must follow His Word on how to handle your current commitments. The above Scripture clearly says that you need to finish what you start. Paul is writing specifically of the incredible amount of giving going on in the churches of Macedonia. Giving generously is never easy because it is not our natural response. Unfortunately, in our flesh, we are more selfish than we'd sometimes like to admit. That's why Paul urges them to finish what they began.

Even Solomon completed the monumental task of building the legendary Temple. (See 2 Chronicles 2-7.) This was not an easy task; it took great vision and commitment. Solomon had the integrity to follow through, no matter what obstacles he encountered along the way. It was a long-term commitment, too—twenty years, according to Second Chronicles 8:1. We need to have that same perseverance in our involvements.

We, too, made a long-term commitment when we became parents. We committed to raise up our children in a godly manner and to equip them to manage life on their own. Approximately eighteen years of teaching, training, guiding and counseling is not a short-term commitment!

Think for a minute about your commitments to outside activities and projects. Do they cloud your vision for the most important commitment you've ever made—that of raising your children properly? If so, it's time to finish up and scale down.

> *Heavenly Father, forgive me when I get so bogged down with outside commitments that I forget my commitment to my children. Help me to be a woman of my word and follow through with what I start.*

June 13

Let us therefore draw near with confidence to the throne of grace, that we may receive mercy and may find grace to help in time of need. (Hebrews 4:16)

A king's life included isolation. No one was allowed in the king's presence or the inner court without his permission. Only select members of his royal court were permitted to be near him at all times. It wasn't like today, where a citizen of this country can speak with a public official with little or no hassle. You probably need an appointment, but it is not impossible to speak with a city council member, the mayor or even your congressman. Yet, in the day of the ruling kings and queens, it was nearly impossible to obtain an appointment to speak with the king or queen. They weren't really interested in speaking with the people over whom they ruled.

In contrast, the Ruler of the Universe, the almighty King of kings and Lord of lords, has made Himself available to us at all times. Anytime of the day or night, if we need Him, we can approach His throne. Wow! What a thought! The one who can give power to a king or take it away in an instant is willing to listen to us, His children, at anytime. Today's Scripture even clarifies that we can approach His throne with confidence that He is ready to listen and respond. We can be confident that He is willing to extend His mercy and grace to us in a moment's notice. All we need to do is reach out to Him in prayer. In those moments, we will find ourselves before His throne.

Are you, as one of the rulers of your home, readily available for your children? Or are you so busy that they don't feel confident they can approach you?

Oh my Lord and Almighty King, thank You for making Yourself available to me at all times. I pray now, as I approach Your throne, that You will show me how to imitate Your loyalty to my own children.

But I have this against you, that you have left your first love.
(Revelation 2:4)

In Revelation 2, the warning of today's verse was directed to the people in the church at Ephesus. Ironically, just thirty years earlier the apostle Paul had commended this church for its love (Ephesians 1:15-16). The love that he referred to is their incredible love for Jesus. So what happened to bring them from commendation to warning? *Busyness.*

The people at Ephesus started out like many Christians do. They met Jesus Christ as Savior and fell in love with Him. That strong love spilled over into all they did. Many churches today, not unlike Ephesus, soon become known for their unconditional love and acceptance. The church grows and flourishes. But often, when growth happens, the focus shifts. It quickly goes from a relationship to a race—a race to get things done. In Ephesus, ministry happened and things got done, but in the process, the people got so caught up in doing that they forgot about loving. They forgot why they were doing it in the first place. They forgot their first love—Jesus.

Do you remember the first time you looked into your child's eyes and fell in love with him or her? Do you remember that feeling? Now, years later, your love is probably even deeper. Do you remember when you first fell in love with Jesus? Have you gotten so busy doing good things for the Lord that you have forgotten to love Him? Are you so overworked that you don't take time to sit at His feet anymore, spending time in worship and prayer? Take some time right now to assess your schedule and ask yourself, "Am I so busy doing that I have forgotten about loving?"

Lord Jesus, help me to remember what it was like when I first met and fell in love with You. Take me back to my original passion and commitment, not to Your service, but to You. Keep my heart sensitive to the times that I get caught up in doing and forget about loving.

But Martha was distracted with all her preparations; and she came up to Him, and said, "Lord, do You not care that my sister has left me to do all the serving alone? Then tell her to help me." (Luke 10:40)

*P*icture this scene: A fire crackles in the hearth and the fragrances of simmering soup and baking bread fill the house. Jesus has just arrived to dine with Mary and Martha. He reclines near the fire, and Mary kneels at her Savior's feet. She wants nothing more than to be with Him. She sits in rapt attention as He talks quietly, the fire popping in the background. They look like two old friends catching up on times past.

Meanwhile, in the kitchen Martha puts the final preparations together for dinner. She sweeps the floor for the third time and peeks in the oven to check the bread. Can't let it get too brown, she frets. Examining the pies that now cool on the windowsill, she catches a dripping edge with her fingertip and brings it to her lips. Hmmm, she frowns. I'm not sure they're sweet enough. Her eyes whisk across the room and fall on the table. Oh no, she worries. The table is not yet set—that was Mary's job. "Everything must be perfect," she reasons. "After all, the Savior is dining with us." She enters the sitting room and suggests that perhaps Jesus could get Mary to help her.

Notice Jesus' response in verses 41-42: "Martha, Martha, you are so worried and bothered about so many things; but only a few things are necessary, really only one, for Mary has chosen the good part, which shall not be taken away from her."

Can't you just picture Mary smiling sweetly and Martha retreating to the kitchen with her tail between her legs? I'd like to know if she got the message and left the dinner dishes for later? When was the last time you spent a few uninterrupted moments just sitting at the Savior's feet? Jesus wants us to spend time with Him more than He wants us to get things done.

Dearest Jesus, how I long to spend undistracted time with You. Help me to gain fulfillment like Mary did by being with You, not by doing for You.

Strength and dignity are her clothing, and she smiles at the future.
(Proverbs 31:25)

ou knew we'd eventually get to her, didn't you? The infamous, Proverbs 31 woman. As I was reading this familiar passage one day, I was particularly drawn to today's verse. This woman is strong, she is dignified and she is smiling.

Why is she so happy? Isn't she overwhelmed like the rest of us mothers? The footnote in my Ryrie Study Bible told me otherwise; it says she has no anxieties. What's her secret? After doing some serious studying of this happy woman, I believe I discovered the truth behind the smile: balance.

Read the entire passage (Proverbs 31:10-31) and see for yourself. She is the picture of balance. She does work hard, but she doesn't spend all of her time taking care of her household, although that is her primary focus. But she also takes time to rest and relax. If you read the passage carefully, you will notice that she spends a little time doing a lot of different things. She is balanced.

I am convinced that most people, including stay-at-home moms, would be much happier if they would just grasp this concept of balance. God intended for us to live a balanced life, making time for Him, family, work, fun, ourselves and friends. Ecclesiastes 3:1 specifically says, "There is a time for everything."

When I spend the bulk of my time in one area and not enough in the others, I get off balance—then I get grumpy. I can eliminate complications when I stay balanced in all my activities. Many moms I know are stressed because they are overcommitted in one area and undercommitted in others. When I spend some time in each of the areas that are important to me, I am very happy. It's as simple as that.

Heavenly Father, thank You for Your model of a Christlike woman
in Proverbs 31. Help me to strive to be more like her in character, and
help me find the right balance of activity and responsibility in my own
life, that I too may smile on the future.

June 17

Yet you do not know what your life will be like tomorrow. You are just a vapor that appears for a little while and then vanishes away. (James 4:14)

$\mathscr{I}$am reminded of a story I recently read of a young mother who died at the age of twenty-seven. Her death was sudden and unexpected. Tragically, she left behind a husband and a two-month-old daughter. How this story jolted me into the reality of our finite state. We often think we have so much time to spend doing the very things we want and need to do, including spending time with our kids. They need our attention and so do many other people and projects. Sadly, in the competition for our time and attention, our children often get pushed to the back of the list. We reason it out telling ourselves, "This other commitment won't take much time and besides, I've got lots of years with my kids, right?" Wrong! The above story illustrates that is just not so. God can take us at any time. We do not know if there will be more tomorrows. So we have to live today like it may be our last. If it was your last day to live, wouldn't you spend your time with the people you most love?

Make a list of all the things you want to do with your children. Include everything from teaching them to finger paint to reading more books to taking them to Disneyland. Don't forget to include plans to introduce them to Jesus as their Savior. Now, make plans and goals to begin accomplishing these things. If you do not make a plan, it will not get done. And your time with them will be gone, like vapor that vanishes before your eyes.

I hope, Lord God, that you will see fit to give me many more tomorrows. But teach me to make the best of each day that I have. Give me wisdom as I plan my time and may I show my kids that they are a priority in my life by the time I do spend with them.

All things are lawful, but not all things are profitable. All things are lawful, but not all things edify. (1 Corinthians 10:23)

There are many worthy causes in our world. Practically every day I get mail from some person or organization requesting money to help fund a cause. Most of these are legitimate programs; all of them are legal—"lawful." But I have to ask myself how many of them are really doing something "profitable." I have heard or read about many so-called "worthwhile" causes which waste much of the money they receive on processing and paperwork fees, with a very small amount of the donations (sometimes as little as ten percent) actually going to the heart of the program—usually the people you think you are feeding or clothing. To me, an organization where so much of the funds get caught up in red-tape procedures is not profitable. We really have to use discernment when deciding where to put our hard-earned money.

The same is true of our time. According to the dictionary the word "edify" means to "instruct or improve." How many times have you been asked to be involved in something that you did not feel was either instructive or would improve anything or anyone? Perhaps it was perfectly lawful, but you didn't see how it was edifying. I have been asked to be involved in many things which I did not feel were necessarily edifying. Ask yourself the next time your time or involvement is being requested—is it edifying for myself or my family? The answer to that single question may be your answer to the request.

> *Teach me, Lord, to discern between what is edifying and what is not. Help me to be selective in my activities and involvements and show me how to distinguish between what is lawful only and what is profitable for me and my family.*

Therefore, since we have so great a cloud of witnesses surrounding us, let us also lay aside every encumbrance, and the sin which so easily entangles us, and let us run with endurance the race that is set before us, fixing our eyes on Jesus, the author and perfecter of faith. . . . (Hebrews 12:1-2)

Have you ever watched a relay race? You may have noticed that each runner's eyes are focused on one thing—the runner in front of him. He has one goal in mind; to pass the baton smoothly and quickly to the runner who will take his place. He is not distracted by onlookers or the cheering noises of the crowd. His eyes are transfixed on his goal. Roaming eyes would weaken his concentration and slow him down. The winning team has the greatest combination of endurance, focus and speed.

Life is like a relay race for Christians. They have carefully charted their course, choosing to follow Jesus Christ, running along the narrower path to Him. In front of each mother, are her children, waiting on the track to be the next to be passed the baton of faith. As we train our children we would do well to emulate a winner's style of focus and dedication. If we get involved in too many other outside interests, we often find we have wasted valuable time, only to look around and see our children grown and much farther down the course of life. We cannot make up for the lost time of teaching, training and guiding. That is a dangerous gamble, because they may be wandering aimlessly without the baton of faith.

As Christians, our goal should be to get from this point, life here on earth, to the next point, eternal life in heaven with Jesus. The shortest distance between two points is a straight line. If we can keep our focus on Jesus then we will achieve our desired end result. There are people watching you every day, witnessing how you raise your children and how you arrange your priorities. Be sure your activities are in line with your priorities and that they won't distract you from your goal.

Lord, help me to keep my eyes on You as I run the race of life. May I remain focused and not become so distracted with other activities that I become encumbered. I want to stay the course and pass along the baton of faith to my children.

The LORD your God is in your midst,
  A victorious warrior.
He will exult over you with joy,
  He will be quiet in His love,
He will rejoice over you with shouts of joy. (Zephaniah 3:17)

Have you ever heard God's silence? There may have been times in your life, maybe even now, that you earnestly sought God in prayer and became discouraged because He did not answer you. This is common in the life of every believer. Take heart—there is always a reason for God's silence.

One of the most crucial reasons that God often chooses to be silent or "quiet in His love" is because He is trying to draw us closer to Him. When I am seeking God's direction for a decision I need to make, or perhaps am in turmoil about some situation in my life, I spend a considerable amount of time talking to Him about it, pouring my heart out to Him. During these times of intense prayer, I feel the closest to God.

It is when I have the answer I seek that I seem to slack off in my prayer time. I think I don't "need" to hear from God as much when things are going smoothly in my life. That assumption is false. We need God every day of our lives. The time we spend with Him in reading His Word and in prayer is valuable because it prepares us for the hard times. We can handle adversities better when we are strong in our relationship with God. The time to prepare for battle is not in the middle of one.

God rejoices in your presence. He longs to draw you close to Him. The only way to develop an intimate relationship with God is to spend time in His presence often. God's quiet way of loving us is often more than our human hearts and minds can understand. It is His way of teaching us to love and trust in Him. He is not silent at times because He does not love you; He is silent because He loves you deeply and wants to draw you close.

Lord, teach me to persevere in my prayers. Even when I am met by silence, remind me of Your Word that says You are in my midst. May I guard my time with You each day and not let the hectic pace of life and the demands of caring for my family crowd You out.

Be careful to listen to all these words which I command you, in order that it may be well with you and your sons after you forever, for you will be doing what is good and right in the sight of the LORD your God. (Deuteronomy 12:28)

There are consequences to the busyness of life. One of the highest prices we pay when we get overcommitted is the price of our dearest relationships. When the events of our day crowd out our time with God, we will soon find ourselves further and further from where He wants us to be. We start following the voices of those surrounding us, and soon the voice of our Savior is drowned out in all the clamor.

Just as we have to train our children to listen to our voices, we have to train ourselves to listen to God's voice. My preschooler naturally tries to tune out my voice when he is watching a favorite television program. I have had to train him to do otherwise. Often that means turning the television off and instructing him to look into my eyes and listen to my voice. Sometimes I ask him to repeat what I have just said to be sure he heard and understood my words.

We need to practice these same exercises when listening to God. Find some quiet moments away from the distractions of life and tune into our Savior's voice. Start by reading His Word. The answers we seek in life are often waiting for us there, but we do not take the time to look and listen. Once we quiet our hearts before Him, we can hear Him. Like the young child who is learning to listen, you may want to repeat aloud what you hear Him saying to you. As you hear yourself repeating His instruction, you are more apt to follow through. Another method of sharpening your listening skills is to record your thoughts in a journal.

Listening takes practice and diligence. We, as children of God, are no different from our own children when it comes to tuning into His voice. With time, we can learn to hear Him above all the distractions of life.

Help me, Lord, to hear Your voice clearly amidst all the noise in my busy life. Teach me to listen for You, and to make time to meet with You, that I may learn to recognize Your voice and respond to it.

But from those who were of high reputation (what they were makes no difference to me; God shows no partiality)—well, those who were of reputation contributed nothing to me. (Galatians 2:6)

Reputation can mean everything, or it can mean nothing. Some stake their lives on their reputations, others lose their lives because of them. Take Jesus, for instance. He was a good man, right? He was without sin! He healed the sick, cast out demons, fed the hungry and brought many people to the saving grace of God. Yet He had a bad reputation. Why? Because the Pharisees didn't like Him. Jesus attracted the attention the Pharisees wanted for themselves, so they set out to destroy Him. They began with His reputation, and it eventually cost Him His life. That was all part of God's plan, but it does bring up the question: How important is reputation?

Reputation is something that is built not necessarily by the person owning it, but by the perception of those who use it. It is your character as viewed by the public. Jesus was an upstanding person, but those who did not like Him, labeled Him otherwise. Jesus always did what was right, in spite of the reputation it earned Him. Others' opinions of us are not always an accurate assessment of who we are.

We should be concerned with pleasing one person above all else—God. Don't be as concerned about your reputation as you are about doing what is right in the eyes of God. Don't put pressure on yourself to commit to every worthwhile activity under the sun. You may make people feel uncomfortable because you are doing the right thing for your family by keeping your outside commitments to a minimum and even by being a stay-at-home mom. Sometimes the truth makes people uncomfortable. But Jesus kept right on promoting the truth anyway.

Today I want to pay tribute to a man who knows how to walk in that truth and doesn't let a little thing like reputation keep him from living out God's principles in his life—my husband. Happy Birthday, Jimmy!

Lord, thank You for sending Your Son in the form of man to live here on earth for a time and spread Your gospel. Help me to promote the truth in everything that I do and say.

June 23

And how delightful is a timely word! (Proverbs 15:23)

My week had been more hectic than usual. I stood at the front door, balancing a child on one hip, groceries on the other, holding another child by one hand and diaper bag and purse with another, clutching my keys in my teeth. I stared at the doorknob and then nodding to my preschooler, motioned for him to get the keys out of my mouth and unlock the door. He understood; we'd been down this road before. It was the beginning of another hectic, frustrating evening.

At nearly midnight, I was finally ready for bed. Turning off all of the lights, I passed the kitchen counter and saw a familiar scrawl on an envelope. It was a letter from my father. And it was addressed to me. Just me. Unfolding the two-page letter, I began to read. My tired eyes absorbed every precious word. When I got to the end, tears now streaming down my cheeks, I turned it over and read it again. Every golden word was like life to me. I slowly folded the letter and carried it to my hope chest, where I stored it with the other letters I have received from my father over the years.

"How delightful is a timely word!" My father had written me simply to encourage me and affirm my worth and value. Every year or so, he has sent me a letter full of words of praise and encouragement to spur me on in all aspects of life. Each letter is different, yet full of the same love and affirmation every time. My father's letters have come at the most amazing times— when I needed to hear his words of encouragement the most.

You may be overcommitted, and you may not spend as much time with your children as you know you need to. Work on it. Pray about it. And communicate your love to them. Every word that comes from your mouth or pen that affirms your child's worth will have profound impact. It's never too late.

If your children are still at home, speak timely words of love and encouragement to them now. You can start a collection of love letters for them too. I write each of my boys a letter on their birthdays every year. Delight your children today with a timely word.

> *Lord, thank You for my father's timely words. Help me to commu-*
> *nicate to my children, their incredible value and worth, the way*
> *my father has. Keep me focused on the things that truly matter.*

"And so in the present case, I say to you, stay away from these men and let them alone, for if this plan or action should be of men, it will be overthrown; but if it is of God, you will not be able to over-throw them; or else you may even be found fighting against God."
(Acts 5:38-39)

Change is a part of life. Every day people change jobs, houses, cars, clothes, breakfast cereals, channels, hairstyles; we change our minds about everything at one time or another. Usually the changes we experience in life are influenced by our own choices. Sometimes, however, we are the victims of change. We desperately try to be in control of our lives, but no matter how hard we try to remain at the helm, we need to remember that we need to let God steer. Our lives are in His hands.

How many times have you planned something only to have God change your plans at the last minute? It happens to me all the time. I used to get frustrated when things didn't go according to my plan, but through the years of growing in my relationship with Christ, I have learned to view change as a tool that He often uses for my own good. A canceled appointment, an unexpected illness, thwarted plans or a change in schedule are all measures God may use to redirect me.

Do you feel like you are constantly fighting against your schedule? Are you easily frustrated by change? Chances are you are entangled in a web of wrong activity for you and have found yourself fighting against God. You may need to make some changes. It may involve denying some of your own desires if you discover they are conflicting with God's will for your life. He knows what is best for you, and His will may be clashing with yours. Change can be puzzling at first, but once you begin to line up your will with His, it is the only thing that makes sense.

Lord, help me to seek out that which You want for my life. Teach me to relax when You bring about change in my life, not fight against it. Bring my will into harmony with Yours, that I might see every event in my life as part of Your master plan.

June 25

*. . . I count all things to be loss in view of the surpassing value of
knowing Christ Jesus my Lord, for whom I have suffered the loss of
all things, and count them but rubbish in order that I may gain
Christ. (Philippians 3:8)*

My oldest son is farsighted. He cannot focus on any object close to
him without his glasses. When he was four, I found him in his
room, face pressed into a book, eyes squinting to see the contents of each page.
I watched him silently for a minute from the doorway. I had just finished
cleaning his glasses, now in my hand. I cleared my throat to announce my ap-
proach and extended the glasses. "Do you need these?" He smiled brightly, re-
plying, "Thank goodness, Mommy. My books are blurry without them!"

He had not quite grasped that it was his view that was blurry, not the
books. He would figure that out in time. For now, it was enough to know
that he needed his glasses to see. Without them, nothing was in focus; his
entire view was distorted.

Many of us go through life with our spiritual view largely distorted. We
plow through life without spiritual focus and end up in an embankment of
fog. Without clear perspective, we soon find ourselves lost in a mist of bad
choices, misarranged priorities and confusing circumstances. The only way
to maintain a clear view is to spend time with God in His Word and in
prayer. This is how He brings everything into focus, making life and all it
holds much clearer, including the decisions we need to make.

Our perspective often gets knocked out of focus when we view every-
thing we are doing as critical. The only real life-preserving activity we need
to be concerned with is the development of our relationship with Jesus
Christ. When He is in His rightful place in our lives, all other events and
relationships fall into place. Their importance or lack thereof can be viewed
with clarity when they are observed from a focused perspective.

*Clear away the fog, Lord. Help me to stay focused on You and Your
plan for my life, in order that I might maintain a clear perspective
of all that surrounds me. Keep my view of You sharp.*

June 26

. . . Yet he will have control over all the fruit of my labor for which I have labored by acting wisely under the sun. . . . (Ecclesiastes 2:19)

Mothers daily find themselves going five different directions at once. While it is part of the "job," we intensify the problem by stretching ourselves too thin. Parenting takes more time, energy and patience than most of us humanly have. That is why we need to continually look to God to help us do the best we can. Part of doing our best includes making wise choices about our activities outside the home. Sometimes the hectic schedule that causes burnout comes not from mom's commitments, but the children's. There are sports, recitals, school plays, church programs, field trips, and much, much more. We are raising a generation of over-achievers who are headed for early burnout if we don't take the reins and slow down the pace.

Just as you need recreation or "play" to bring balance to your life, so do your children. But as we limit our own outside activities to avoid exhaustion and stay in line with our priorities, we need to guide our children in setting similar limits. By doing so, they will learn how to be effective in balancing both work and play.

One wise mother of three active teenagers has come to an agreement with her children that they must limit their activities and sports to two each. This system works well for their family. The limitations they have set allow for enough time to enjoy both planned and spur-of-the-moment outings with the whole family. In addition, these restrictions have forced them to consider how they want to spend their time. The kids have grown emotionally by learning to focus on what is really important to each of them. And, they are discovering the value of time.

Do your children's schedules keep you on the run? By teaching your children early on to choose their activities carefully, you are providing a frame of reference for learning self-control and wisdom. Overcommitment at any age is a destructive practice.

Lord, thank You for showing me the value of time by helping me to set my own limitations and realign my priorities. Give me guidance as I seek to do the same with my children.

June 27

As each one has received a special gift, employ it in serving one an-other, as good stewards of the manifold grace of God. (1 Peter 4:10)

Each of us has special gifts that God implanted in us—He created us each uniquely. The Scriptures command us to use our gift(s) to serve others. We are not being responsible with what God has given us or gifted us with if we are not using those gifts. That does require being involved in the lives of others and being committed to outside activities. Yet, we throw ourselves off-balance when we begin committing to too many areas of service, especially those that may not be in the area in which God has gifted us. So how do we discover our gifts?

For some, discovering their gift is easy and may even be obvious. Someone with the gift of mercy for example, usually has a deep compassion for people that comes naturally and shows up easily in their desire and ability to help and pray for others. For others, discovering gifts takes some searching and praying. (Read 1 Corinthians 12 for a description of the various spiritual gifts.) Some churches have networking classes designed to help you discover your spiritual gifts and then channel them for proper service. Ask your pastor about starting one if there is not such a class currently available at your church.

Uncovering your spiritual gifts can be the weight you have long been searching for to help you balance out your scales. If you are overcommitted in outside service and activities, knowing your gifts will help you to assess what areas you will be most effective in. If you have a hard time saying "no," this knowledge can give you the confidence you need to discern where your involvement should be. Then you can truly be a good steward with what God has given you.

Thank You, God, for making me special and gifting me uniquely. I want to serve You with my gifts. Help me to discover them and then use them for Your glory. May I find balance in my commit-ments as I seek to honor You in all of my activities.

Like apples of gold in settings of silver
Is a word spoken in right circumstances. (Proverbs 25:11)

Ah, the power of the word "no." By it wars are ended and without it, sin began. Have you ever thought about that? If Eve would have just said "no" to the serpent, we wouldn't be in such a sinful state. Unfortunately, I think her lack of courage in this area was handed down when she ate the apple. Why is it so hard for us to say "no?" Maybe it's not hard for you. I have a terrible time saying that two-letter word because by so doing, I feel that I am sending out a message of personal rejection.

Instead of recognizing that I am simply passing on a request for my time or services, for many years I was under the guise that I was rejecting the person who was requesting it of me. In actuality, I am rejecting the request, not the person. It took me awhile to figure that out. Do you ever feel like that? If so, you need to re-train your thinking like I did. Otherwise, that incorrect line of thought will get you way in over your head and suck the life out of you!

If we perceive that the answer to a specific request should be "no," then we need to learn to think of it as "a word spoken in right circumstances." Inevitably, when we commit to something under the wrong circumstances, we end up regretting it. Sometimes we even end up paying for it. Or our children do, because it is our time with them that often gets shorted as a result of taking on another commitment.

The years we have with our children are like precious treasure, growing more valuable with each passing year. Just like silver requires a lot of time in polishing to maintain its luster, so do our children. If we neglect the real needs of these tiny nuggets the Father has entrusted in our care, they will become dull and lifeless from just plain doing too much! Learn to say, "no!" when you need to and the whole family will shine like apples of gold in settings of silver.

Lord, I want my children to shine before You. Help me to be committed to them by learning to say "no" under the right circumstances. Give me discernment that I might know what my answer to a request should be.

> *Then I will make up to you for the years*
> *That the swarming locust has eaten. . . . (Joel 2:25)*

A dear friend of mine has one of the most beautiful relationships with her parents I have ever witnessed. Recently, she went to her parents home for dinner after a particularly stressful day. Upon her arrival, her father immediately sensed her tension and invited her to sit in his lap. There he held his twenty-something daughter, tears now streaming down her cheeks, while she poured her heart out. He nodded in understanding and prayed for her. Her heart lightened and her perspective was refreshed.

This scene touches my heart. What makes it more incredible is that her earliest memories are of an empty chair. For years, he had been an alcoholic and devoted his time to any place but home. The thread that held the family together was their mother. She was committed to keeping them secure by relying on Christ for strength. She taught them to do the same. Together they believed that God would bring their father home. He did.

When my friend was eight, her father returned. He accepted Christ as his Savior and Lord, and his life was forever transformed. Today, he cherishes all four of his children and loves his wife deeply. Putting together the pieces of a broken family has not been without its struggles, but God has been the glue that keeps them united. In the words of my friend, "God is making up for the years that the enemy stole from me. Those years that the locusts had eaten, God has returned to me tenfold."

There is hope for your situation, too. God can make up for the years that the locusts have eaten. Remain steadfast in your commitment to Him and your children. Stay faithful to your husband. God can restore all relationships. It is never too late.

> *Lord, You are faithful, even when we are not. Strengthen my commitment to my family so we can withstand the attacks of the enemy. Draw my children and their father close to You in such a way that our faith is increased beyond measure. Make up for any years that have not been the best.*

June 30

So teach us to number our days,
That we may present to Thee a heart of wisdom. (Psalm 90:12)

Once when my husband and I were balking to our pastor at the exces-sive amount of time it takes to properly parent small children he shared these words of wisdom with us, "When your kids are little they are begging to get on your calendar; suddenly, they become teenagers and you are begging to get on theirs." Words to heed from a man who knows—at the time he had one son preparing for marriage and two teenage daughters preparing to leave the nest and head for college.

Our pastor's words made me realize that I can't ever turn back the clock. Watching someone else's children grow up and leave the nest solidified that truly we need to number our days and use them wisely. I often find myself frustrated by the demands that parenting young children entail. Because their neediness during their early years can be exhausting, some days when my energy is at a low, I find myself longing for the days when my kids won't "need" me so much. My pastor's perspective of longing for the days again when his children needed him more than they now do has changed my frustration into appreciation.

You may have read all of the devotionals this month all the while think-ing, "Well, thank goodness overcommitment is not a problem for me. I spend plenty of time with my kids." If this is the case, I commend you. Continue on the path you are now traveling. It is the smoothest and straightest path to God's best. If, however, you are among the many moms who choose the rockier road of overcommitment then be warned: I know many stay-at-home moms who now have teenage children and are in utter despair over the lack of time and attention they gave to their kids when there were younger.

Lord, I want the time You have given me with my children to count. Help me to number my days wisely and take seriously my limited time. Give me focus as I dedicate these years to my children and seek to raise them up in You.

July:
On-the-job Training

*There must be an instruction manual
around here somewhere . . .*

good employer sets up a training program for his employees. I worked a variety of jobs before becoming a full-time stay-at-home mom. Some of the jobs included training, some did not. In the jobs where I was left to figure things out on my own, I quickly became frustrated and unproductive. On the other hand, when someone worked with me and trained me in my duties, I flourished. Just knowing that someone was available as a resource greatly boosted my confidence.

Many stay-at-home moms feel they have been thrown into the job of parenting with no training, no direction and no one to turn to for guidance. They believe there is no "instruction manual." Fortunately, that assumption is not true.

God did not create the job of motherhood and then leave us on our own to muddle blindly through the task. He provides on-the-job training in His Word. This month we look at the Bible as God's instruction manual for stay-at-home moms.

My prayer is that God will give you a new desire to search for the answers to your parenting questions in His Word. In this resource, the author makes Himself totally available twenty-four hours a day. You can go to Him anytime you need guidance, and He will show you the way.

All Scripture is inspired by God and profitable for teaching, for re-proof, for correction, for training in righteousness. (2 Timothy 3:16)

*I*f there is any doubt in your mind that the Bible is an instruction manual, today's verse should clear it up. Another word for instruction is "teach."

One of the best ways to teach children is through example. Children are imitators, and the Bible is full of wonderful examples. The story of David and Goliath exemplifies David's courage and faith in God to supply his needs; Daniel in the lion's den demonstrates his unshakable faith in God and commitment to worship God alone; Joseph illustrates steadfastness, patience, kindness and forgiveness. The Bible also includes instruction on how to reprove, correct and train. If you want to know what God says in those areas, use a concordance to locate verses that talk about a specific word. Most Bibles have a small concordance in the back.

Use God's Word to teach your children. Try to set aside time every day when the whole family is together to read a passage from the Bible and then discuss it. Ask the children how the passage applies to them and their lives. Get a discussion going. If you have small children with short atten-tion spans, focus more on stories about specific people. Stick to a single point. As you include God's Word in your home on a daily basis, God will use the knowledge of His Word to begin training your children in righ-teousness.

Lord, thank You for making the Bible available as a teaching tool. Show me how I can utilize it in creative ways to make Your Word come alive to my children.

And be kind to one another, tender-hearted, forgiving each other, just as God in Christ also has forgiven you. (Ephesians 4:32)

Scripture memory is a great way to teach our children. When we help them to memorize the truth of God's Word, it will become a part of their lives, even from a young age. Just in case you think this discipline is only for older children, read on. Today's verse is a principle that a good friend taught her four-year-old. By helping him memorize the verse, they could then bring it up if he was not being "kind" or "forgiving" with his younger sibling. If Jordan acted out, Dawn would simply say, "Jordan, what does the Bible say about being kind to one another? Are you being kind right now?" Little Jordan would then recite the familiar passage and they would discuss his behavior.

Dawn felt this internalizing of godly character was working very well. She realized how much Jordan understood the principle one day when she was running short on patience and snapped at Jordan unnecessarily. He looked up at her with serious blue eyes and very quietly and respectfully said, "Mommy, you are not being very kind to me right now and the Bible says to be kind." You can imagine Dawn's surprise and delight at her young son's ability to apply this principle so early in life—even though it was directed at her! Needless to say, she apologized to her son for her lack of kindness toward him.

If we use God's Word to instruct our children, the results will be godly men and women. What you put in is what you will get out.

> *Help me, Lord, to apply Your Word to my children's lives. Show me how I can help them memorize Scripture and internalize Your truth. I am committed to instructing them according to Your ways.*

July 3

There is a way which seems right to a man,
But its end is the way of death. (Proverbs 14:12)

Today's world has many theories about how to raise children. Bookstores are crammed with books on child-rearing. Unfortunately, not many of the philosophies of these books are biblical. Satan is the master of deceit and the Bible says in Second Corinthians 11:14 that he "disguises himself as an angel of light." If our enemy can make something look like the truth, then he can deceive even followers of Christ. We really have to be on guard about what we read when it comes to child-rearing philosophies. Check the advice against the Bible. Do the theories and ideas match God's Word?

Sometimes something can sound good and be totally out of line. For instance, there is a popular theory today that children are innately good. The belief is that when they are small, they should be allowed to do whatever they please—everything from throwing temper tantrums to throwing food—because they don't "know any better." If you test that theory against God's Word, a warning light flashes. The Bible says we are born with a sin nature (Psalm 51:5). That discredits the theory of children being innately good. So, if every child is born with the natural instinct to sin, then we need to train them to discern right from wrong behavior.

The Bible also says to "train up a child in the way he should go" in Proverbs 22:6. If we allow them to do whatever they want, then we are training our children in self-indulgence, disobedience, disrespect and impatience. The goal is to bring insight and spiritual life to our children. Ignoring that responsibility will only lead to catastrophic consequences, possibly for all eternity.

Lord God, may I forever take seriously the responsibility of raising my children in a godly fashion. Give me insight and wisdom as I seek out teaching tools. Help me to discern the light of Your truth in what I read and hear.

July 4

"And you shall know the truth, and the truth shall make you free." (John 8:32)

What better day to reflect on the truth than Independence Day—the day that we celebrate our social, cultural and religious freedoms. Of the fifty-five men who formed the Constitution, fifty-two were active members of their churches. Thomas Jefferson called the Bible "the cornerstone for American Liberty." Patrick Henry said, "Our country was founded on the gospel of Jesus Christ." James Madison said, "We've staked our future on our ability to follow the Ten Commandments," and in his farewell address, George Washington said, "You can't have national morality apart from religious principle."

National morality today is far from "religious principle"; legal abortions, drug abuse, rape, murder and violent crime are rampant. Many national leaders have demonstrated total disregard for the Bible's standards. Even prayer is outlawed in many schools. In the 1940s, teachers dealt with gum chewing, talking in class, running in the hallways and littering. Now the issues are teen pregnancy, rape, murder and drug abuse.

What has happened to our schools, our cities and our nation? We have left behind God's law. So what can you as a stay-at-home mom do? Know the truth. Learn God's Word. Live by His commands. Teach them to your children. Change takes place one person at a time—one family at a time. You and your family will be free from the hands of the enemy because the truth shall make you free.

Lord, may I live in the unchanging freedom of Your truth, teaching my children to do the same.

July 5

But one who looks intently at the perfect law, the law of liberty, and abides by it, not having become a forgetful hearer but an effectual doer, this man shall be blessed in what he does. (James 1:25)

The Bible provides a freeing way to parent. As today's verse states, it is really "the law of liberty." There is freedom in doing what is right. When we take God's commands seriously and put them into practice, the result is blessing—for us and our children.

Parenting correctly takes time, but we are too busy doing other things. If you are trying to teach a whining two-year-old patience and self-control, it takes time to stop what you are doing and correct the behavior by appropriate discipline. What about the third grader to whom you are trying to teach self-discipline? When you are not home after school to be sure he does his homework and monitor what he watches on television, what patterns might he fall into? If you are not there, you cannot correct unacceptable behaviors.

It is vital to be a doer of the Word. As stay-at-home moms we have ample opportunity to teach our children both by example and instruction. Although it is tough at times, you will be blessed. And what greater reward is there than seeing your children grow up to be doers of the Word?

Teach me, Lord, to be a doer and not just a hearer of Your Word. Thank You for showing me that obedience to Your Word sets me free.

July 6

All discipline for the moment seems not to be joyful, but sorrowful; yet to those who have been trained by it, afterwards it yields the peaceful fruit of righteousness. (Hebrews 12:11)

When my son, Seth, was a little over two-years-old, he decided to test a new word he had learned—"no." When I told him to pick up his toys, something he had been doing on his own for months, he looked at me, tilted his head, planted his feet in front of him and shouted "No!" I was shocked. Considering that he had never done this before, I decided to give him a warning. I firmly but gently said, "Seth, you may not talk to Mommy that way. Now, please pick up your toys so we can get ready for lunch." "No" again tumbled out of his mouth. I picked him up, swatted his bottom and placed him in his crib for a time of isolation.

He cried and shouted his protest for several minutes. When he had quieted down, I returned to his room and talked to him about his behavior. At two, he may not have fully understood the need for respect of parental authority, but he did realize the consequences of his actions. They were painful, and he did not wish to repeat them.

When I correct my children, it is not a joy-filled moment. Sometimes it is as painful for me as it is for them. Still, it is necessary. Right from wrong is learned by instruction. Instruction involves correction and discipline. It is a learning process, and sometimes being consistent in correction is tough. The result of such training will be worth the effort, however, when the crop becomes the peaceful fruit of righteousness.

Help me, Lord, to discipline my children appropriately and to train them up to yield the fruit of righteousness. Give me the courage to follow this instruction in Your Word.

July 7

. . . {F}or the inward thought and the heart of a man are deep.
(Psalm 64:6)

*A*child's behavior reflects his heart. Our actions are in direct correlation to our thoughts. As parents, we have a God-given opportunity to shape the thinking of our children and, in turn, their behavior. It is our responsibility to teach our children to think before they act. But our world says, "If it feels good do it!"

Even much of the public school curriculum teaches a lifestyle without consequences. Much of it blatantly opposes biblical values. The trouble is that teachers alone cannot change the curriculum. Parents have to get involved and, sadly, most Christian parents are unaware of what their children are taught.

If the schools teach your children one thing and you are teaching them another, can you imagine the battle in their young minds? That is why an increasing number of moms have turned to homeschooling. If this is not an option for your family, you can make a difference by getting involved in your child's school. Volunteer one afternoon a week. If you hear or see something that contradicts your value system, you have every right to speak out. Politely suggest an alternative. Get involved with the PTA or run for school board. Talk with your children about what they are learning at school.

Oh Lord, how I want to teach my children to think and act like a
servant of Christ. I pray that You will show me how to plant You
deep into their hearts and minds.

. . . {S}he took from its fruit and ate; and she gave also to her husband with her, and he ate. (Genesis 3:6)

*L*et's face it, even though we know what we should be teaching our children, we sometimes blow it. It is difficult to feel like a successful mother when you have a temper-tantrum prone toddler or a rebellious teenager. In the midst of those situations, you may feel like all of the godly instruction in the world has failed. Your child is not behaving in a godly manner, and you are not responding in a godly manner! My first child went through a tough period of testing when he was two years old. After one particularly difficult day I plopped on the couch and cried out to God, "What do You want from me? I'm doing everything right according to Your Word. Why won't my son obey me?"

In the quiet of my heart, God answered me. My son is human—he has a sin nature, just like me. God showed me that my relationship with Him is no different than Seth's relationship with me. God did everything right, has given me instruction and still, I disobey and misbehave at times. God was the perfect parent, and yet Adam and Eve disobeyed Him. Yet God didn't give up on them or stop loving them—neither does He with us today.

Dr. James Dobson has said that today's kids respect strength and courage. They will disobey parents sometimes to test their determination and toughness.

Testing is a normal part of growing up. Our persistence in instilling godly instruction in our children will pay off. Repetition is the mother of learning, so keep repeating—you will be heard!

Thank You, Lord, for modeling perfect parenting. Teach me to be a better mother and help me to never give up doing it Your way.

He has told you, O man, what is good;
And what does the LORD require of you
But to do justice, to love kindness,
And to walk humbly with your God. (Micah 6:8)

Today's Scripture explains exactly what is expected of us as believers. When the people of Israel tried to make amends for their disobedience and disbelief after God delivered them into the promised land, they questioned what God wanted of them. They tried to figure out how they could make up for their mistakes and bad behavior. God's reply was simply, "to do justice, to love kindness, and to walk humbly with your God."

He wanted only their obedience.

When it comes to our children's well-being, we are often like the Israelites who stomped in disbelief at God's promise. He has provided His Word for us as moms to properly raise our children. Still, we grumble and complain and seek answers elsewhere. What a foolish mistake! God's way is the best way. The justice He speaks of is simply doing the right thing. What else could be more right than His Word?

If we just walk humbly with Him, display kindness and seek justice as we raise our children, we have done what He requires of us. The rest is up to Him.

God of justice, teach me to walk in humility with You. I don't
want to be full of myself but full of Your Holy Spirit. Empower me
to raise my kids right and to seek only what is good in Your sight.

And why do you call Me, "Lord, Lord," and do not do what I say? (Luke 6:46)

The title of "lord" denotes complete devotion and service. To "lord" over someone means to totally rule in every area of that person's life. Is Jesus your Lord? Have you given Him complete control of your life—even of your parenting? For many moms, "Lord" is an affectionate term used when they pray and talk about the God whom they serve. When it comes down to headship though, God is not truly lording over their lives. If He was, they would submit to His authority in every area, including His commands on proper parenting. The Bible gives very specific instruction on how to discipline. (See Proverbs 13:24, 22:15 and 29:15-17.) Yet, many parents ignore those commands. Aren't they then ignoring Him as "Lord"?

If we cannot do what He tells us to do in His Word, then we should not call Him our "Lord." God's Word instructs us in every area of parenting. We just need to take the time to seek the answers to our questions. Take some time to reflect on your parenting methods. Are you getting your principles from Scripture or another source? Do you do what He says to do with your children? ("Train them up in the way they should go . . ." Proverbs 22:6) Do your actions justify calling Him your "Lord"? If not, take this opportunity to get right with Him.

Lord, I want You to be just that—my Lord in every area of my life. Forgive me for sometimes giving You the title. Direct me as I seek to give You lordship over my parenting. I want to do it Your way.

Obey your leaders, and submit to them; for they keep watch over your souls, as those who will give an account. (Hebrews 13:17)

Do you ever feel like a soul keeper? I want to be sure my children lead godly, productive lives and make it to eternity. Part of that achievement is in training them to understand and submit to God's authority. He is their ultimate Leader. In the process however, they have to learn to submit to other authority in the form of parents, teachers, pastors, police, even coaches. If they can learn to submit to these earthly forms of leadership, they will be better able to submit to God. In teaching them to follow their authorities, we are preparing them for a lifetime of serving Christ.

Obedience is characterized by submission. The dictionary defines it as "giving in to the orders or instruction of one in authority." Do your children obey your orders? Your instruction? Or are they constantly challenging your authority? If so, then how will they be able to obey the One in ultimate authority over their lives, Jesus Christ?

Once your children turn their hearts and lives over to God, they are responsible for being obeying His instruction. If they have never come under your authority and acted in obedience, especially when it's against their desires, how then will they submit to the Savior when confronted with all of life's temptations? Your children will have many choices to make. Will you have properly prepared them to make the right ones? What account will you give to God for the responsibility of the children that He bestowed upon you?

God, You are my ultimate Authority. Help me to teach my children to obey You, me and all those in authority over them. Give me insight on how to prepare them for a lifetime of serving You.

Do all things without grumbling and disputing; that you may prove yourselves to be blameless and innocent, children of God above reproach in the midst of a crooked and perverse generation, among whom you appear as lights in the world. (Philippians 2:14-15)

Instructing a child how to properly conduct himself is probably the single most important thing on any parent's mind. But just teaching your kids the right thing to do is not enough. It is just as important to teach them why they should do the right thing. I told my two-year-old son not to throw his toys. When I watched, he didn't do it. But when he thought I was not paying attention, he would throw a toy or two. I tell him not to throw his toys (the what), and that if he does, he may break them and he may hurt someone (the why).

Teaching a child both the what and the why can change his conduct, over time. Seth had to test my instruction but he no longer throws his toys. In fact, he now tells other children not to throw toys, and why. By teaching them why, we enable our children to understand the possible consequences of their actions. If we tell our teenagers to save sex for marriage but don't explain why it is the best thing to do, will they be able to say, "no" when faced with the temptation?

God instructs us in the what and the why. Philippians 2:14 tells what to do: "Do all things without grumbling and disputing;" and verse 15 tells why: "That you may prove yourselves to be blameless and innocent, children of God above reproach." If God believes in equipping us, shouldn't we do the same for our children?

Thank you, Lord, for showing me how to teach my children not only to act, but to think morally and responsibly. Give me opportunities to help them apply Your Word to all situations.

July 13

He who dwells in the shelter of the Most High
Will abide in the shadow of the Almighty. (Psalm 91:1)

Of all the important lessons we teach our children, one is paramount. God is our ultimate Security. If we instruct our children that their security lies in God alone, they will be self-confident, self-sufficient and yet, self-less. When we depend upon God as our Source for all things, we learn to reap security in who God is, rather than in who we are, and what we accomplish. Our character and accomplishments change, but God's character is unchanging. We can depend on His constancy. When hard times befall us, we can be secure in the knowledge of who God is and His care for us.

This is a hard lesson to apply when you're thirty-something, married with 2.5 children, a mortgage payment and summer vacation plans when your husband announces that he's lost his job. If your security is in the Lord, you will pray. If it's not, then you will panic!

Teach your children in their early years that Christ created them special and unique; they are more precious than the finest gold to their Creator and to you. Reinforce their value often. They will develop an inner peace and security that brings stability and steadfastness. No matter what the peer group says or what tragedy swarms them, they will be able to say "no" when they know God loves, accepts and promises to provide for them.

Lord, I pray that You will help me to instill a true sense of security in my children. May I instruct them to depend solely on You in all things and to dwell in Your shelter at all times.

July 14

Children, obey your parents in the Lord, for this is right. (Ephesians 6:1)

Instructing our children to do what is right is part of God's plan. Children are to obey their parents not only when it is convenient, or the parents are fair and just or if the children feel like it. Children are to *obey* their parents. Instructing our children to obey begins early. A toddler who does not learn to obey may run out in the street. Obedience is not only a heart issue, but a safety issue at times. It's important, however, to teach our children to obey us not out of the fear of reproof, but out of the love of virtue. We are training them not only to do, but to think. Our children must learn to do what is right out of the simple pleasure of right itself. If they only obey you out of fear of disciplinary action, then you are not training their hearts.

I can recommend a great learning tool to help you in the instruction of your children. *Growing Kids God's Way* is a biblically based parenting program including books, audio and video tapes to assist you in your quest to train your children's hearts. Many churches around the country even teach parenting classes using this material.

When we begin to instruct our children early, we set the stage for their obedience to God later in life. If we have not taught our children to obey us, how can we expect them to obey a God they cannot see?

> *Lord, help me to obey Your commands and then to teach my children to obey me—and ultimately You. Show me how to train their hearts in the love of virtue, so that they learn to make the right choice every time.*

July 15

———— ❧✿❧ ————

But a natural man does not accept the things of the Spirit of God; for they are foolishness to him, and he cannot understand them, because they are spiritually appraised. (1 Corinthians 2:14)

When you seek to raise your children according to biblical standards, there will always be opposition. We live in a world ruled not by God's standard, but by self-imposed morals and values. When my husband and I became parents, some people we deeply respect openly disapproved of our chosen child-rearing techniques. Their concern was that we were "too hard" on our first-born and "too stringent" in our disciplinary methods.

At first, we allowed these opinions to cause us to doubt our parenting skills and applications. It didn't take long, however, for us to realize that the methods we chose in training our children are strictly biblical and our antagonists were not like-minded. Our goal is to raise our children to be morally responsible and biblically responsive. They could not understand that line of thinking. Something wonderful happens when we turn our lives over to God; He opens our eyes to the truth of His Word. Until then, the Bible doesn't make much sense to us. Even after we become believers, we have to seek God on the meaning of the Scriptures. Therefore, we cannot expect an unbeliever to understand our methods if we're raising our children according to biblical principles.

My husband and I learned not to be dissuaded by well-meaning objections. We have a responsibility to raise our children properly, and we are the ones who will answer to God for our choices. As long as we do what is best for our children in God's eyes, it doesn't matter what anyone else sees.

Lord, help me to run my household and raise my children according to Your Word. Give me strength to stand firm in my parenting methods against the opposition of those who do not share my philosophy.

Also it is not good for a person to be without knowledge,
And he who makes haste with his feet errs. (Proverbs 19:2)

I would never attempt to fix my car without reading a manual or try to install an electrical appliance without first looking at the manufacturer's instructions. Similarly, I would not attempt to raise children without acquiring some knowledge on the subject. The best place to glean information about any subject is from the person who created it. God, our Creator, knows us best. Consequently, He gives clear direction and insight into the conditions, habits and nature of man in one place: the Bible. If we proceed without caution or direction, we are headed for trouble: "He who makes haste with his feet errs." You wouldn't build a house without a blueprint, would you? Neither should you build a life without a plan. God has a plan detailed for us in His Word if we'll just take the time to read it.

I heard about a woman who had eighteen children. The only alone time she could find with God was when she pulled her apron up over her head. Those kids learned that when Mama had the apron over her head she was praying and they had better not bother her. She managed to steal several five-minute sessions with God a day, and she swears it was those minutes under her apron with God that gave her the wisdom, the knowledge and the patience to go on.

Find some time each day to read the parenting manual God wrote for you.

> *Forgive me, Lord, for not making time for You. Give me the discipline to spend time daily in Your Word and in conversation with You. May I acquire the knowledge I need to raise my children in a manner that is pleasing to You, that I may not act in "haste."*

July 17

So shall My word be which goes forth from My mouth;
It shall not return to Me empty. . . . (Isaiah 55:11)

If we saturate our children in God's Word, we can be sure that sooner or later it will soak in. If we pour God's Word into our children, when life squeezes, God's Word will flow out. Our children are eager to soak up anything we are willing to teach them. As they grow and mature, our teaching has to become more creative to keep their interest. As stay-at-home moms we have an incredible opportunity to teach our children. As their first teachers, we can also be the most influential.

I was raised in a strict Christian home. My parents took every opportunity to train me in biblical standards. When I went off to college, however, I strayed. To my folks, it appeared their efforts in raising me in a godly manner were null and void, but they continued to pray for me and love me in spite of my rebellion. It didn't take long for God to bring me back to a lifestyle that honored Him.

During my rebellious behavior, I was bombarded with thoughts of my wrong behavior. Bible verses from my childhood flashed through my mind—the Holy Spirit was at work in me! My parents had taken the time to buid a moral warehouse in me.

Lord, help me to build a moral warehouse of biblical knowledge
and principle into my children. I thank You for Your promise that
once activated, Your Word is never dormant.

But the Helper, the Holy Spirit, whom the Father will send in My name, He will teach you all things, and bring to your remembrance all that I said to you. (John 14:26)

When I was a rebellious teenager, God brought to remembrance the things I had learned in His Word. At the time it was a message of conviction; as a parent I find it a message of comfort. God will use His Word however necessary to keep us close to Him. I find that reassuring. As a mother who wants what's best for my children, I take great comfort in knowing that God has sent a Helper, the Holy Spirit, to work with me in raising godly children.

There have been times when I want to find a specific Scripture passage to use in teaching one of my boys, but I cannot remember where to find it. I have unsuccessfully searched my concordance. I have called upon God to help me remember. And many times, He will bring to my remembrance where to find it. Other times, He has answered my plea for help through a friend or my husband.

God is the greatest Teacher. He is the One who inspired men to write the Bible. He sent His Son to communicate many of its truths here on earth. And He still teaches us through the wisdom in His Word and the help of the Holy Spirit.

Do not hesitate to ask God to send the Holy Spirit to help you raise godly children. After all, today's verse claims that He will teach us *all* things.

Thank You, God, for sending the Holy Spirit as a Helper. I acknowledge that parenting is a huge responsibility and I want and need Your help in raising children who will be committed to You.

July 19

> ... {B}ut let everyone be quick to hear, slow to speak and slow to anger. . . . (James 1:19)

Sometimes the most powerful words of instruction we can give to our children are no words at all. Silence can speak. Many times we jump to conclusions and falsely accuse them before we know all the details of a situation. When Seth was three, I found him bent over the cat's food dish which is off-limits. Seeing cat food scattered all over the kitchen floor, I gave him a tongue-lashing. I discovered after I sliced him with words of reproof that he had been picking up pieces of food and putting them back into the dish because his dad had unknowingly backed his chair into it and spilled the contents.

My quick-to-speak reaction doesn't build my children's trust that they can always talk to me about anything. I definitely want to win their confidence, especially for those upcoming teen years! I have learned the hard way to ask questions and then carefully listen to my children, never assuming that I know exactly what happened.

I always try to sneak in a lesson on God's forgiveness of our sins when I make a mistake with my children. If I look at my mistakes as opportunities rather than as failure, it lessens the sting a little! Jesus is also a great Example of the "quick to hear, slow to speak" model. He always listened intently when someone spoke to Him. He never interrupted, and His words were few but full of meaning. And sometimes, He was silent.

> Slow down my tongue, Lord. Often times, I am slow to hear and quick to speak and that is not how it should be. Give me self-control in this area and show me the power of instructing my children as much in my silence as in my words.

———— ❧❀❧ ————

For the word of God is living and active and sharper than any two-edged sword, and piercing as far as the division of soul and spirit, of both joints and marrow, and able to judge the thoughts and intentions of the heart. (Hebrews 4:12)

God's Word is powerful! When God's Word is studied and internalized, its power is activated in our lives. God uses the truths of Scripture to build character. It becomes our conscience in a way. What better conscience could we have than the Bible itself. Much more effective than Jiminy Cricket! He has the right idea: "Always let your conscience be your guide." This isn't a bad sentiment, particularly if your conscience is run by the Holy Spirit and fueled by God's Word. This makes a powerful combination.

The real beauty of God's Word comes alive when we see our thoughts and motives through the internal conscience that has been woven into us from His Word. We can stop ourselves before wrong thoughts turn into wrong actions.

If we will take the time to educate our children in God's Word, they too, will develop a conscience based on the Bible. Their moral warehouses will become full of the knowledge of right and wrong based on what God says. As they begin to make their own decisions, they draw on their moral warehouse or conscience. Don't misjudge the power of instructing your children in God's Word. If you don't have a regular family devotional time, start one today!

Thank you, Lord, for giving me Your Word as a way to instill Your standard of conscience into my children. May I use the Bible as the most important instructional tool in my kids' education. May they always call upon the knowledge they glean from it.

July 21

Establish my footsteps in Thy word,
And do not let any iniquity have dominion over me.
(Psalm 119:133)

here is no right time or place to teach the Scriptures to our children. Neither is there a specific way to do it. Anytime is the right time, anywhere is the right place, and anyway that we can get the message across is the right way to teach God's Word. We should take hold of the opportunities God gives us every day to weave spiritual lessons into life's experiences.

While walking through our neighborhood one evening, my older son admired the colorful flowers in a neighbor's yard. He wanted to pick one. Instead of just saying "no" and closing the discussion, I took the opportunity to talk about respecting others and their property and what the Bible says about respect. From there, we discussed God's beautiful creation and His role in our lives as the Creator. The entire discussion took less than five minutes. I have learned that my children will absorb much more if I take hold of the everyday moments when they are open to learn. When children ask questions, it is a teachable moment. Many parents find teachable moments at the end of the day as they tuck their children into bed. In those quiet moments with your child, some of the deepest and most important discussions take place. Don't brush off their questions, even if it's late at night and you are tired.

Most teachable moments come when you are doing everyday kinds of things. If you seize the moment, God can seize their hearts.

> *Help me, Lord, to use the everyday opportunities You give me to teach Your Word to my children. Show me how to listen to them, not only with my ears but with my heart.*

July 22

But let all things be done properly and in an orderly manner.
(1 Corinthians 14:30)

God modeled orderliness in Genesis when He created the world. He had a specific order in which He worked. His manner was not chaotic or whimsical. He even had structured time for rest. In the same way, it will save you and your children much frustration if you establish some kind of a routine. A routine naturally brings order to your day. If children know what to expect, they usually respond positively.

By nature, I am not a person who likes routine. I love variety and spontaneous activity. Fortunately, the job of a stay-at-home mom is full of surprises. However, I have realized that when there are constants in my children's lives, they are much happier and more secure. We have some structured playtime at our house every day. We try to eat meals at about the same time. We have time reserved for an afternoon nap. There are exceptions when the routine is broken, but they are just that—exceptions. You don't want so much structure that your children cannot be flexible because life does not always follow a pattern or routine—and flexibility is an important life skill. But so is orderliness, which breeds organization, responsibility and accountability. These are all strong character traits for our children to learn.

There are constants to build into the lives of older children as well. Set regular curfews. Establish a central place to keep track of appointments and messages. Plan family meetings. Orderliness provides a certain security.

> *Lord, thank You for modeling order in Your creation of the world. Help me to live my life properly and in an orderly manner according to Your Word. Show me the proper balance of routine and flexibility that will bring security to my children.*

See to it that no one takes you captive through philosophy and empty deception, according to the tradition of men, according to the elementary principles of the world, rather than according to Christ. (Colossians 2:8)

There are many books and programs on the market promoting the raising of "happy, healthy, well-adjusted" children. Unfortunately most of them are foundationally incorrect because they don't use the Bible as the basis. From just a surface glance, however, it can be difficult to detect whether a particular child-rearing program or philosophy is unbiblical. The author of such material knows how to catch your interest by using words and phrases like "emotionally healthy," "well-adjusted," "happy," "independent," "creative," "resourceful" and "positive." There is nothing wrong with any of these qualities. But are they really the most important ones for your children? What about obedience, self-control, patience, respect, joy, kindness, gentleness and faithfulness? The Bible mentions these as desired character traits. They are endorsed by the greatest child-rearing Expert of all—Jesus Christ.

It does help to have other books to read and glean ideas from, as well as practical application in raising our kids. (You're reading this book, aren't you?) But, other books should be only supplementary to God's Word; they should never replace your regular reading of the Bible. Be selective when you choose a book to read on raising children. Don't be lured into worldly thinking by nice-sounding buzz words and philosophies. So what if it sounds good—is it biblical? If it's not—put it back on the shelf. Don't let worldly philosophy take you captive.

Lord, give me discernment as I raise my children by Your standard. Remove the blinders from my eyes, so I will not be fooled by the world's deceptive philosophies wrapped in attractive packages.

July 24

For the time will come when they will not endure sound doctrine;
but wanting to have their ears tickled, they will accumulate for
themselves teachers in accordance to their own desires; and will
turn away their ears from the truth, and will turn aside to myths.
(2 Timothy 4:3-4)

This Scripture brings about the reason for yesterday's reflection. People do not always want to hear the truth because it can be difficult or uncomfortable. Instead, they want something that feels good, that gives the sensation of being "tickled." The world's philosophers know this. They have written books and programs which feel good when it comes to raising our children. These feel good philosophies that have captured the hearts of many parents, and in turn, the next generation.

In staying home with our children, we have made the choice to spend a lot of time with them. A mother that has been with energetic preschoolers or challenging teenagers can wear down. The task is exhausting, emotionally and physically. If mom is tired, she can easily be sucked into something that looks as if it would save her a little time and energy. That is why such philosophies as "parenting made easy" have become popular. Let's face it, parenting is not easy. Nothing ever worth having comes easy; and biblically responsive, morally responsible children are worth having.

So, be warned. There are many people who would like to "tickle" your ears with the myths of today's child-rearing practices. Do not be fooled. Remember to check every philosophy and every idea against God's Word. If it doesn't check out, then chuck it!

Ground me in Your truth, Lord, so that I might recognize the
myths in child-rearing philosophy. Keep me close to You and renew
my spirit when I grow weary.

For whatever was written in earlier times was written for our instruction, that through perseverance and the encouragement of the Scriptures we might have hope. (Romans 15:4)

There are those who will try to tell you that the Bible is a great book, but it is outdated. They will tell you it is old-fashioned and was never intended for use today. Today's verse should dispel that argument. I find great encouragement in knowing that God specifically inspired the Bible for our use yesterday, today and tomorrow. It doesn't matter who you are, where you came from or what era you live in; God's Word is for you. And today's verse specifically points out that it was "written for our instruction, that through *perseverance* . . . we might have hope." To persevere means to continue doing something in spite of difficulty, to remain steadfast in purpose.

God never intended for life as a Christian to be easy. He knew it would be tough to endure the opposition of the world. He knows the struggles you go through as a stay-at-home mom. He sees your frustrations and hears your cries. And He authored the book just for you—not only to give you instruction in how to raise your children, but also to offer you hope.

So carry on with your head held high and hope in your heart, knowing that you are not alone. Many other women endure the same trials you do. God loves you and offers instruction, as well as words of encouragement, on every page of the greatest book ever written. Read it.

Thank You, Lord, for showing me that Your Word is not only filled with instruction for me as a stay-at-home mom, but also with hope. Thank You also for the assurance that the Bible is relevant not only to my life today but for whatever I will go through tomorrow.

———————— ❧❀❧ ————————

The things you have learned and received and heard and seen in me, practice these things; and the God of peace shall be with you. (Philippians 4:9)

he Bible is full of the promises of God. Today's Scripture is just one of them. Some of His promises contain conditions, others do not. This particular promise has a condition: "The things you have learned and received and heard and seen in me, practice these things." In other words, we must practice what He's preached.

We must live out what we learn. If we do, then we receive the promise: "the God of peace shall be with you." Carrying the peace of God in our hearts can be a life-changing experience. The peace that God brings is different than any other kind of peace. The difference is found in Philippians 4:7: "And the peace of God, which surpasses all comprehension, shall guard your hearts and minds in Christ Jesus."

The difference between the peace of God and the peace of mind we try to attain on our own is that God's peace surpasses all comprehension. It will come and envelope us during the most difficult of circumstances in life. We won't comprehend our own untroubled spirit! Our lack of fear and anxiety will amaze others, even bewilder some. The peace of God just takes over and guides us.

I want that kind of peace. Don't you? All we have to do is exercise God's Word in our lives. That doesn't mean we will sail through life without a hitch. Parenting exasperates us all at times. We will make mistakes. But God's peace comes to us as we strive to live according to the principles in His Word.

> *Lord, I want Your perfect peace—a peace that surpasses all comprehension. Fill me with Your Spirit and Your peace as I seek to parent according to Your Word.*

And those who have insight will shine brightly like the brightness of the expanse of heaven, and those who lead the many to righteousness, like the stars forever and ever. (Daniel 12:3)

This Scripture is actually a prophecy concerning the pending return of Christ. The notes in my Ryrie Study Bible indicate that this passage refers to those who will see through the antichrist's deception and lead others to the truth during the Tribulation period. I find this interesting in light of our study about the Bible as our God-given instruction manual for parenting. The people in this Scripture verse "who have insight" are those who know the Word of God completely. It is not indicated that these people whose knowledge causes them to "shine brightly like the brightness of the expanse of heaven" are select clergy or other spiritual leaders. They can be anyone who loves the Lord and knows His Word. That means you could be one of those to whom the prophet is ascribing. How well do you know God's Word? You have to know it to teach it to your children. The only way you will know it is to read it.

As a stay-at-home mom, this is your chance to shine brightly before your children and to lead them to righteousness. What higher calling could there be? All you need to know is contained in the pages of God's Word. Although this Scripture is prophetic, it can also apply to your life today. Will you be a shining star for Jesus?

Lord, give me the discipline to study Your Word so that I might be filled to shining with the knowledge of it. Show me then how to instruct my children in Your ways so that they too, might shine for You.

Hear, O sons, the instruction of a father,
And give attention that you may gain understanding,
For I give you sound teaching;
Do not abandon my instruction. (Proverbs 4:1-2)

*J*often worry that I will forget to teach my boys a major piece of information that will make a huge difference in their lives. Most of us have our children at home with us for at least eighteen years; it goes by quickly. I have decided that I am going to keep a journal for each of my boys with all of the ideas, thoughts, truths, beliefs and philosophies that I want to pass on to them. When they leave home, I will give them the collection of my thoughts as a final memento.

Many parents have done the same thing. You may be familiar with the series of books entitled, *Life's Little Instruction Book.* It began as a gift from father to son. The son was preparing to leave home and attend college. His father wanted to "jot down a few observations and words of counsel" for his son, and ended up with a binder full. His son said, "Dad, I've been reading the instruction book and I think it's one of the best gifts I've ever received. I'm going to add to it and someday give it to my son." I'm certain his father is still smiling.

You too, can pass your heart's reflections to your children. Begin writing today. The years will fill the pages before you know it. You don't have to be a professional writer, just a mother. That qualifies you to share your heart with your children. The goal is to express to your children what you hold most valuable and what you want to pass on to them in thought and word. Even if theirs are the only pair of eyes that ever see it, you have written your own proverb.

Lord, continue to give me wisdom and guidance as I instruct my children. Show me how to capture my thoughts today for my children's understanding tomorrow.

Although He was a Son, He learned obedience from the things which He suffered. (Hebrews 5:8)

Sometimes being a parent means we have to let our children make mistakes. Then we have to let them suffer the consequences of their inappropriate actions. It is part of the learning process. Many times, their suffering is a consequence of their disobedience. If we do not allow them to suffer that consequence, they may not learn the importance of obedience. I personally find this part of parenting painful. Sometimes consequences for disobedience come naturally. For instance, my son, Seth, was running down a gravel hill. Seeing the potential danger, I instructed him not to run. He chose to disobey, however, and wound up with a knee full of gravel and torn skin.

Other times, the consequence must be imposed by the parent. One steamy July afternoon I was swimming in the pool with my boys when the automatic cleaning heads popped up. Seth, then three, was fascinated by their bubbling action and wanted to push and poke at them. I instructed him not to, however, as doing so could send the entire cleaning system into disrepair. Again, he chose to disobey. The consequence? He lost the privilege of being in the pool and our afternoon of swimming came to an abrupt end.

Even our heavenly Father let His Son suffer in order to learn ultimate obedience. Jesus did not want to endure the horrendous death that was in store for Him. He even asked God to change His mind and cancel the whole deal. (See Matthew 26:39.) But that was not part of God's plan, and so Jesus obeyed. His obedience saved us all from eternal death.

Lord, give me discernment to apply the appropriate consequences for my children's disobedience as I seek to train them in righteousness. I pray that they will learn ultimate obedience to You.

> *Thy word I have treasured in my heart,*
> *That I may not sin against Thee. (Psalm 119:11)*

Christian values have to be both taught and caught. Our role in the home is to do just that—teach and model biblical principles to our children. Our culture is full of anti-Christian social pressures that find their way into the lives of our children. But, if we have instructed them well, then instead, God's Word will thrive in their hearts. The heart is the place to start.

Children like to have fun. So, if we make learning God's Word fun, then they will want to be involved. Many parents gather the family into the living room before bedtime to sit and listen to dad read the Bible. There is nothing wrong with this approach, but if you ask a kid what he thinks about this method of instruction, you will probably hear a resounding "Boring!"

There are a myriad of fun ways to hide God's Word in your kids' hearts. One of the best ways for kids to memorize Scripture is by fun activities and games involving everything from flash cards to sidewalk chalk. You can take advantage of family vacations, holidays, birthdays and other special occasions to teach godly values. To stimulate your creativity and give you plenty of great ideas for hiding God's Word in your children's hearts, I recommend *Let's Hide the Word* by Gloria Gaither and Shirley Dobson. It is full of ideas for building biblical principles firmly into the lives of your kids. *Let's Hide the Word* provides great ideas for truth-building at all ages and levels of learning. God will honor your commitment to teach them His ways, and He will bless your efforts. His Word is timeless, so it's never too late!

> *Lord, how I want to hide Your Word in my children's hearts!*
> *Give me guidance as I seek to make learning fun for my kids. Most*
> *of all though, help the truth to permeate their lives in such a way*
> *that they learn how to live according to You.*

July 31

Therefore, to one who knows the right thing to do, and does not do it, to him it is sin. (James 4:17)

We have spent the entire month studying how and why to use the Bible as an instruction manual for raising our children. I hope by now you see the benefit of doing so.

So, what will you do with your newly acquired knowledge? The Bible is clear that God holds you accountable only for what you know and what you do. You are not responsible for the thoughts or actions of your husband, your friend, your neighbor and ultimately, even for your children. There will come a time when they will make their own choices; you are training them to make the right ones.

This great responsibility became yours the minute you gave birth. It is part of the role of a Christian mother. The child who is very young and is still learning right from wrong has more margin for error than a teenager, who knows the difference. The Christian who is young in her faith has more margin for error than the one who has had a relationship with God all her life.

You now know, after our month-long devotion to the subject of instruction, that God's Word is the ultimate authority on right and wrong. It is the one dependable and foolproof resource you can use for raising godly children who will live by biblical principles. Because you know this, you are now held accountable before God to do the right thing—to use it!

I urge you now to search your heart. Spend some time with God and ask Him to help you use His Word to raise morally responsible, biblically responsive children. If you have not sought to do so in the past, forgiveness is yours. All you have to do is ask, and God will give you a clean slate to start afresh. Remember, it's never too late to do what is right!

> *Lord, I commit to training my kids according to Your Word, using the Bible as my ultimate guide. Be with me and help me to always do what is right where my children are concerned.*

August:
Performance Reviews

How do I know if I'm doing a good job?

All of us like to be given a pat on the back for a job well done. Words of encouragement go a long way, especially praise that gives meaning to what we're doing. Most jobs outside the home have some type of performance review system.

In the jobs I've held outside the home, I achieved much more when I was formally reviewed against specific objectives and rewarded accordingly. The job of stay-at-home mom does not include a formal annual performance review, however. So what is a mother to do?

God's Word will provide the source of evaluation. It is full of the expectations and goals God has for us, and He, after all, is our rightful Employer. He tells us what we are to do not only in our role as a mom, but as a wife, a friend and a servant of Christ.

This month we'll take a look at how to evaluate yourself against God's Word, the myth of "measuring up" and even how to enlist your husband's help in achieving your goals. But most importantly, we will learn what it means to truly find the joy of praise for a job well done in God alone. If you've been in need of some reassurance that you're doing a good job, then this month is full of little blessings for you. I pray God will lift you up as you look to honor Him.

August 1

*For God is not unjust so as to forget your work and the love which
you have shown toward His name. . . . (Hebrews 6:10)*

The first thing we must remember as we serve our families is that
God will ultimately reward us for our work. It may not come in the
form we would like—such as a day off with pay, but He will reward us. It
may be in this lifetime, and it may be in eternity. Regardless of the timing
or the vehicle used, we will be rewarded for our work as a mother. Some-
times He allows us to reap some of the reward almost immediately through
little things like a hug or a "thank you" from one of our kids. For me, those
little things make a big difference. Sometimes they keep me going just
when I think no one appreciates me or my efforts.

Regardless of whether we get the words of encouragement or pats on the
back we so long for now, we will receive all that and more from our heavenly
Father later. It may seem as if no one notices all our hard work, but God does.
His Word says He does and that He will not forget. That means all of our
hours of teaching, days of training, months of travailing and years of sacrific-
ing will be noted and rewarded. Staying home to work and train up godly
children is a great gift of love, both to our children and to God. He has en-
trusted our kids to our care only for a short season, and He is carefully watch-
ing to see how we make use of that time.

On the days that you are frustrated and feeling like no one cares what you
do, open your Bible to Hebrews 6:10 as a reminder that God sees, and He
cares. Sometimes this job means that we must deny ourselves the immediate
gratification we so crave. We must hold out for the reward at the end of the
job, when the account is closed and the keys have been turned in. It is then,
when we turn to switch off the lights, that God will sneak in and flood us with
the light of His presence and a pat on the back for a job well done.

> *Lord, help me to remember that I work for You and that You see all
> that I do. May I keep focused on the fact that even when I am feel-
> ing unappreciated that You appreciate my work and that my re-
> ward will come in time through You.*

For I am confident of this very thing, that He who began a good work in you will perfect it until the day of Christ Jesus. (Philippians 1:6)

In my quest to raise godly children, I can put too much emphasis on each little bit of progress my sons are making or not making and forget the big picture. I recently heard that football players score three times as much in the final two minutes of each half than the entire rest of the game. The reason is simple. Their focus at that crucial point is on the end zone only. If they gain a few yards in the process, great, but their minds stay focused on the goalposts until they reach them. It requires incredible concentration.

Good parenting also requires tremendous concentration. When it would be much easier to hang out on the sidelines and run in once in a while for a few achievements here and there, we will not accomplish our goal of having godly children if that is our mind-set. If we get wrapped up in our comfort zone, it keeps us from aiming for the end zone. That sometimes means giving up a little pat on the back here and there for a few yards gained in exchange for bigger celebration when the end result is accomplished. I'm not saying we shouldn't celebrate the little victories in our parenting process. It is important to stop along the way and assess our progress. I am saying that we shouldn't get so caught up in the victory over making it to the fifty-yard line that we lose sight of the end zone before the game is over.

Don't be distraught if you don't see much enthusiasm from your teammates (your family) when you've gained a yard or two. Just keep concentrating on getting your kids to the end zone and God will take care of the rest: perfecting His workmanship.

Lord, give me concentration as I focus on raising my children in a godly manner. Remind me of the end zone and motivate me when I am tempted to stay in my comfort zone. Thanks for being my Coach.

August 3

---

*But let each one examine his own work, and then he will have rea-
son for boasting in regard to himself alone, and not in regard to
another. (Galatians 6:4)*

A dangerous game to play is that of comparison. When things are
going well with our children, it is easy to get a little
self-righteous and begin to brag about their good behavior and accom-
plishments and about our parenting skills.

When you see a friend struggling in a specific area with her child, and
you're tempted to share your own success with your child in this area be-
cause you want to help . . . don't! I have seen this kind of "helping" part
friendships. The Bible tells us to "bear one another's burdens," and if a
mom is having a difficult time and seeks your advice or support, then you
should offer whatever words of wisdom you can. One word of caution
though: Don't give this kind of advice unless you are asked. If the advice is
unsolicited, the mom who has the "problem child" usually reacts defen-
sively to her friend's enthusiasm, taking it as a personal attack. When you
are asked, "How do you do it?", remain humble and stick to God's Word
when sharing bits of wisdom on your parenting practices.

Be excited about your children's progress in every area of life, but be
humble about it as well. Be careful not to compare one child's achieve-
ments with another. Treat each child's accomplishments and character de-
velopment with equal enthusiasm.

Remember, your task is to focus on your own children, not your friends.
Your job is not to give performance reviews to other mothers. You are to
examine your own work only, lest you find yourself out of work and out of
friends!

> *Lord, help me to keep my opinions to myself about how other moth-
> ers raise their children, and may I walk in humility as I seek to
> raise children who will love and serve You. Keep me from the dan-
> ger of comparing my methods or successes with those of other moms.*

August 4

Do not be deceived: "Bad company corrupts good morals."
(1 Corinthians 15:33)

Friends of ours have five children, ranging in age from seven to seventeen. The second oldest, Jacob, was in high school, and came to his father for permission to attend a New Year's Eve party hosted by a fellow classmate. As Alan posed questions to his son about the party, he began to feel uncomfortable. Although Jacob promised not to partake in any of the drugs or alcohol that would be present at the party, Alan still did not want his son to go. Jacob admitted that he wanted to go to the party because the "whole school" would be there, and he didn't want to be left with nothing to do on New Year's Eve.

Alan came up with an alternative plan. He proposed to host a party at their house. He offered to purchase all of the refreshments the kids could eat and drink, let them play loud music, shoot pool, watch movies and play games. Jacob finally resigned himself and spread the word that he would also be hosting a party at his house. He felt sure only his best friend would show up. Much to his surprise, however, the evening of the party arrived and his house swarmed with kids! Teenagers from around the city laughed, celebrated and enjoyed themselves into the early morning hours at the Goddard house.

Alan told us that his son thanked him for pushing the issue and standing so firmly in his convictions that the other party would have been a bad choice. He also told his father that many of the kids had really wanted an alternative to the other party.

Make your home a safe and fun place for your kids to be. Allow them to invite their friends over. Invest in a VCR, a stereo, a pool table, computer games, board games or whatever else your kids like to do. If you have the money, add a game room on to your house.

Lord, help me to stand firm in teaching my children that bad company corrupts good morals.

"Let your light shine before men in such a way that they may see your good works, and glorify your Father who is in heaven." (Matthew 5:16)

One of the interesting things about light is that it is silent yet illuminating. Light can penetrate the darkness and expose the truth in any situation. Without ever uttering a word, light shatters the myths that blind and bind us in the darkness. That kind of powerful testimony is what this Scripture verse refers to: a kind of silent courage in the way you live life. Sometimes God uses the things you do with your children as a testimony to others. Silently, and yet powerfully.

We have encouraged our boys to pray from the moment they learned to speak. A friend of ours, who had a six-year-old at the time, noticed that our three-year-old said grace one day when he joined us for lunch. He asked us how often our son prayed. We told him we gave Seth the opportunity to pray at every meal, at nap time, bedtime and any other time we were praying. Sometime later, our friend told us he determined that he was going to work with his son in encouraging him to pray. He never thought it was important for a six-year-old until he witnessed the enthusiasm with which our Seth prayed. When he began to train his son in prayer, he was amazed at how enthused he too became about praying.

The light of a child's faith, because it is still so untainted by doubt or confusion, shines so brightly that it will certainly glorify God and may even witness to your friends and neighbors. When God uses your children to teach an adult something, you have just received a rave performance review!

Let my light shine brightly, Lord, before my children, lighting their way to You. May the good works of our family encourage others to develop a deeper relationship with You.

August 6

Beloved, do not imitate what is evil, but what is good. . . .
(3 John 11)

Children learn best by example. One drawback is that they don't know a good example from a bad one. My husband has unintentionally taught our oldest son a few habits that I prefer he hadn't! The actions themselves may be innocuous, but become detrimental when a young child cannot reasonably assess the context of a situation in order to decide when a particular action would be acceptable and when it would not.

Take spitting, for example. Not a pleasant habit, in my opinion. My husband, however, does it often to clear his throat. Of course, he uses discretion and is tactful about it so that it never comes across in an offensive way. One day though, when my firstborn was two, he was working outside with my husband in the yard. Jimmy paused to take a break and "clear his throat." He cleared it all right, and launched it about ten inches from where he stood. I watched from the window as my young son followed suit, only his attempt landed on his chin, dribbling onto his shirt. My husband thought this was hysterical until he saw my disapproving frown in the window and decided he had better correct the situation. We are still working on it!

Children imitate the people they love and respect. If you want to see what you look like, watch your child; if you want to hear what you sound like, listen to your child. Most children that get caught stealing confess that they learned the behavior from a parent or older sibling. Those who abuse are often the victims of abuse themselves. Children who continuously lie have usually learned from an untruthful parent. When the telephone rings and your child answers it and says it's for you, do you tell them to say that you're not home? That's lying! If you are unsure about whether or not you should do something, think about this—would you want your children to do it?

Lord, help me to be a good example for my children, carefully considering my words and actions. Teach me to be an imitator of You, so that my children will mimic godly behavior.

Some boast in chariots, and some in horses;
   But we will boast in the name of the LORD, our God. (Psalm 20:7)

When it comes to parenting, what do you put your faith in? Better yet, who do you put your faith in? Do you put your faith in the philosophies of the so-called child experts known as modern-day psychologists? Do you rely on the advice and opinions of your friends and relatives? Or do you put your faith in God? Most of us say we put our faith in God. But what do your actions say? Where do you run when things aren't going well with the children? Do you run to your husband, your best friend, your mother? Or do you run to God? If you don't run to God first, then you aren't truly putting your faith in Him when it comes to raising your kids. I find it easy to go to God first when I need guidance with a ministry decision, help with my attitude or wisdom when facing a dilemma in our business. But I confess that when I need guidance in raising my kids, I seek the counsel of others first.

God always knows what I need, even before I ask. His solutions are always best—for me and my kids. You will know you are growing as a mother, and as a Christian, when you find yourself going to God before you talk with anyone else. Many times I am frustrated and want an answer right away, so consequently I talk to someone else rather than God. I know that with God sometimes I have to wait for an answer. And I'm not the most patient person. I need to remind myself, though, that God will give me the answer in His perfect timing. He will show me what to do when I need to know. Maybe I don't need to know as soon as I think I do! I must trust Him and put my faith in Him by seeking Him first, not last.

> *Lord, forgive me for not always seeking You first when I am looking for answers regarding my kids. I want to put my faith in You alone when it comes to raising them. Show me how to wait patiently for Your guidance.*

. . . {A}ny kingdom divided against itself is laid waste; and a house divided against itself falls. (Luke 11:17)

These words of Jesus should ring in our ears as a warning of what can happen when the parents in a household do not hold one another in mutual respect. Research has shown that one of the biggest dividing factors between husband and wife are child-rearing issues. This argument starter is second only to financial issues. It is easy to see why Jesus put so much emphasis on the relationship between husband and wife. It is the central relationship in the home—at least is should be. When the relationship between husband and wife is not running smoothly, the other family dynamics are going to suffer.

In light of the importance of the husband-wife relationship, we are going to take several days to study it and how it relates to your role as a mother. Most stay-at-home moms rely on their husbands for positive reinforcement; some get it and some do not. We are going to talk about how to handle the disappointment of a nonsupportive spouse, and then we are going to explore how to gain his support. We will uncover some ideas for strengthening your marriage, and as a result, your relationships with your kids. We will look at the portrait God paints in His Word of a godly wife and how it affects your role as a mother.

For today, begin by going before God and asking Him to prepare your heart for what He wants to show you about your marriage in the coming days. Your relationship with your husband is one of the most important points in this book. If your marriage is not where it should be, then your relationship with your children will never be as good as it can be. Take some time now and search your heart. How is your relationship with your husband? Ask God to be specific in revealing things to you.

Lord, please show me specifically how I can strengthen my marriage. I pray You will teach me to stand in unison with my husband so that our household will stand firm.

Then the LORD God said, "It is not good for the man to be alone; I will make him a helper suitable for him." (Genesis 2:18)

When God created the world, He made man to take care of the world. And then, God created woman. He had a specific role in mind for the woman; she was to be a "helper" for man.

What does it mean to be a helper? By definition, a helper gives assistance or shares in the labor of something. To be a helper means there must be a colaborer. So, in the area of parenting, you are colaboring with your husband. This means it's a joint venture. It does not mean you are a doormat, but an equal partner. What does that say to you? To me, it means I can respectfully disagree with my husband in matters, but then always leave the final decision to him. God created the man to be the head of the household, not the woman. I need to respect God's order if things are to run smoothly in my home. In the area of raising children it may seem as if I am the leader because as a stay-at-home mom I naturally put more hours into the task than my husband.

Because we own a small business, my husband has seasons when he has to work a lot of hours. Sometimes that means he's not around much during the kids' waking hours. During these times, I have to constantly remind myself that God made me to be Jimmy's helper, not the other way around. When I keep things in the proper perspective, however, and show my husband respect and support his position of authority in the family, I am amazed at how he lifts me up to a position of authority with him. We are partners. Many times, he will revert to me for a final decision on a child-raising issue, realizing I am more familiar with the circumstances. This only happens, though, when I willingly place myself under his authority.

Lord, thank You for creating me to be a "helper." Remind me of my role when I begin to think too much of myself. Show me how to support my husband as head of our home. I pray that You will help him to earn that position and be all that You created him to be.

For this cause a man shall leave his father and his mother, and shall cleave to his wife; and they shall become one flesh. (Genesis 2:24)

You have probably heard today's Scripture read at many wedding ceremonies. I wonder how many newlyweds consider the impact of these words. I certainly didn't understand them until I'd been married several years. I thought that I would live in wedded bliss for the rest of my life. But then life happened, and so did our conflicts. Our relationship has grown stronger with every problem we solve, every obstacle we overcome. But we must be willing to put the time in to talk it out. A good marriage takes huge quantities of two things: time and effort. Today's verse emphasizes the coming together of two distinct persons into a permanent union. But note the time it takes to form the union. The word "become" notes that it is a process.

You and your spouse will have many conflicts to work through in your role as parents. Kids often try to divide their parents on issues, stripping away the unity mom and dad work so hard to achieve. Do not allow your children to do this. Always support each other in front of your kids, whether you agree with your spouse or not. Discuss the issue later in private. Children whose parents stand together are much more secure. But they will still try to test your loyalty to each other.

Rekindle your marriage vows and plan a romantic date for your husband this month. Take time to look at your wedding album together or view your wedding video. Let your husband know how much you love him. Read Genesis 2:24 together and review your progress in "becoming one," discussing ways you can continue to fuse your union in the future.

Thank You, Lord, for blessing me with a wonderful husband. Bless our marriage and stay in the center of it as we seek to become one in You. Help us build the kind of marriage that stands the test of time.

An excellent wife is the crown of her husband, but she who shames him is as rottenness in his bones. (Proverbs 12:4)

This verse motivates me to strive for excellence in my marriage. To think that my husband would view me as "rottenness in his bones" if I did otherwise is a sobering thought.

My husband has told me that one of the most effective ways of showing him that I care about him is by showing him respect. Showing him respect means that I lift him up in front of others and in private. It means that I support him and help to bring out the best in him—not by nagging, but by encouraging him to always do his best. It means I will show my admiration of him and his achievements. If I disagree with Jimmy, which I sometimes do, I try to show my support of him in public regardless, and then discuss my reservations with him in private.

When you become a mother, you are modeling the role of a wife to your children. If you have a daughter, she will learn what it means to be a wife by watching you. Her treatment of her future husband will be determined by how you treat yours. She will bring into her own marriage a preconceived idea of her role as a wife based on what she witnessed in you. If you have sons, they will search for someone whom they feel will treat them just as you treat your husband. They will look for a woman who has your qualities. There is great potential here to steer our children onto the path of a healthy marriage—if yours is healthy.

Take a minute to consider the condition of your marriage. Would your husband classify you as his crown, or better yet, as his queen?

> *Lord, I want to be the crown of my husband. May I be the kind of wife that brings him honor and blessing all the days of his life. And Lord, I pray even now for the perfect mate for each of my children. May they wait for Your best.*

August 12

Do two men walk together unless they have made an appointment?
(Amos 3:3)

When was the last time you sat with your husband and had a long, uninterrupted discussion? When was the last time you had even an uninterrupted five-minute discussion? Recent statistics report that on the average, most married couples spend less than ten minutes a day in meaningful conversation together! No wonder the divorce rate is over fifty percent! If we don't spend time with each other, how are we supposed to build a strong and lasting relationship?

Often in the first few years of marriage and before children, couples spend a great deal of time sharing meaningful conversation. When children arrive most couples sigh heavily, wave romance good-bye and put their relationship on the back-burner for the next eighteen years. This is dangerous to your marriage.

Talk with your husband about the amount of time you spend together in conversation and how often just the two of you do something fun together. Is it enough for both of you? Come up with a plan of how to spend more time together. Learn a hobby that you can do together. Set a weekly date night and arrange for a regular baby-sitter. Take turns planning the dates. Most major cities host marriage encounter-type weekends designed specifically for building and strengthening your relationship. Try to attend something like this every couple of years.

On a daily basis, try to spend at least twenty to thirty minutes discussing the daily happenings of your life. If you can, spend some time in discussion while the children are awake; it is good for them to see mom and dad communicating.

Lord, give my husband and me the discipline and commitment to schedule time together. As we share time and conversation, strengthen our marriage.

However, in the Lord, neither is woman independent of man, nor is man independent of woman. (1 Corinthians 11:11)

Marriage is a partnership. Parenting is also a partnership. Have you ever noticed that when things are going really well in your life you become more independent? Independent of God, independent of your spouse. It is easy to think we don't really need anyone when we have everything under control. God never intended for us to be completely independent. However, there is a healthy balance to be found in marriage. We don't want to be so dependent on our husbands for reinforcement that when we don't get it, we teeter on the edge of emotional mayhem.

Many stay-at-home moms struggle with this distinction because they so desperately need someone to verbalize that they are doing a good job. We have to first tell our husbands that we need their positive words. Many times, it is simply a case of the husband being oblivious to his wife's need, and once he understands, he is happy to oblige. Some men, however, even after being coached by their wives, still do not respond favorably simply because they have a difficult time with this form of communication. As a rule, it is a struggle for men, more so than for women, to verbalize their feelings.

So what do you do if you're frustrated by your husband's lack of positive strokes? Be patient with him and don't whine or nag. Pray! Ask God to change your husband's heart and show him your need for his support. Focus on your role as a wife and mother and concentrate on how you can improve, rather than on how your husband can improve. So many times, we go to God and ask for His help with something, but then we jump right back in and tell Him how to do it. True dependence on God means being independent of our desire for approval from anyone but Him.

Lord, help me to develop a healthy dependence on my husband and a total dependence on You.

August 14

Let all bitterness and wrath and anger and clamor and slander be put away from you, along with all malice. (Ephesians 4:31)

itterness is an incredibly destructive emotion. It begins very subtly and disguises itself in things like bad attitudes, unforgiveness, pain and disappointment until it grows and festers to soon take over someone's life. A beautiful garden can be taken over and quickly destroyed by weeds. The weeds must be pulled from down deep, removing the root and not just the stalk on the garden's surface. If only the visible weed is removed, the root will grow and another weed will pop up. This cycle will continue until the root is removed. Similarly, if a root of bitterness is allowed to remain in a person's life, it will rapidly spread, destroying a once beautiful and positive outlook on life.

Christians have every reason to be positive and joyful. They have a Savior who loves them unconditionally, wants the best for their lives and will help them to achieve it. The enemy, Satan, loves to sneak in and destroy a Christian's joy by slowly overtaking it with bitterness. Bitterness in our lives begins as a root from some event that caused us anger, pain, hurt or disappointment. Forgiveness must take place before the root of bitterness can be removed. Many times it takes some digging to uncover the problem that started it all, because most people bury painful situations deep into their memories.

Many marriages are destroyed by bitterness. Couples cause each other pain, anger or disappointment and then never resolve these situations. If you are aware of some unresolved pain that you have caused your spouse, you need to go to him and ask for his forgiveness. If your husband has hurt you and the event(s) have never been resolved, you need to forgive him. Unforgiveness provides fertile soil for bitterness to grow. De-weed your marriage today, and watch it flourish!

Lord, may forgiveness be at the forefront of my marriage, so that bitterness can never take over.

I will heal their apostasy, I will love them freely,
For My anger has turned away from them. (Hosea 14:4)

The chosen nation of Israel is called "the bride of Christ" in God's Word. Although the people of Israel, in general, were unfaithful to God and fell into all kinds of sin, including worshiping other gods, God remained faithful to Israel. This verse's statement of unconditional love and forgiveness is one that we should model. God remained passionate and faithful in His commitment to Israel despite their unfaithfulness to Him.

Do not let the enemy divide you and your husband. He does not want Christian marriages to work because two believers standing together in devotion and service to God are stronger than one. The enemy will use the very things and people closest to you in an effort to destroy you—including your children. Don't let him do it! Keep lines of communication open with your spouse about the rearing of your children. You are both human, so you will make mistakes. Let forgiveness flow between you; administer grace freely in your home. If you live in this kind of atmosphere, the enemy cannot consume you.

Remember, love is not a feeling—it is a commitment. Remain committed to your husband despite your feelings. If your husband is not a believer, do not give up on him and your hope for a strong Christian marriage. It can happen. Pray for your husband's salvation daily. Continue to serve God and to love your husband unconditionally. No matter how poor the condition of your marriage, no matter what the circumstances, God can save it. Complete healing and restoration between you and your husband is possible with the Lord. He has a purpose for your being together, and He will accomplish it if you remain faithful.

I want to be committed to my husband, Lord, no matter what the cost. Give me the fortitude to do so. Keep our marriage strong and steadfast and keep us wise about the schemes of the enemy.

. . . {F}ear God and keep His commandments, because this applies to every person. (Ecclesiastes 12:13)

Abraham Lincoln once said, "Let us have faith that right makes might; and in that faith let us to the end dare to do our duty as we understand it." Lincoln fought for what was right and he pursued justice at all costs.

This is what we, as Christians mothers, should be doing for our children. President Lincoln followed the principles of the Bible in running the country, and he happened to be one of the most popular, and more importantly, successful presidents in our nation's history. He got things done. And he did them the right way—God's way. This should serve as an example to us: If we run our home by biblical principles, then we too will be successful in getting the right things done. That doesn't mean it will be easy. On the contrary, doing the right thing is usually more difficult than doing the wrong thing.

In President Lincoln's day, he didn't have political opinion polls to gage his success. He had only the measuring stick by which he began—the Bible. He had to make some tough decisions, and his choices weren't popular with everyone. As mothers, we often have to be the "bad guy" and say no to some of our children's desires and requests, but being more concerned with doing what is right for our children and less with popularity actually makes us the "good guy."

When we are unsure of what is "right" for our kids, we need only to look. The answers are all in God's Word. When we keep His commandments, we are always doing the right thing. That is the only assurance we truly need to know we are leading our children in the right direction.

Lord, thank You for giving me the Bible to guide me in my parenting. Show me how to find the answers I'm looking for in regards to making the best decisions for my children. Remind me that Your Word is the only measuring stick I ever need to check my progress.

"Heaven is My throne,
And earth is the footstool of My feet;
What kind of house will you build for Me?" says the Lord;
"Or what place is there for My repose?" (Acts 7:49)

One of the fond memories I have is of my father and his special chair. After a long day at the office, he would stroll in the door, deposit his briefcase in the den and loosen his tie. He would seek out my mother and give her a big hug and kiss. Then he headed straight for his "throne," as my mother called it. He kicked off his shoes and plopped down in that comfortable old chair, resting his weary feet on the footstool. As he sank down into its comfort, you could almost see the arms of the chair wrap around him, as the worries and pressures of the day fell from his shoulders. I loved to climb up into his lap. He would read to me or we'd share a television program.

God views our home as His footstool. Our home is to be one of His resting places. Is your home a place of peace and rest, or is it one of chaos and turmoil? My mother always managed to make our home a sanctuary. It was a place where I knew I was loved and accepted, no matter what. I was expected to live according to the principles my parents set forth, and yet my home was a reprieve from the world.

Would Jesus find rest and peace if He stepped into your home? Do your husband and children find peace there? If so, then this is a good indication that you are building the kind of house God desires. Do everything you can to make your home a household of peace. If you do, your children will find what they need within those four walls.

Lord, may my home be a place of peace for You and for my family.
Help me to make it a place of love and acceptance. Dwell within
our walls, Lord. I pray that when my children need rest and peace,
they will always find it in our home.

Therefore, do not throw away your confidence, which has a great reward. (Hebrews 10:35)

Drama is used regularly at our church in Yuma to reinforce the message that is being communicated by the pastor or other speaker. One year at our women's retreat, a drama was performed in the form of mime. This particular drama, "Measuring Up," was the story of a character searching for her identity. She wandered from clique to clique, desperately trying to make friends, but every group rejected her. A measuring tape was held up to her in mime action and, with the shake of a head, indicated that she just didn't measure up. Even her own family rejected her. She couldn't measure up to their expectations either.

In the end, this character, now totally void of all confidence in herself or her abilities, stood on a chair to hang herself with all of the measuring tapes of rejection. God intervened just in time, communicating to her that she didn't have to measure up to be a child of God; she only had to accept the free gift of salvation in God in order to be a part of God's family. In the Lord, she found total acceptance and confidence. As I watched, I couldn't help but draw a parallel to the main character in this mime drama with myself as a mother. All too often, I feel rejected in my parenting practices by various "groups": other mothers, friends, relatives, even my children! Feeling I don't "measure up" to others' expectations for me as a mother, I begin losing confidence in my abilities as a mom. Doubt and confusion enter my mind. This downward spiral leads to despair and self-destruction. There is reward for the one who trusts God when she parents her children according to God's standard. If I keep my eyes on Him, I will not end up hanging by a thread!

Lord, give me confidence in You that I can transfer into my abilities as a mother. May I focus my attention on Your approval and not the approval of others.

And to make it your ambition to lead a quiet life and attend to your own business. . . . (1 Thessalonians 4:11)

No one likes a busybody. There are plenty of people who are more interested in the affairs of others than those of their own household. They know what the neighbor's kids are doing, but they don't know what their own children are up to.

One mother was on the telephone constantly, gossiping about everyone she knew. She was so wrapped up in the fact that a friend's teenage son had gotten involved with the wrong crowd and was taking drugs that she didn't even see the warning signs of the same trouble in her own home. Her son grew more distant and spent a lot of time in his room, but she brushed it off as part of his blossoming adolescence. She didn't bother to investigate, so she didn't know that he wasn't in his room, but was sneaking out the window to go party with his friends. She wasn't aware because she was usually on the phone late into the night discussing some detail of someone else's problems. She discovered much too late that her teenage son was also running with the wrong crowd and severely hooked on drugs.

The heartbreak this family experienced might have been avoided if this mother paid as much attention to the condition of her own children as she did to everyone else's kids. All too often, when we involve ourselves in the tragedies of others in a judgmental way, they become our own. The Bible says we are to lead a quiet life and attend to our own business. In short, that means don't be a busybody!

Lord, help me to resist the temptation to gossip and get wrapped up in the business of others. Keep my focus on my own family, and make me sensitive to the needs of my children, so that I am ready to attend to them at the proper time.

Watch yourselves, that you might not lose what we have accomplished, but that you may receive a full reward. (2 John 8)

Before I became a stay-at-home mom, I was a manager in a large department store chain. This company had a monthly award called "Employee of the Month" (EOM). The recipient had his or her picture taken, which was mounted on a plaque and hung in a prominent location for all to see, and he or she received a gift certificate in a sizeable amount to spend in the store. The award meant being the center of attention for an entire month. Those who received the award beamed every time someone slapped them on the back and declared, "Great job! You're an asset!" Interestingly enough, after a person received the honor of EOM, an intriguing phenomenon began to take place. After being a shining star, many of these employees became lax in their standards and turned into falling stars. Their source of motivation was gone. There were no more handshakes and cheers of admiration and appreciation.

When we stay home with our kids during their early years, we have every reason to be motivated. Our task is clearly outlined before us: to mold and shape these curtain-climbing toddlers into respectable men and women of God. Once their kids toddle off to school, however, many moms lose their motivation to spend time with their children. This is tragic, because it is when our children enter the world of outer influence that they need our time and attention the most! The pressures to disembark on a wayward journey from the straight and narrow is enormous.

There is no "Mother of the Month" award to keep you motivated. The calling is higher—the reward eternal.

> *Lord, keep me focused. Give me the endurance to continue in my role as a mother at all times. I pray my kids will be strong in character and strong in You, outlasting the strength of the world.*

"Behold, how happy is the man whom God reproves,
So do not despise the discipline of the Almighty." (Job 5:17)

Sometimes I have to discipline my children. Some offenses call for a verbal reprimand, some for the suspension of privileges, and more serious acts for an even greater punishment. Whatever the context, I try to be sure the punishment fits the crime. I do not particularly enjoy this aspect of parenting. In fact, I don't like it at all. Yet I know if I want them to grow into godly men, reproof is sometimes necessary. It is part of learning—so is making mistakes. We have to allow our children to make some mistakes; then we must correct them accordingly.

Similarly, as a mother I am learning and growing. That means I too will make some mistakes in my parenting. Thankfully, I have a loving heavenly Father who will correct me when that happens. Just as our children have to submit to our authority when it comes time for discipline, so do we have to submit to God's authority. His correction may hurt, but it is only for my benefit, to make me a better person—a better mom. When I am in fellowship with God, if I have made some bad choices, I know almost immediately. I get a check in my spirit. Something doesn't feel right. At times God allows me to suffer the consequences of a wrong decision.

God does provide us with a kind of performance review on a continual basis. But just as with any job, we must accept constructive criticism and be willing to admit when we make a mistake. Sometimes the process can be painful, but the end result is a better woman—and a happier mom!

Lord, I thank You that You love me enough to hold me accountable
to Your standard. Through Your correction, equip me to be a better
mother to my children. May I discipline them with as much wis-
dom and love as You discipline me.

*"The Rock! His work is perfect,
    For all His ways are just;
A God of faithfulness and without injustice,
    Righteous and upright is He. (Deuteronomy 32:4)*

While on a business trip with my husband at a beach resort, I felt the sunrise beckoning to me. I slipped out of bed, dressed and met the sunrise at the water's edge in time for a bursting display of orange and red. I took a deep breath of the salty air and began to stroll the beach. This was heaven on earth.

I was bouncing along, singing and collecting sea shells when I spotted the perfect shell. Part of it was buried in the sand, so I started to uncover it. All the others I had in my hand had missing edges or a hole in the middle. This one appeared to be perfect. When I dug the shell out, I lifted it up to admire it in the bright sunlight. It had a chipped edge. Not quite perfect. Close, but not quite. As I continued to search for the "perfect" seashell, I suddenly realized I was not going to find it because it didn't exist. There are no perfect seashells. God reminded me that there are no perfect people either. Christ is the only Model of perfection there is.

As I rested on a big rock, I fingered each shell in my collection, noting each imperfection: each chip, each hole, each odd color marking, each broken edge. *How very much like people these shells are*, I mused. We all have our own imperfections. Some are noticeable right away; some are more subtle. Still, we lack perfection, and that's why we need Christ. He finds us beautiful in spite of our oddities, frailties, flaws and brokenness.

I put a lot of pressure on myself to perform perfectly as a mom. My seashell collection reminds me that there are no perfect mothers. But God is faithful, and He will do perfect work in and through me in spite of my defects. All I need to be is willing, not perfect.

> *Lord Jesus, thank You for being perfect so I don't have to be. Remind me each day to strive for excellence in all I do, not perfection. May Your grace cover my shortcomings.*

———— ✿❀✿ ————

*For what credit is there if, when you sin and are harshly treated,
you endure it with patience? But if when you do what is right and
suffer for it you patiently endure it, this finds favor with God.
(1 Peter 2:20)*

I'll never forget my firstborn's first preschool experience. He was invited to go to preschool for a day as a special guest of his cousin. Seth was so excited he was jumping up and down. I was both excited and nervous. I was worried about how he would behave.

My husband picked Seth up from school and when they walked through the front door, Seth greeted me with a big hug and began reciting his day to me. "Mom! I went to school and I got to see a turtle, and I petted him, and we had snacks, and I colored, and we played on the playground." He looked at me with serious eyes and said, "Hope hit me and she broke my glasses—see?" he said, taking them off to show me. "And I got a bloody nose too," his chin jutted in the air to reveal dried blood around his nostrils. "She didn't like me," he said matter of factly. "You didn't do anything to prompt her to hit you?" I questioned. "No," Seth said. I looked at my husband for confirmation. "True story," he said, looking rather amused.

"Well, Seth, what did you do when Hope hit you?" I asked. "I told the teacher," he announced. "And I cried." I let out a relieved laugh and grabbed him and hugged him. "Well, of course you cried, honey, but you didn't hit her back, right?" He looked at me again with serious eyes, "Nope," he said simply, "that wouldn't be kind."

I was overjoyed! Not that my son got slugged by a girl, but that he didn't hit her back. I praised Seth again and again for doing the right thing.

*Lord, strengthen me and affirm me as I continue to walk in the
path You have chosen for me in being a mother. Help me to remember that the time I spend training my children in Your ways now
will last their entire lives.*

Martha therefore said to Jesus, "Lord, if you had been here, my brother would not have died." (John 11:21)

As women, we are used to being the ones who fix things. We fix skinned knees, broken dolls and squabbles between siblings. If something is not right, we will fix it—or die trying! Women are fixers. It is part of our genetic make-up. Many of us, then, become easily frustrated when we cannot fix something. Martha found herself in that situation. To enable you to understand today's devotion, read the account of Lazarus' illness and miraculous resurrection by Jesus in John 11:1-44.

Martha and Mary loved their brother very much. They wanted him to be well again and so asked Jesus to heal Lazarus. Even though these sisters did everything right and had unshakable faith, they did not receive the miracle they were seeking. Lazarus died. We read later, however, that Jesus chose to resurrect Lazarus from the dead. Jesus could have healed Lazarus at any time. He had the power. But Jesus was waiting to display this act of His power, waiting for a moment in which it would receive the greatest attention and God would receive the greatest glory. Which do you think would get more attention: healing a sick man or resurrecting a dead one?

Sometimes when we seek God in prayer, we become frustrated because we can't "fix" whatever it is we're praying about, and we don't see God fixing it either. Often we cannot see past our own worries, fears or frustrations to see God working in our lives. Martha could not see past her own grief to realize that God had a greater plan. He may be waiting for the right moment to answer your prayer, a moment when He can receive the greatest glory for His act of grace in your life. Wait . . . and you just may experience His resurrection power too!

Lord, I realize that Your plan in working out the details of my life may be different than mine. Help me to relinquish control of every circumstance in my life to You and trust You completely.

*Therefore I ask you not to lose heart at my tribulations on your be-
half, for they are your glory. (Ephesians 3:13)*

The best way to teach our children how to persevere through the tri-
als they will inevitably face is to let them watch us persevere
through some. During the writing of this book, my husband and I under-
went a major transition that turned into a time of trial. We bought the
family construction business. We were suddenly responsible for the welfare
of many families. We watched our finances diligently and were prudent in
our spending. Still, a time of great financial need arose. We were in need of
work and there was none on the horizon. We felt the full weight of respon-
sibility for others on our shoulders. We had to lay off some employees. We
continued to seek out work, but nothing materialized. We waited and
prayed.

During this famine of work, we learned a great deal about putting our
faith and trust in God. We prayed together as a family for God to provide
for us. We explained the situation to our oldest son, then three, and he
prayed simple prayers of faith: "God, please help Dad get some work.
Amen." He would beam after he prayed and pat his dad on the back, say-
ing, "Don't worry, Dad. God will take care of us."

Through this time of tribulation, our sons were learning to pray, rather
than panic. When Jimmy would walk in the front door at the end of an-
other distressing day, our three-year-old would give him a hug and an-
nounce that we should pray because "Dad had a bad day." His young faith
was being shaped in the face of adversity.

We have discovered that periods of testing strengthen not only our faith
in God, but our children's. We have learned not to be so quick to run from
our trials. We have chosen to fall on our knees and seek refuge from the one
who can give it.

*Lord, thank You for taking care of my family in great times of
need—and at all times.*

August 26

For as he thinks within himself, so he is. . . . (Proverbs 23:7)

Words are powerful. They can build up or tear down. Most of us are the product of the words our parents directed toward us as we were growing up. If they told you that you were smart and very resourceful, you more than likely believe that about yourself. Unfortunately, some children grow up in a much less positive environment. Many insecure adults are a product of a parent's negative words: "You're stupid" or "You can't do anything right" or "You'll never amount to much." We become what we think we are, and as young children, we are like wet clay, easily molded by the words of those we love and respect the most.

I try to speak words of encouragement to my children: "You are so smart," "That was a wise thing to do" and "Way to use your head." My son Seth, then three years old, was playing in the family room while the air-conditioning repairman worked close by. Seth decided to "greet" our visitor by body slamming him! Seth let out a big friendly "Hi!" as I let out a big gasp. The repairman looked down at Seth and said, "Well, that wasn't very smart, young man." To which Seth immediately replied, "I am too smart. I am Seth Donald Riley and I am very smart!" I apologetically smiled at the now perplexed repairman and explained Seth's outburst as "self-confidence in the making."

Encouraging words do make a difference in our children's beliefs and attitudes about themselves. Make every word you speak to your children be a building block on their tower, so that when your job is completed, they will be skyscrapers of greatness, with an image that resembles the Master Builder—Jesus.

Lord, give me many kind words that will build my children up and none that will tear them down. Show me how to build their confidence in You.

. . . {F}or the intent of man's heart is evil from his youth. . . .
(Genesis 8:21)

Sometimes our children display surprising behavior. One summer afternoon my four-year-old was hurrying through his peanut butter and jelly sandwich and pears. Itching to go outside and enjoy the warm sunshine with his younger brother, who had already finished his lunch, he declared that he was finished and asked to be excused. I instructed him to eat his pears and then he could go outside. A few moments later he said he was done, and I saw that indeed the pears were gone. He scooted off to play.

Thirty minutes later it was time for a nap. After reading a story and tucking both boys neatly into bed, I tackled the lunch dishes. As I picked up the remaining half sandwich on Seth's plate I discovered his pears hiding underneath.

When Seth awoke and asked for a snack, I asked if he would like to finish his pears. A baited question, you can be assured. I held my breath as he smiled brazenly and replied, "Oh, did you find them?" I stared at him in disbelief. Exasperated, I sighed and explained that what he had done was the same as lying. We talked about the importance of honesty and trust. He lost the privilege of a snack, and his hungry tummy at dinnertime assured that he would hide no food. His plate was clean. *But what about his heart?* I wondered.

Some things are just inherent. Like sin. Children don't have to be taught how to do wrong; it just comes naturally. We have a responsibility to teach our children how to be victorious over that sin nature and train their hearts to do right instead. After the pear incident, any questions in my mind of Seth's comprehension of such concepts as lying, cheating and stealing were cleared up. I will keep working on training his heart in the right behavior, and sooner or later, that little heart will quit telling him to hide his pears!

Oh Lord, give me insight into the heart of my children that I might know how to train them in Your ways. I pray that as they grow, their intentions will be a reflection of Your truth.

Wise men store up knowledge. . . . (Proverbs 10:14)

*J*was watching the women around me stamping furiously. We were having a D.O.T.S. (Dozens of Terrific Stamps) party. Women were stamping cards, stationery and scrapbook pages. What caught my attention in all of this was the proliferation of color. With each dip in the ink pad, the stamp left a more intense impression. The harder we pressed, the deeper the color we produced.

I was impressed that the imprint our Maker leaves on our hearts is similar in relationship. God longs to leave an imprint on our hearts. Our lives can be full of vibrancy and a deeper meaning if we are willing to use the tools He has given us. We have God's Word, full of knowledge and color, to apply to our lives. But to use it, we have to dip into it. We have to press it into our minds, storing it up so we can later use it to make an impression. The more knowledge we have, the more vibrant God's imprint will be. But if our heads are empty, so will our hearts be.

We have all seen people who seem to walk in complete peace all the time. When the circumstances of their lives are falling apart, they stand steadfast, trusting God. God has made His mark on the hearts of such believers through the vibrancy of His Word. The harder life presses in on them, the deeper they go into God's Word.

As dozens of women and I filled the pages of cards and letters with impressions of colorful flowers, teddy bears and warm greetings, I determined to store up knowledge of God's Word in my heart diligently. I want His mark of peace in my life.

> *Keep me disciplined, Lord, in storing up the knowledge in Your Word within my heart. I pray that I would press into You more deeply when life presses in on me. Imprint Your peace firmly on my heart, Lord, that I may bear the mark of a true believer.*

But let him who boasts boast of this, that he understands and knows Me. (Jeremiah 9:24)

Iused to be what I call a "pleaser." I would do just about anything requested of me—all in the name of "God's work"—if it would please the requester. Only recently have I discovered that true security in who I am comes from God alone. It took me many years of searching for the "real me" before I finally discovered, while listening to a speaker one day at a women's conference, that I have strived to please others all my life. I realized that trying to please everyone else didn't please God! We cannot be all things to all people. We can and should only try to be who God intended us to be.

Once I established who God created me to be, I felt free to say "no" and learned to better balance my life with right priorities. I no longer felt such a need to please others by doing everything requested of me. Rather, I had a longing to please God. I cannot tell you the sense of freedom that came with finally being comfortable in knowing exactly who I am in Christ! I felt secure in the assurance of His love and no longer needed affirmation and pats on the back from others to feel loved and accepted.

When we stand before God someday, He is not going to be impressed with the number of committees we served on. He will, however, be delighted with our devotion to our families. They are our most important project. The only way to give the kind of commitment to our children that they deserve is to understand God's plan for us. When we know Him, we know what He has called us to do. And we will then know our limits. Serving Him is the only task that knows no bounds and that is something to boast about!

Lord, keep me humble in my service to You. I pray that I would keep my focus upon You so that I may know what You want me to do with my time. May the assurance of Your love alone always be enough for me.

August 30

❧✿❧

"This book of the law shall not depart from your mouth, but you shall meditate on it day and night, so that you may be careful to do according to all that is written in it; for then you will make your way prosperous, and then you will have success." (Joshua 1:8)

*I*n a frenzied world where everyone seems to be searching for prosperity and success, usually ending their journey frustrated, this Scripture is like a neon light from heaven. When I first discovered it, I wanted to engrave it on the highest mountaintop for all of the world to see! I have always believed that the secrets to success are all in the Bible, and now here is a Scripture that states just that.

My husband has said that even unbelievers who use the principles of the Bible do well on earh (though not in heaven!). It gives clear direction on how to be successful in everything from marriage and parenting to finances to how to run a business.

As Christians, we measure our success not by how big a house we own, how nice a car we drive, how well dressed we are, how high on the corporate ladder we have climbed or even how well behaved our children are, but by how well we follow the principles of the Bible. The times I diligently work to apply God's Word to every aspect of living, my life runs much smoother. When I take God and His standard out of the equation disaster is the result.

I often hear people say they struggle to see how the Bible, written centuries ago, is relevant to their lives today. That confusion comes from the enemy—who does not want people to put God's Word into daily action. If you are questioning how relevant the Bible is to your life today, I challenge you to try living by its principles for six months and to discover for yourself a simpler life. Look at it this way, if the Bible is wrong, you have nothing to lose by applying its principles to your life. If it is right, you have everything to gain.

Lord God, show me how to apply the Scriptures to my life. Bring me Your success.

August 31

Wives, be subject to your own husbands, as to the Lord.
(Ephesians 5:22)

*B*iblical submission bestows honor upon the woman. It builds confidence and secures her identity. Biblical submission promotes women and their families and, because it is done out of obedience to God, it always brings a blessing.

The first few years of our marriage, submission was a bomb just waiting to explode. Every time we had a decision to make that we disagreed upon, we argued until I was screaming. We had constant discord until I came to understand biblical submission.

Then when an issue came up that required a decision and we had contrasting views, I gave my opinion and then ended the conversation with a statement such as, "That is what I think we should do, but you are the head of this house so I will leave the final decision to you. I will support you in whatever decision you make." Notice I did not say I would support the decision, but my husband. It is important to let our husbands know we have more confidence in them than in the decisions they make. The first time I used this statement my husband was surprised, to say the least, but he swelled with pride and thanked me for showing him "respect." As I allow Jimmy the authority that God has already granted him, he in turn desires to show me respect for my opinions.

Joy comes when we live according to God's plan. The idea that women who submit become slaves to their husbands is a lie. By submitting, we actually are freed to live a life of peace and harmony. Bondage occurs when we seize authority that never belonged to us in the first place—then we become slaves to our own selfish desires, and we all know where that leads!

> *Lord, thank You for setting up a clear model of authority in the home. Help me to uphold my husband as head of the household, whether he deserves that place or not. Raise him up to be a godly man.*

September:
Job Satisfaction

I'm sure I'll love working here!

So much of what we get out of life is dependent upon one little thing—attitude. Our attitude affects how we make decisions, how we treat others and how we parent our children.

If I am going to enjoy my job as a stay-at-home mom, I need to have a positive attitude. Lack of contentment is a real killer of family cohesiveness. Unfortunately, many young moms are not grateful for their families because they have a bad attitude about being at home. I constantly battle a restlessness to "do" something besides dishes. That feeling of being trapped within the walls of my house has imprisoned me in a bad attitude. The positive attitude comes when I acknowledge my discontent, disown it and move on.

Regardless of your circumstances and the reasons why you are at home, whether willingly or begrudgingly, this is the month that can make a big difference in your life. It all comes down to one thing—attitude. You can find joy in your situation and rise above your undesirable circumstances or you can suffer in self-pity. The secret is in being content where you are. True contentment and satisfaction are found in the Lord. Ask Him to develop an attitude of joy in you that goes deeper than your circumstances.

September 1

Behold, children are a gift of the LORD;
The fruit of the womb is a reward. (Psalm 127:3)

o you perceive your children as little presents from God? Your answer would probably depend upon the day, right? Well, despite good days and bad days, that is exactly how God views them. Each child is a precious gift, handpicked especially for you by Him. Each gift comes to us wrapped in unique packaging with distinctions tailor-made by the Creator Himself. Some of those distinctions are harder to appreciate than others.

I remember when my oldest son was having a myriad of health problems during the second year of his life. His bouts with croup, ear infections and asthma attacks wore me out! After one all-night session of croup, I received a card in the mail from a friend. She wrote, "God must have known Seth would need very sensitive and loving parents when He chose Jimmy and you to be his caretakers."

Her words not only uplifted me, but they also changed the way I saw myself. God chose me to be Seth's mom. That realization brought new value to my role as a mother. For whatever reason, God knew I would be the mom Seth needed. This fresh way of thinking bolstered my exhausted attitude. I had been growing weary of taking care of my precious gift! After reviewing my friend's thoughts, I began to view even those twilight hours in the rocking chair, holding a wheezing toddler, as a special assignment from God.

Do you appreciate the gifts God has given you? God loves each one of us uniquely and has matched each of us up with the perfect children for us. We are responsible to take good care of the ones whom God has entrusted us with. The value of a human soul is priceless. Give a gift back to God by training your children in His ways.

Thank You, Lord, for giving me the beautiful gifts of each of my children. Help me to treat them as precious treasures. Show me how to be the mom You know they need.

We are destroying speculations and every lofty thing raised up against the knowledge of God, and we are taking every thought captive to the obedience of Christ. (2 Corinthians 10:5)

A friend was struggling with her youngest teenage son. He was not behaving the way she wanted him to, and she was having some pretty "un-Christian" thoughts regarding his well-being. When she found herself caught in this destructive cycle of negative thinking, she would recite today's verse, asking God to take captive her wrong thoughts and attitudes and to destroy them. Then she sought to replace them with thoughts and attitudes that would be pleasing to God. I have followed her example, and when I am having negative feelings toward my children, I too have used this exercise to get my thought life back in line with God's Word. It works!

Taking every thought captive means that I don't allow my thoughts to control my actions or my feelings. I let God control them. A wrong thought doesn't become dangerous until I hold onto it long enough that it turns into destructive anger or bitterness or until it drives me to do something inappropriate.

When a pot is left on the stove to simmer until it boils, it often bubbles over, leaving a sticky mess. We leave behind a mess when we allow our wrong thoughts to simmer and boil into an outburst. The mess is usually emotional in nature, caused by careless words that spew out and scald the soul. Don't leave any emotional scars on your children as a result of your negative emotions. Prevent it by "taking every thought captive to the obedience of Christ," as soon as you begin to think wrong thoughts.

Lord, keep my mind pure and make me sensitive to the knowledge of inappropriate thoughts and feelings toward my kids. Give me the sense to take those thoughts captive before they become destructive.

Blessed are those who hunger and thirst for righteousness, for they shall be satisfied. (Matthew 5:6)

Being content or satisfied with your job as a stay-at-home mom will come from only one source: God. Contentment with your place at home is a direct result of a close relationship with God. When we get to know Him, we begin to see His heart's desire, and Scripture makes it clear that His desire is for us to be at home with our children as much as possible. When we hunger and thirst for God, and for His righteousness in our lives, we want to do what's best.

A hunger and thirst for righteousness is different than a physical hunger and thirst. Our need for God is insatiable. The more we receive, the more we want. In contrast, when we eat physically, we become full, and when we do not eat, we become hungry. With God and His truth the opposite is true: When we eat spiritually, we become more hungry, and when we do not feed our spirits, we lose our appetite for God. That's why it is so dangerous to go too long without reading the Bible and praying. The absence of it causes a lack of craving for it. Attending a Sunday church service is not enough. You wouldn't eat only once a week, would you? You'd starve!

Just as we eat food daily, we need to partake of God's food daily. This is difficult with small children—believe me, I know! Try to grab fifteen minutes in the morning before the kids wake up, or if you're not a morning person, try nap time or later in the evening when everyone else is in bed. God looks at the heart, and He will honor your intentions, no matter what time of day it is. You will become close to God and begin to hear and understand Him in a new and exciting way. And a sweet spirit of contentment will creep into your life.

I want to make time, Lord, to spend time with You. Make me hungry for Your Word and bring me contentment as I feast on Your truth.

September 4

Rejoice in the Lord always; again I will say, rejoice!
(Philippians 4:4)

When I was in the second trimester of pregnancy with my second child, I opened up my closet door one morning and groaned with disappointment. I was in between my regular clothes and maternity clothes. My round belly had outgrown the last pair of pants in my wardrobe, and maternity fashions made me feel like a beached whale. A sense of panic began to well up in me. I stood for a moment in the doorway of my closet lost in self-pity. A Bible verse crept into my thoughts: "Rejoice in the Lord always; again I will say, rejoice!" The word "always" hung before me.

"OK, Lord," I said aloud. "I need to rejoice even in this depressing circumstance. Help me to focus on something positive." Instantly, He brought the little life growing inside of me into my thoughts. As I began to reflect on the wonderful baby that would soon join our family, I decided to focus on what I could wear in waiting of his arrival instead of what I couldn't.

I spent the next two hours rearranging my closet. I examined each item of clothing and arranged all of the items I could wear into a special section. That way, when I opened the closet each morning for the next five months, I would focus on all of the things I *could* wear. To my surprise, I discovered I had quite a few appropriate things that would actually fit me far into my pregnancy.

What began as a depressing event turned out to be a pleasurable experience when I focused on the positive rather than the negative. The silver lining is usually there, shining behind the dark clouds of our negative attitudes.

May I rejoice in You, Lord, for all things at all times. Right now I rejoice in my beautiful children—may I teach them to rejoice in You always and in all ways.

Then He said to His disciples, "The harvest is plentiful, but the workers are few." (Matthew 9:37)

One afternoon I was sitting in the play area of a fast-food restaurant watching my three-year-old run and jump and climb, hoping he would wear himself out before we went home. I struck up a conversation with the woman next to me and discovered she was a full-time missionary! She and her husband and four children were traveling on furlough from their mission base in Ethiopia.

I listened intently as this missionary mom told me about the spiritual need of the people in Ethiopia and the spiritual warfare they were up against. It was obvious their needs were many, but there weren't enough workers to meet all of those needs. Suddenly, the words Jesus spoke to His disciples in the above verse became real to me. A comment she made impacted me perhaps because it hit closest to home. She simply said, "The need is always great, but the time I have to give to the village people for now is limited because I have my own mission field at home," as she gestured to her children playing. "They are my mission field."

I look at my children differently now. It took a conversation with a missionary mom to show me that I was a missionary too! I don't have to look very far to see souls who need guidance, direction and care.

We are preparing our children for the Lord's harvest and the season to harvest is brief. In one fleeting moment, just as the chaff is sifted from the grain, so will the souls of our sons and our daughters be filtered through the Father's hands. That which falls to the threshing floor is swept away forever.

Lord of the harvest, help me to take my work at home as seriously as a full-time missionary. Remind me daily that my children are my mission field. Be with me as I prepare them for Your harvest, and guide me as I guide them to You.

September 6

Where there is no vision, the people are unrestrained. . . .
(Proverbs 29:18)

*L*ife without objectives is pointless. Most people don't travel unknown territory without a road map. The sensible thing is to choose a destination and then chart a course before departing. But many of us try to journey through life without even setting a destination, much less charting a course.

Have you ever set a life objective? It is different from setting a goal. Goals relate to distinct areas of life, such as career, family and finances. But a life objective marks the direction for your entire life. It is your road map. It is the bigger picture; it complements and actually helps you to accomplish the goals you set.

Knowing what your life objective is can help you in your role as a mother. It simplifies decision making because when you are faced with such choices as sending your children to home, private or public school, you will have a standard by which to evaluate your choices. Having a life objective will also keep you motivated. Setting a life objective will help you to stay focused, since success is largely the result of focusing on one thing and doing it well.

If you are caught in a fog of uncertainty, not sure what you want from life, setting a life objective will help guide you out of it. Give some serious thought this month to what you want to accomplish. What is really important to you? Take some time to think about this quote by the well-known psychologist William James: "The best use of your life is to invest it in that which outlasts it."

> *Lord, give me clear direction as I seek to set a life objective. Show me where being a mother fits into my objective. Speak to my heart so that Your vision for me becomes my own. Keep me focused as I strive to become all You want me to be.*

━━━━━━━━ ❧✿❧ ━━━━━━━━

For God has not given us a spirit of timidity, but of power and love and discipline. (2 Timothy 1:7)

Has fear ever stopped you from doing something you wanted to do? Real fear can be immobilizing. The enemy often uses fear in an attempt to keep God's people from being effective in their work for the Lord. Fear can be blown so out of proportion that it becomes debilitating. Raw fear, the kind that keeps you tied in knots, does not come from God. The only kind of fear that is useful to God is a reverent fear, such as a sense of awe and respect for God.

As a mother, I have often been afraid of my responsibility. Doubt and a sense of incompetence have plagued me. *What if I don't do a good job as a mother? What if my children fall into harm or make bad choices because of my failure as a parent?* These kinds of thoughts can push me into ineffectiveness if I am not careful. The fear of failure keeps many people from even trying to accomplish what they desire. The fear of inadequacy drives many women out of the home and into the workplace.

Being a full-time mom is the most significant job a woman can have. But there is a great fear of failure in motherhood plaguing today's generation of moms. We need to remember that the one who tries is never a failure; it is the one who fails to try. The enemy plants the seeds of doubt in a woman's heart because Satan does not want moms to stay at home with their children.

When I begin to fear the awesome responsibility that God has given me as a mother, I need to give myself a reality check with Second Timothy 1:7. God has not given me fear; He has given me power and love and the discipline to do my job. He has fully equipped me. If you feel weak in your fear, then you will know it is not from God. He does not bring His followers weakness but strength!

Lord, thank You for reminding me that You bring strength, not weakness. I know that fear is not from You. Fill me with Your power, Your love and Your discipline to be the best mother I can be.

September 8

With a long life I will satisfy him. . . . (Psalm 91:16)

Sometimes the aspects of motherhood we think we will enjoy the most are the very things we enjoy the least! I remember being so anxious for my oldest to begin preschool. He was a handful for me—his boundless energy and demanding nature exhausted me.

Seth's first day of school went well. He waved to us happily as he skipped off with his teacher. The second day was not such a euphoric experience. "Don't leave me, Mommy," he whined. I knelt down and looked into the eyes of my fearful four-year-old. "Mommy will stay for five minutes, but then I have to go and you have to stay. But I will be back at noon to pick you up just like yesterday, OK?" He nodded.

Five minutes later, I reassured him of my pending return and quickly turned to leave the playground. To my surprise, Seth did not cry—*I* did. Was I a terrible mother? Had I placed my child prematurely in a situation he wasn't ready for?

I poured my heart out to God and as I did, I began to feel some sense of relief. When I returned at noon to pick Seth up, he ran into my arms and just as the day before, began chattering excitedly about his morning at school. Each day got easier after that. One morning I looked at my younger son. Soon he too would be the one skipping off to learn new things and make new friends. I felt a sense of remorse that I hadn't enjoyed the days more with both of them skipping around me. I vowed to get more satisfaction from my time with them.

Lord, bring me satisfaction with my life at every stage. Help me to appreciate the time I have with my children; although some days it seems long, I know in the end it will not seem long enough.

September 9

. . . {A}s for me and my house, we will serve the LORD.
(Joshua 24:15)

*H*ow often do you say or hear the phrase, "I'll pray for you"? How many people really mean it when they say it? Do you? Chances are, most of us say it more often than we actually do it. It becomes a cliché, spoken loosely in many Christian circles. But the person to whom you speak it may really need and depend on your prayers. Prayer is one of the most important tools in a believer's life. It is our direct line to God. We learn and grow closer to God by spending time in prayer. Prayer can change hearts. In the book of First Timothy, Paul reminds Timothy that his mother and grandmother have been faithful in their prayers for him (1:5). Their faith was that of endurance and perseverance; they did not give in easily to discouragement. It was clear that theirs was a household of faith.

A friend from college called me a few years after we had graduated. She told me she had received Christ as her Savior and that her grandmother had been praying for her salvation for twenty years! Never underestimate the power of prayer. The faith of my friend's grandmother is the kind of faith I want to model to my children. She never gave up.

If you are discouraged because one or more of your children is not walking with God, don't give up! Keep praying for them. Every prayer for every child is of value to God. If you serve the Lord in your home and stay committed to Him no matter what the cost, soon your entire household will be saying, "As for me and my house, we will serve the LORD."

Lord, may I be committed to prayer. I ask right now that You would bring each of my children to a knowledge and acceptance of You as Lord and Savior. May ours be a house that serves You forever.

September 10

---

*The faith which you have, have as your own conviction before God.
Happy is he who does not condemn himself in what he approves.
(Romans 14:22)*

True faith in God matures and grows. The longer we have had a relationship with Christ, the stronger our faith. Long after we have stopped growing physically, we continue to grow spiritually. Our walk and the development of our faith in the Lord is a lifelong process. As our children grow and mature, their understanding of the world we live in and the rules that govern it develop. We need to help our children grow spiritually and yet be patient as they learn. It will not all make sense to them right away.

God is very patient with us, isn't He? We, as full-grown adults, still don't completely understand His ways. Sometimes I'm sure that He shakes His head in frustration at how dense we can be. His Word says He loves us, yet we feel sometimes that no one loves or appreciates us. His Word says He sees all and knows all, yet we attempt to hide our sin from Him. His Word says He cares for us, yet we don't trust Him with the everyday circumstances of our lives. You may be on a different level of understanding than a friend, so be careful not to be judgmental. You may have a friend who feels it is wrong to spank her children; you, on the other hand, may feel that spanking is a right and necessary form of discipline. If you judge your friend, then you are condemning yourself in your own belief.

God brings us all around to the same answers; the right ones, in His time. Sometimes we are stubborn and don't want to listen to Him. But that is between God and the one who is acting deaf. Be content to grow in your walk with God; don't try to walk someone else's.

> *Lord, help me not to judge others with different convictions. May I be busy examining my own life, not the lives of others. Give me patience with my children as they grow in their faith too.*

—————— ✦🌹✦ ——————

Let the words of my mouth and
   the meditation of my heart
Be acceptable in Thy sight,
O LORD, my rock and my redeemer. (Psalm 19:14)

When Seth was three, he was playing in his room one day when I heard some loud banging and shouts of frustration. I hurried to his room to witness him hurling a container of blocks to the floor saying, "Come on you stupid thing, open up." He looked up and saw me standing in the doorway. "Mommy, I can't get these stupid blocks out of the stupid container." Trying to see this as a teachable moment, I sat on the floor beside him and said, "Seth, I understand that you are frustrated, but do you think it's helping anything to yell and use words like 'stupid'?" He looked at me and said, "Well, Mommy, you say it."

Instantly humbled, I tried to defend myself. "When did Mommy say 'stupid'?" I honestly couldn't remember. I try to be very careful with my words around my kids. He shrugged nonchalantly, replying, "Yesterday when you couldn't get my seat belt on, you called it a stupid seat belt." I sighed in embarrassment. He was right. (I hate it when that happens!)

Sometimes being a parent means admitting when you're wrong. Many times we guard our words around our children, though inside we are seething and want to verbalize our anger or frustration. Choosing not to pour it out to our children is wise, but we do need to pour it out to God. Our words reflect what is in our hearts. We may be able to guard our words and hide our hearts from our kids, but we can't hide them from God.

> *Lord, I make today's verse my prayer that "the words of my mouth*
> *and the meditation of my heart be acceptable in Thy sight." I pray*
> *also for my children, that they will meditate on the pure and good*
> *things of You. May their words reflect honor in their hearts.*

September 12

Therefore I say to you, all things for which you pray and ask, be-
lieve that you have received them, and they shall be granted you.
(Mark 11:24)

I have learned that I will never be satisfied with the job as a
stay-at-home mom if I don't believe I will be satisfied. There are
days I awaken, after too little sleep, believing I'm going to have a terrible
day, and then I do! When I expect the worst, that is usually what I get.

God says we must believe that we will receive something before we actually
will receive it. The same is true of happiness and contentment. Have you ever
met someone with such dynamic faith that she amazes you? She is always ex-
cited about God and what He is doing in her life, and the most intriguing
thing of all—this person receives everything she prays for? "It isn't fair," you
grumble. The difference of the outcome may be in the depth of faith. A faith
so strong that it believes in God and His promises regardless of the situation is
the kind of faith God answers.

How strong is your faith? When you pray and ask God for something,
do you really believe He will deliver? Or are you doubting that He even
hears you or, furthermore, cares about your problems? Today's Scripture
verse proves that God is ready and willing to grant our requests, but we
must first believe. Jesus scolded Peter for not believing that he could walk
across the water to meet Jesus (Matthew 14:31). And Peter was even
face-to-face with Jesus when he got tripped up by doubt.

When we believe that our worth is beyond measure, then it will be.
When we believe that we can be fully satisfied being keepers of the home,
then we will be. And when we truly believe that God can meet all of our
needs and provide us with complete and total happiness, then He will.

Lord, thank You for loving me enough to listen to me when I pray
to You. Give me faith, Lord, faith that believes in Your promises.

Through all this Job did not sin nor did he blame God. (Job 1:22)

ob was a man of integrity. He went through the ringer of life, yet he never wavered in his faith and trust in God. There is an old saying that when bad things happen to us, we have two choices: We can become bitter or we can become better. Job chose to become better. With each trial he suffered, he moved closer to God.

In contrast, some people who have experienced tragedy or loss become bitter and blame God for all of their problems. Many of us like to make someone else responsible for our happiness because it's convenient. Certainly we all have people or circumstances in our lives that make it difficult to live joyfully, but no one or nothing can "make" us happy. We are each responsible for our own happiness. Others may do things to us that result in pain, but we choose how we are going to react to each and every situation in our lives. Job never blamed his misfortune on a workaholic father, a disconnected mother or a God who didn't care. He knew the real culprit—Satan.

Everything that Satan does to a Christian is under God's watchful eye. He monitored every attack against Job—Satan wanted to strip Job of everything he had in order to show God that Job was only serving God because God had given him wealth. God was so confident of Job's unwavering faith, He allowed this attack on Job to prove Satan wrong and for Job to grow in his faith in God. Job's faith in God was undaunted; this attitude of gratitude no matter what happened to him was Job's choice.

You too have a choice each time you become the victim of an unfortunate circumstance. You can become bitter or better. You can trust God or turn from Him.

Lord, like Job, make me better and stronger in my faith through all I endure.

———— ❧✿❧ ————

*"For our gospel did not come to you in word only, but also in power
and in the Holy Spirit and with full conviction. . . ."*
(1 Thessalonians 1:5)

I sat in rapt attention at a women's conference, listening in amazement to the speaker. This woman gave Scripture references for every point she made, but not once did she read from the Bible. She had them all memorized. She rattled off reference after reference, getting more excited with every Scripture she applied. Her enthusiasm was contagious, and I found myself more uplifted with every word she spoke. I realized afterward how little Scripture I had memorized. I could give a paraphrased version for lots of verses, but I didn't know many of their references. I walked away from the workshop feeling somewhat humbled and very challenged.

Every time Satan tries to steal our joy or send us into discouragement, we can whip off a Scripture to counteract his attempts. Memorizing Scripture gives us an unbeatable sense of joy, because for every word the enemy has, we know that God has an even greater, more powerful one.

A friend who attended the conference with me decided immediately to apply this Scripture memory principle to a specific problem in her life. She had been having trouble with her stomach for years. She had daily pain and was constantly on medication. She memorized several Scriptures about God's healing power and began to recite them aloud daily. The first day she did this she had no pain. She continued to do this for weeks, still with no pain. Today she still enjoys great health. Scripture memorization is a practical way to show our faith in the God who keeps His promises.

*Lord, give me the discipline to memorize more Scripture. Unleash
the power of Your Word.*

September 15

---❦---

Therefore I am well content with weaknesses, with insults, with distresses, with persecutions, with difficulties, for Christ's sake; for when I am weak, then I am strong. (2 Corinthians 12:10)

How often do you hear yourself or others say, "If only things were different, I'd be content. If only I had more free time, if only I had more rest, if only we had more money, if only I had better friends, if only my children would obey me, if only my husband showed me more support—then I'd be happy." Living with an "if only" attitude is the very thing Paul warns the Corinthians about in today's verse. Contentment is an attitude. We need to learn to be thankful for what we have instead of complaining about what we don't have.

A pastor's wife once told of a time when she and her husband had to go without a salary because of a church split. Both of their cars were repossessed. Someone arranged for them to rent a car, but it was old and clunky. It often broke down in main intersections. This woman confessed that she hated the car and had a bad attitude about it. One day, the Lord convicted her and showed her that she was not grateful for what He provided for her. That old clunker was better than no car. She cleaned that car up so it was shining brightly and gave it a tune-up. She started blessing that car and thanking God for it. About a month later, God provided her with a much better and newer car!

The best definition of contentment I've heard is this: Contentment is living independent of the circumstances. This isn't always easy, but it's necessary if we are going to live a life blessed by God.

Lord, teach me to be thankful. Help me to focus on what I do have instead of on what I do not.

Because you did not serve the LORD your God with joy and a glad heart, for the abundance of all things; therefore you shall serve your enemies whom the LORD shall send against you. . . . (Deuteronomy 28:47-48)

This Scripture motivates me to serve God joyfully. It makes it clear to me that if I don't, there will be consequences. Serving God halfheartedly leads to our discontent and God's displeasure. No one who truly loves God and desires to live life as a follower of Christ is seeking to displease Him. But that is exactly what we do when we demonstrate half-hearted faith.

Do you know any halfhearted Christians? Do you walk around with a long face, complaining about how life's got you down? Many of us want things from God, and when things don't happen the way we'd like, we become frustrated and get mad at God. We say He's not listening. He's listening, but He is not going to make good things happen in our lives if we're not serving Him joyfully when things aren't going so well. Many stay-at-home moms are not serving the Lord or their families in joy and gladness. Instead, they complain about their circumstances. That kind of attitude influences other mothers who are contemplating leaving the workplace to stay home with their kids.

There are many women who long to be at home with their kids but they can't because they are single parents or because of some other circumstance. So when God provides a woman with the choice to stay at home, and then she is negative and crabby about being there, it is a tragedy. Let's be excited about this opportunity God has given us. Consider it a privilege and an honor. There are many women who would love to take your place.

> *Lord, may I be ablaze with excitement in serving my family for You, doing so with great joy.*

September 17

It is better to live in a corner of a roof,
Than in a house shared with a contentious woman.
(Proverbs 21:9)

have always been a happy person by nature. Our home is filled with joy and laughter. But when my husband began taking over his father's construction business, the atmosphere of our home changed.

Jimmy was familiar with construction, but managing and operating a business was new to him. He had to put in long hours during those early months. I was home with a strong-willed two-year-old and a baby on the way. Several nights a week Jimmy wouldn't arrive home until after Seth's bedtime and many times long after mine! I'd have dinner on the table only to receive a phone call from him saying he wouldn't be home until late. While dinner turned cold, I turned steaming mad. My husband is a very focused individual. He couldn't see anything except the mammoth objective in front of him. In my frustration and despair, I became the contentious woman; I managed to find fault in absolutely everything. We began to fight—often. Even when Jimmy tried to make peace, I turned our discussions into another war. I was miserable, and I wanted him to be too.

One day I stumbled across today's verse. As I read it a second time aloud, I choked on the words. I realized I was a contentious woman in the worst way.

I asked Jimmy for forgiveness. God gave me the words to tell him that I wanted him to succeed, and if it meant long hours for a while, we would get through it. Within a few months, Jimmy began to cut his hours so he only worked late one night a week and rarely worked on weekends.

Lord, thank You for showing me my discontent. Fill my heart instead with joy.

* ❧❀❧ *

And He said to them, "Follow Me, and I will make you fishers of men." (Matthew 4:19)

*I*t has been said that to know the will of God is the greatest knowledge, but to do the will of God is the greatest achievement. The world is full of people who believe they should do one thing, when God has another plan in mind. Such was the case of the apostle Peter.

Peter was a fisherman and content in being such until God planted another desire in his heart. Jesus told Peter He wanted him to quit catching fish and start catching men. What a job offer! Peter immediately dropped what he was doing and followed Jesus. This detour was not part of his original life objective, but he followed Jesus anyway. His obedience brought about a life of blessing and honor and a special place in God's heart for Peter. His obedience was not without cost, however. He gave up his life's ambition and received trials and persecution. Peter felt it was worth it, however, and his devotion developed into a very special relationship with Jesus.

When you become a mother, Jesus says something to the effect of "Follow Me, and I will make you mothers, worthy of My name." It might not have been in your original plan to be a stay-at-home mom, but your obedience to His call will be worth the change in plans. God's plan for your life may be different than what you envisioned. But the key to great blessing is in being willing to adjust your plan to God's. What greater call on your life can there be?

> *Lord, give me contentment daily in my life as a stay-at-home mom. May I continue to listen to Your voice. Help me to be obedient and to do Your will, no matter what the cost.*

———— 🌺🌹🌺 ————

For there is a proper time and procedure for every delight, when a man's trouble is heavy upon him. (Ecclesiastes 8:6)

God's Word tells us to delight in trials, trouble and persecution, for it makes us stronger in Christ. This is a tough lesson to teach our children. Unfortunately, it is something they often have to learn on their own.

One afternoon I was playing with my three-year-old. He could not get one of the Lego® pieces to fit into the other. "Mommy, you do it—I can't." "You can do it Seth. Keep trying." I demonstrated how to do it, but then immediately took the pieces apart again and handed them back to Seth. "Here, now you try." Several attempts later, Seth fit those pieces together and the look of satisfaction on his face was worth the wait. "I did it Mommy, see!"

No mother enjoys seeing her children unhappy, in pain or frustrated. But if we know they will benefit from their distress, it helps to allow them to go through it. Just as God does not eliminate every problem from our lives, neither can we eliminate every problem from the lives of our kids. As children approach adolescence, the ability to cope with frustration and problems becomes increasingly important.

The ideal environment for our children is not one void of trial and difficulties. Our job is not to eliminate every challenge in our child's path, but to gently encourage them through their problems, giving guidance and support along the way. We should teach our kids to look at the end result and at what is accomplished by walking through a trial. The satisfaction they will feel and the confidence they will gain as their character is strengthened will be worth the tears of frustration they may shed in getting there.

Show me, Lord, how to help my children develop a confidence in problem-solving. May I provide them not only with the proper tools to conquer their trials but also with encouragement.

September 20

I will bless the LORD at all times;
His praise shall continually be in my mouth. (Psalm 34:1)

This command is easier said than done. Patience is not a character quality that comes naturally to me. Since patience is listed as one of the fruit of the Spirit (See Galatians 5:22-23.), I know I need to make it a priority to develop more of it if I want God's blessing in my life. When I get impatient with my kids, I begin to yell. The tone of voice I use and the words that come out of my mouth would not be classified as "praise." I am not blessing the Lord or my children when I demonstrate impatience.

I generally run out of patience when I forget to ask the Lord for a generous portion each day. I have learned that in the face of frustration, when my patience has run out and I feel a scream welling up inside of me, there is one thing that helps curb my temptation to yell. I start blessing and praising the Lord. I shout, "Praise You, Lord! Thank You for children who are healthy and vivacious and have more vigor than I know what to do with!" Once I have started praising God, my patience almost immediately returns and instead of yelling, I can then calmly instruct my children.

Learning to praise God continually is a process. I am still working on it. With practice, I know I will soon have an attitude of praise. So can you, with practice. Through the process, it will become easier and easier to be satisfied and joyful at all times, even in the midst of children who have more energy than the Energizer® Bunny.

I bless You and thank You, Lord, for my children. Develop in me an attitude of praise that flows out of my heart and mouth at all times.

And whatever you do in word or deed, do all in the name of the Lord Jesus, giving thanks through Him to God the Father. (Colossians 3:17)

Fresh out of college in his first corporate job, Jimmy was eager to please and to move up. He shared his ideas for improvement with his supervisor. He quickly discovered, however, that his boss did not take pleasure in Jimmy's "ideas," and he went to great lengths to keep Jimmy's suggestions from reaching the next level.

Jimmy's boss was jealous of many of the zealous new recruits, and he did not want any of them to outshine him. If they looked too good, he might look bad in comparison. He wanted things done one way—his way, and any ideas other than his were taken as direct challenges to his authority. Eventually this man's employment there was terminated. The higher-ups didn't want someone who was not interested in the company's progress. He wasn't making things happen; he was keeping them from happening.

One of the benefits of being a stay-at-home mom is that you don't have some paranoid boss trying to douse any flicker of excitement you may ignite. God is our Boss, and He encourages us to grow and improve, both in our relationship with Him and with our kids. The only requirement: "do all in the name of the Lord Jesus." There are no rigid programs or formats. But there is plenty of room for variety, creativity and change. If we don't like the way things are being done in our home, then we have the freedom to change it.

Basically, there are three kinds of people in life: those who make things happen, those who watch things happen and those who say, "what happened?" Which kind of person are you?

Lord, thank You for giving me freedom in my job! Help me to enjoy my role as a stay-at-home mom and to have fun training my kids in Your ways.

—— ❦ ——

Be anxious for nothing, but in everything by prayer and supplication with thanksgiving let your requests be made known to God. (Philippians 4:6)

Are you a "worry wart"? My friend Missy worried about everything. She worried if she didn't have anything to worry about. Her anxiety was the cause of many health problems as well, although she didn't make the connection until God transformed her worry-wart heart into a prayer-filled heart.

Missy was a new Christian, and having a desire to get to know God better, she agreed to attend a weekly women's Bible study with me at my church. One morning about halfway through the study, the lesson centered around Philippians 4:6. After some discussion, Missy realized that rather than being anxious for nothing, she was anxious about everything. I remember her amazement at the word "everything": "in *everything* by prayer and supplication with thanksgiving let your requests be made known to God." She couldn't believe that God would actually want to hear about absolutely everything in her life, down to the smallest detail!

Missy set to work turning her worries into prayers. It took time to abandon her old habit. She constantly had to remind herself that God wanted to know everything that was bothering her. In time, as she worried less and prayed more, her health began to improve as well.

Remember, God wants to know all the details of your life. If you are a worrier, you will teach your kids to worry. If you are a warrior, taking all your worries to God in prayer, you will teach your kids to pray.

> *Lord, help me to be a warrior, not a worrier. May I worry about nothing and pray to You about everything. Thank You that no detail of my life is too insignificant for You to take care of.*

September 23

You do not have because you do not ask. (James 4:2)

I awoke at 3:30 a.m. to the sobs of my three-year-old. Stumbling from my bed in bleary-eyed confusion, I made my way to Seth's room. "What is wrong, honey?"

He burst into further tears, "I'm crying because I'm thirsty!"

"All you have to do is ask. I'll go get you a drink." I shook my head all the way to the kitchen. Upon returning with a cool glass of water, I asked, "Why didn't you simply call out to Mommy and ask her for a drink instead of sitting here crying about it?"

He blinked back the tears. "Because you should have known I was thirsty and you didn't bring me a drink."

It is silly for a child to assume that his parents know all of his needs. We shake our heads in frustration when this happens, yet we do the very same thing to God.

Unlike earthly parents, our heavenly Father does know what we need before we ask; He is omniscient. Even so, God wants us to come to Him and present our specific requests to Him. The interaction that happens when we ask and God gives creates a closer relationship. That doesn't mean that He will give us everything we ask for; He knows what is best for us and sometimes it is not what we want! Often when I have a lot of needs, I feel better just talking to God about them. Then, as I watch Him respond to meet my needs, I generate an attitude of appreciation for His loving care.

Lord, thank You for Your promise that if I ask, I shall receive.

Be of sober spirit, be on the alert. Your adversary, the devil, prowls about like a roaring lion, seeking someone to devour. (1 Peter 5:8)

A television documentary featured the migration of wildebeests in Africa from a desert plain to more fertile land. The herd remained tightly knit as it covered many miles; the wildebeests ate, drank and slept together. As the camera followed the fascinating journey of these creatures, it often swept to one side or another, revealing other creatures migrating along with the wildebeests—lions silently followed the herd's every move. The lions hid themselves in the brush, waiting and watching for any wildebeests that strayed from the herd. The lions never attacked the entire herd. As long as the wildebeests stayed together, they were safe.

This scenario is hauntingly similar to our condition as Christians. God created the church body for our protection. Through the body of Christ, or the "herd," we can be fed spiritually as well as find the rest we need to grow and thrive in our walk with God. If we will stay close to other Christians, we have a network of other believers who will seek to protect us spiritually. It is when we leave this umbrella of protection and become a lone ranger Christian that we often get in trouble. Satan will seek to destroy us when we are alone and vulnerable.

Don't be a lone ranger mom either. If you are not attending a local church where you can meet other stay-at-home moms, then find one. Seek out other Christian moms and start a weekly play group. The opportunity for regular interaction with other moms who have the same priorities as you can be lifesaving! There is strength in numbers. And where there is strength, there is survival.

Lord, keep me safe from the enemy, who seeks to destroy me and my family. Show me the wisdom in staying connected with a body of believers, both large and small. As I remain committed to You, strengthen me, in my walk with You. Show me how I can protect other believers as well.

September 25

———— ❧✿❧ ————

Therefore comfort one another with these words.
(1 Thessalonians 4:18)

My husband and I were planning our annual Mommy-Daddy getaway when three-year-old Seth informed us that he was very sad we were "going away." We reassured him that we would be back in three days and he would have a wonderful time at his grandparents. For days all he talked about was how sad he would be when we were gone.

In seeking for something we could leave with Seth to remind him of our love and commitment to him, I came across a fabulous idea in a book called *Creative Family Times* by Allen and Connie Hadidian and Will and Lindy Wilson. The book advocated making your children a "Mommy and Daddy Tape." It can include such things as Scripture verses, Bible songs, godly character definitions, the ABC's and 1-2-3s, as well as any other material that you think is appropriate for your child.

Jimmy and I set to work immediately. We presented the special tape the day before we left, explaining that even though we would not be with him physically, he could listen to our voices anytime he wanted. He played the tape several times that day even though we were still home. When we left, he was no longer anxious about our departing. He waved happily out the window as we drove away. My parents reported that he played it several times a day, and it seemed to comfort him if he started missing us. There is something about the sound of a parent's voice that is soothing to a young child.

Lord, may the sound of my voice always bring comfort to my children. I pray that they will learn to listen and respond to Your voice and Your instruction.

I can do all things through Him who strengthens me.
(Philippians 4:13)

I'll never forget the look on each of my boys' faces as they took their first steps. When you are a stay-at-home mom, you are the one who witnesses these fabulous "firsts." Seth, my oldest, became easily aggravated at trying to master the skill of walking. No amount of smiling, encouraging words or clapping of our hands would bring him to his feet to try again. We learned that Seth was not extrinsically motivated; he was not driven to perform out of the encouragement of others. His motivation to do something came from within.

Our second child is different. Levi is driven by a desire to please others. When he was learning to walk, his extrinsic motivation became clearer as he would take another step with every "Hooray for Levi" we sounded.

Learning to work with your children in developing their skills, according to the temperaments given to them by God, is very important. God has wired each of us differently; our temperaments were formed right along with our physical features in our mother's womb. There is one common thread in our training, however, and that is Philippians 4:13. We want our boys to learn that they can do all things when they rely on Christ as the source of their strength. When either of them becomes discouraged while learning a new skill, we gently remind him that he can do all things through Christ who strengthens him. As we discover the varying temperaments of our children, we can help them best by teaching them how to excel by working with their God-given strengths, not against them.

Lord, I thank You that Your strength is all I need to do all things. May my children learn to lean on You as the Source of their strength. Give me an appreciation for their unique temperaments. Guide me in training them for the purpose of serving You and being the best they can in all they do.

She rises also while it is still night,
And gives food to her household,
And portions to her maidens. (Proverbs 31:15)

When's the last time you rose before dawn and made your family a four-course breakfast? If you're like me, you're still hitting the snooze button long after daybreak! Well, today I have great news for you. A closer look at today's Scripture will reveal to you that the supposed "perfect" woman in Proverbs 31 had a lot of help. She didn't do it all herself after all!

I recently went through a season of life where I had two small children, and doing weekly errands such as grocery shopping and banking was a nightmare. One more trip to the post office trying to balance packages and children and I feared I would crack up. I telephoned a girlfriend and cried in her ear. "I can't do all of this by myself. How am I supposed to get my haircut with a three-year-old and a six-month-old?"

"Why don't you just hire someone to watch the boys one morning a week for a few hours so you can get all of your errands done?" she said. "There's nothing wrong with admitting you need a little help."

She was right. I did have the wrong attitude—I felt I had to do everything myself or I wasn't a good mother. I took my friend's advice. A few hours a week alone was all I needed to save my shopping list and my sanity!

I was pleased to discover about the same time that the so-called queen of perfection called on a little help too. You know why she arose before the sun? To give orders! She had maidens. The maidens were the hired help, and the "portions" she passed out to them were their share of duties for the day. Doesn't that make you feel better? Even the Proverbs 31 woman shared the load.

Lord, thank You for helping me to see that saying I need help does not mean I am weak.

This will be written for the generation to come;
That a people yet to be created may praise the LORD.
(Psalm 102:18)

God loves our praise. The Bible tells us that He inhabits the praises of His people. That means He lives where praise dwells. Wherever you find people praising the Lord, there you will find Him. All too often we run to God in times of need only. Our children will not learn to live a life of praise and thanksgiving to God if they learn this attitude from us.

To get in the habit of praising God, begin by making a list of all of the things God has blessed you with: health, food, shelter, your husband's job. Build your list with your child's help. Ask him what he would like to praise God for. Work from the tangible things to the intangible, such as your faith and the freedom to worship God. Add all of the attributes of God that are praiseworthy: mercy, compassion, kindness, patience, provision, forgiveness and so forth. Post the list in a prominent place where you will be reminded daily to praise God. Ask your children to pray and to praise God for one thing. Each time you ask God for something in prayer, give Him praise for something as well.

Praise is something we have to train ourselves and our children to do. When we get into the habit, it develops a heart of gratitude instead of the "gimmies"—give me this and give me that. Every time we praise Him for something, it is like laying a little package down at His throne. He loves to receive our gifts of praise! We are living in a generation where children are programmed to focus on themselves. That only breeds selfishness. We need to train them to put God first. Praise is a start.

> *Lord, I want to thank You for Your mercy and praise You for Your goodness. You have blessed me with a loving husband and beautiful children. All that I have is a gift from You.*

September 29

Jesus wept. (John 11:35)

When my first son was nearly three years old, we were preparing for the birth of our second child. At the time, we had a dog. Although the dog had been a good playmate for Seth, she was becoming more of a nuisance than a benefit. We found a good home for her, and carefully prepared Seth for her departure. The day she left he took it quite well.

The next day Seth looked all over the house for the dog. When I reminded him that she had a new home, he cried. "It's OK to be sad, Seth," I said, stroking his hair, "and it's OK to cry. Mommy understands." Understanding was all he needed, and the freedom to cry. Twenty minutes later he was ripping through the backyard once again, and he never shed another tear over that dog.

As the mother of two boys, I realize the importance of allowing our children to show emotion. The old stereotypical idea that "big boys don't cry" only brings emotional baggage and damage. Jesus gives us a model that weeping is a normal and healthy emotion. The Savior experienced great pain and loss when he took the form of flesh and dwelt as man among us on the earth. He felt and expressed his emotions, to the fullest. He created us with the ability to cry for a reason. Tears can be very cleansing. They can release stress and pent-up emotions.

As you raise your children, steer clear of the attitude that crying is for the weak. Jesus had a tender heart. He wept, and He is as mighty as they come.

Lord, thank You for reminding me that tears serve a purpose. May I raise my children to be emotionally healthy adults, full of compassion and hearts that are not afraid of tenderness.

September 30

———— ❧🌹❧ ————

But the lovingkindness of the LORD is from everlasting to
everlasting on those who fear Him,
And His righteousness to children's children. (Psalm 103:17)

I was raised in a Christian home. Growing up, I was secure in my parents' love and commitment for each other and our family. My father served his role well in our home.

I have many friends who were not as fortunate and lacked the security of a father figure. The way we perceive our earthly fathers is generally the perception we carry onto our heavenly Father.

Psalm 103 is a beautiful portrait of God's attitude toward us. Focusing on the truth of its words can shape our attitudes toward God. If your father has never brought you any sense of security, comfort or compassion, you can look to your heavenly Father to meet those needs instead. God has many qualities that make it easy to hold Him in this kind of esteem. Psalm 103 is a wonderful illustration of those qualities. Take time to read the entire psalm.

Every time I read this psalm, I end up on my knees, with tears streaming down my face—the words impact me that much. This is who God is! I am overwhelmed with gratitude at His attitude toward me—a sinner.

You may have married a man who has not turned out to be the kind of father that Scripture depicts—the kind you want for your children. Whatever your situation, God can meet your children's securities, as well as yours. Continue to look to God to meet the needs that are not currently being met by a father in your life, and teach your children to do the same. Your perception of our heavenly Father will be handed down to them and will shape their own attitudes about who God is.

> *Heavenly Father, You have demonstrated Your lovingkindness to*
> *me over and over again. Overcome any misconceptions I have about*
> *You and heal any wounds.*

October:
Opportunities for Advancement

What's my next step up?

*M*any jobs outside the home are dead-end jobs with no room for advancement. Being a stay-at-home mom is exciting work because there is always room for advancement. God turns many women who have made a career out of being a stay-at-home mom into speakers, authors and teachers. You can speak, write or teach on the subject of being a stay-at-home mom in many settings. It can be as simple as encouraging a friend who is questioning her own validity as a stay-at-home mom and instructing her in the value of her job. You can teach a Bible study or Sunday school class, write a magazine article or book, or even start a ministry or baby-sitting co-op for stay-at-home moms.

As you read this month's devotionals, think about who has helped to encourage and guide you in your role as a stay-at-home mom. Is there someone special you look up to who has been supportive? Send her a note of thanks. Ask God to show you how He may want to use you to possibly teach, train or communicate what He has taught you in your own parenting experiences. Be open to His leading—the next step up in His service.

October 1

. . . {H}e who sows sparingly shall also reap sparingly; and he who sows bountifully shall also reap bountifully. (2 Corinthians 9:6)

Have you ever tasted a ripe, juicy tomato fresh from the vine? Or bitten into an ear of tender sweet corn picked at the moment of perfection? I grew up in the Midwest where farming is the main source of income for many communities. The farmers had to plant in abundance to harvest in abundance. I learned to appreciate the commitment and dedication it takes to grow a successful crop.

When we, as stay-at-home moms and servants of Christ, sow lovingly into the lives of others, our rewards are also abundant. Just as corn kernels take time, sunshine and water to grow into a healthy crop, so do we as Christians take time, encouragement and instruction to grow into healthy, fruit-producing believers. Once I got past the stage of needing mostly to receive input in order to grow in my walk with Christ, I began growing more by giving—giving back to God by serving others. My life took on a whole new dimension of purpose.

My eyes were opened to the women around me who were hurting and needed validation as women, wives and mothers. Just like planting a crop, sowing into the lives of others is time-consuming, but the rewards are abundant and eternal. God can use you to help another mom grow in her faith. You may be just the source of water or sunshine He has in mind. You only need to make yourself available. What are you sowing into the lives of others? Remember, what you sow, you shall reap.

> *God of the harvest, just as You water the crops to help them grow, shower my life with love and kindness so that it overflows to others. Help me to be a source of encouragement to other moms and show me specifically how I can serve You, sowing the seeds You gave just to me.*

*But encourage one another day after day, as long as it is still called
"Today," lest any one of you be hardened by the deceitfulness of sin.
(Hebrews 3:13)*

God uses all of us if we allow Him to. I have many stay-at-home
friends who have encouraged me when I have felt defeated in my
role as a mother. Many of these women thought God would never use them
to do anything "significant" for Him. But encouraging another
stay-at-home mom is important. Often, it is in the early years of staying
home with children that a mother gets the most frustrated.

In my early years as a mom, I had a friend who was a role model for me. I
watched her closely and learned from her as she raised three sons. I have
gone to her countless times for support, advice and prayer in my own frus-
tration with raising children. Because she was willing, God opened a door
for her to teach a Bible study on parenting at our church, and she has been
able to share her wisdom and experiences with many other moms.

Another friend of mine told me she would have given up being a
stay-at-home mom and gone back to working outside the home if it hadn't
been for the faithful support and prayers of a special friend in her life. This
friend constantly encouraged her and reinforced her important role as a
stay-at-home mom when she was feeling worthless.

Are you a veteran stay-at-home mom? There are probably many new
mothers around you who could use some support. Ask God to open your
eyes to the possibility of encouraging others. Your support can make the
difference in the life of a young mother who needs to hear your tender
words of affirmation.

*Lord, thank You for sending other women before me in my quest to
be the best stay-at-home mom I can be. Help me to find someone I
can learn from and receive support from when I am frustrated. And
in turn, use me to encourage new young moms.*

——— ✦ ———

Do not merely look out for your own personal interests, but also for the interests of others. (Philippians 2:4)

art of the growth process in your job as a stay-at-home mom is stretching yourself in the area of serving other women. The Bible tells us to "look out for the interests of others." Surely there should be no tighter group than the body of Christ; yet sadly, that is not true today. Christians spread gossip and strife just as quickly as non-Christians. Instead of protecting each other, we often stab each other in the back. And words leave scars that can last forever. As stay-at-home moms we need to spend less time on the telephone spreading rumors and more time defending each other and building each other up.

A true servant puts others before herself. The Bible is full of one anothers: love one another, encourage one another, help one another, serve one another. It is obvious that having an other-centered mentality should be a goal. When we model this type of behavior, our children will learn from our example. They will adopt an other-centered mentality by watching you.

By simply being a stay-at-home mom, you are already putting others first: your children. Even though children often miss the point in your sacrifices for them, they will usually catch a glimpse of a servant's heart when they see you reach out to someone else in need. So watch for opportunities to serve and protect the interests of others, especially your Christian sisters. In a me-first world, our kids need to see other-centered attitudes just as badly as we need to experience them.

Lord, I want to be a protector, a servant to my sisters in Christ. Help me to put others' needs above my own and to look for opportunities to model other-centered behavior to my children.

Wherefore, accept one another, just as Christ also accepted us to the glory of God. (Romans 15:7)

have a friend who raises her children differently than I do. We have different ideas about discipline, correction, training, schedule, routine, even education. Yet, this woman is a wonderful person. She is warm, sincere, tenderhearted, funny and kind. She has been a good friend to me.

When I began to realize the vast differences in our parenting methods, I became quite bothered and even talked to my husband about it. After some consideration and prayer, God showed me that I needed simply to accept her just the way she is, including her views on child-rearing. I knew that we both wanted to raise morally and spiritually responsible children, because we had talked about it many times. We were just using different means to get there—sort of like taking two different vehicles to reach the same destination.

My friend and I may have different ways of teaching God's principles, but we have the same goal in mind. And that is all that matters. Jesus doesn't tell us to love and accept one another only if we agree with all of the other person's ideas or philosophies. He just tells us to love—that's it. If I had based my acceptance of this woman only on what little I have in common with her, I would be missing out on a fabulous friendship.

Are you missing out on a friendship because you can't get past someone's differences? Are you limiting yourself by not accepting that person just as she is? Take some time right now to ask God to speak to your heart and open it up to someone you may be shutting out.

Thank You, Lord, for accepting me just as I am. I know You love me, even when I let you down or do things a different way than You would prefer. Help me to love and accept others unconditionally, just as You do, regardless of our differences.

October 5

For whatever is born of God overcomes the world. . . . (1 John 5:4)

One of the great things about being a follower of Jesus Christ is that we don't have to give in to the world's deceptions. We can overcome all of the temptations the world throws at us by leaning on Jesus. The world takes many ugly philosophies and paints them a pretty color to try to entice us. One such philosophy is that working outside the home brings more reward than working in the home—being a stay-at-home mom. Advertisements of impeccably dressed female executives are used to entice our flesh. It may look appealing to spend your days that way, but I have done both, and trust me, the rewards of being at home with your children are far greater. They may not be as immediate as the new car or addition onto the house, but they are of eternal value.

Of course, I have to remind myself of this when dealing with a whiny preschooler or picking up toys—again. Some days I don't feel like an overcomer, so I have to look at Scripture to refresh my sense of worth. When we enter into a relationship with God (being "born of God"), we also become overcomers. God gives us all of the tools we need to overcome the enticements the enemy dangles before us. Someone who is an overcomer no longer looks at things such as riches, possessions or promotions as appealing. It takes power to overcome. God supplies each of us with the power of His Holy Spirit when we invite Him into our lives. We just need to learn to tap into that power and call upon Him when a situation arises that we need the strength to overcome.

Don't let the world overcome your faith or your belief that God has called you to be at home with your children.

> *Thank You, Lord, for the reminder in Your Word that You have given me the power to be an overcomer of the world. Help me to exercise the authority You have given me and call upon Your Name when I need it.*

Be imitators of me, just as I also am of Christ. (1 Corinthians 11:1)

Paul's challenge to the Corinthians in the above verse is a pretty tall order. His example of living was sacrificial. But then, he had the goal of imitating Christ, the picture of sacrifice. If you study Paul's life, you will see that he did a pretty good job of imitating Christ's behavior.

I can be selfish. Part of my struggle is that I sacrifice my time all day long. I want to read a novel; instead I read *Winnie the Pooh and the Honey Tree*. I want to go shopping for a new outfit; instead I stay home and wash the old one. I want to go to lunch and the theater with a girlfriend; instead I take the kids to the park for a picnic. My time is not my own. I am sacrificing it and my desires all day for my children. That is part of being a stay-at-home mom.

Although it may not seem that these sacrifices mean anything except depression, that is not true. They mean everything to God, because He knows all of the sacrifices we make. And it pleases Him. Your husband and children may not seem to appreciate you, but God does. Now I understand the sacrifices my mom made for me. She was an imitator of Christ. And now I find myself imitating her, following in her footsteps as a stay-at-home mom.

Our children will imitate what they see in us. What kind of example are you to your children? Are you imitating Christ? Or are you acting selfishly? By watching our kids, we can see our own behavior. Do you like the reflection you see?

> *Lord, I want to be an imitator of You. I pray that You would humble me through the sacrifices made for my children, and help me to do so in love. I pray they also would be imitators of You.*

Do not withhold good from those to whom it is due,
When it is in your power to do it. (Proverbs 3:27)

Shortly before our second child was born, I received word that my grandmother was ill and not expected to live. A surge of guilt ran through me—I had not seen my grandparents since I was sixteen. What do you say to someone you haven't seen in fifteen years? This time, despite the expense and the inconvenience, I needed to go. My husband confirmed my feelings and, after making the necessary arrangements, I was on my way three days later.

As we flew, I thought of all the childhood family vacations to their tiny little house. I laughed as I remembered their old concrete basement. My brothers and I used to play dungeon there. Grandma always made cherry pie and ice cream.

My son would never get to taste Grandma's cherry pie or play dungeon in her basement. The thought brought tears to my eyes, and I reprimanded myself for waiting so long to come back.

My trepidation at seeing Grandma melted as I stood in the doorway of her hospital room, and she extended her bony hand to me. "I've been waiting for you," she whispered. Grandpa looked the same, only much frailer, but not bad for ninety-five years. He chuckled at the two-year-old bundle of energy I sat on his lap and Grandma's eyes had the same sweet sparkle I remembered as a child. And that sassy laugh! We laughed a lot over the next five days as we recalled many moments shared from days gone by.

A few weeks after our visit, both my grandma and my grandpa passed away. I was so relieved that I had gone to see them.

Lord, give me a sense of otherness so that when someone needs me I can see it. Make me sensitive to Your Spirit that I might do the right thing and do good to others at every opportunity. Forgive me for the times when I put myself first, neglecting someone else's need.

October 8

---✦❋✦---

Light arises in the darkness for the upright;
He is gracious and compassionate and righteous. (Psalm 112:4)

Have you ever noticed that when there is a single candle burning in an otherwise dark room, you don't see the blackness surrounding the flame? Your eyes focus on the source of light. So it is with our Christian walk. When we do the right thing, attention is drawn not to the negative circumstances swirling about us, but to the good deed. Good always outshines evil. And when the spotlight is on, there is no better time to give the glory to God.

Not too long ago, there was an amazing story of one soldier's survival that swept the nation. He was a U.S. Air Force pilot whose plane was shot down over enemy territory. Every newspaper, radio and television station aired this man's incredible story of how he escaped the hands of the enemy virtually unscathed. He was a hero. I sat teary-eyed yet smiling as I listened to this man on national television give praise and thanks to God for watching over him and keeping him safe. He said he would never have made it out of enemy territory alive without God's provision and watch care.

What a beautiful testimony! And what a glorious occasion to give the glory to God. This man was humbled and didn't take any credit for his own intelligence and survival tactics; instead he gave all the credit to the One who gave him the wit to escape. His story reminded me that I need to give the glory to God when I do something that attracts attention or is tagged as a "good work." It is then that people who have been living in the dark can get a glimpse of His light.

Help me, Lord, to give You the glory and honor for all good that is
accomplished in my life. May Your light shine brightly through
me, attracting others to You.

And let us consider how to stimulate one another to love and good deeds. (Hebrews 10:24)

Part of your opportunity for ministering to others as a stay-at-home mom involves being an encourager. Encouragement is listed in the Bible as a spiritual gift (See Romans 12:8.) and is also referred to as exhortation. While true exhortation in the biblical definition is the ability to reassure, strengthen and affirm those who are discouraged in their faith and is definitely a gift, speaking encouraging words is something we all can do. Most people can accomplish just about anything if they are encouraged by someone. At the same time, there are many people who never reach their full potential because someone has damaged their confidence with discouraging words. Our words are powerful. To underestimate them is foolish. The impact our words have on our children, our spouses, our friends, is phenomenal.

In her book *Silver Boxes*, Florence Littauer gives account after account of the power that our words, encouraging and discouraging, have on people. She says our words should be "like little silver boxes with bows on top"—presents that we give when we speak to people.

I began to think about words before I spoke them, and when needed, changed them to be more encouraging. We can stimulate others to love and speak kindly and do good deeds by first loving and speaking and doing kind things ourselves. Our children especially will respond to our words, whether kind or unkind. Many times, it is what we say that determines what they do. Think before you speak.

Lord, may my words be encouraging and my actions be exhorting to all those around me, both family and friends. Help me to stimulate others to do good through the power of my speech.

So then, while we have opportunity, let us do good to all men, and especially to those who are of the household of the faith.
(Galatians 6:10)

We have a wonderful ministry in our church called the Ruth Ministry. It is a network of women serving women. We do such things as set up child care, make and deliver meals, find and disperse needed clothing and personal items. Most of the time we are serving when there has been a surgery, the birth of a new baby or even such tragedies as fire or theft. All of the time and most of the resources are donated by this group of women.

The above Scripture illustrates the fact that God sees the importance of helping anyone we can, and the priority we are to take in helping other believers is quite clear. Not long ago, a woman in our body received word that her mother had cancer and was going to undergo some intense chemotherapy treatments. She wanted to go and be with her mother, but the distance between them was great, the trip expensive. So we took up a collection for a plane ticket. She was able to minister to and serve her mother, which blessed them both.

So many times we have opportunities to do good, especially to fellow believers, and yet we are blinded by our own busyness and neediness. Ask God to show you how you can better minister to your Christian sisters. Think about starting your own Ruth Ministry. You never know—someday you may find yourself, in your darkest hours of need, the recipient of the services from the very ministry you helped pioneer!

Lord, help me to see the opportunities that You put before me to serve others, especially my Christian brothers and sisters. Show me how I can serve specifically in a special ministry within our body designed to meet the needs of others.

. . . {A}nd it came about, that everyone who sought the LORD would go out to the tent of meeting which was outside the camp. (Exodus 33:7)

oses was one of the greatest leaders of all time. He was not a particularly gifted man by the world's definition: He wasn't a public speaker, he had no political agenda and he had no real leadership experience. Part of Moses' success as a leader was that he was willing to be the facilitator—he let God lead. Moses sought God daily in prayer, asking for direction and guidance as he was entrusted with God's chosen people. His time with God was so important that he erected what was called the tent of meeting until the tabernacle could be constructed. He made sure that there was a special place where all of God's people could go to seek His face.

God honored Moses' earnest desire to glorify Him; He began to speak to Moses in a special way: "And it came about, whenever Moses entered the tent, the pillar of cloud would descend and stand at the entrance of the tent; and the LORD would speak with Moses" (Exodus 33:9). What a powerful picture! Can you imagine God descending to you in a tornado-like cloud and speaking to you? God's relationship with Moses was so important, and the task at hand so crucial that He felt it necessary to speak with Moses face-to-face. I'm sure Moses was both humbled and blessed.

You are a leader. You are leading your children. You may also be a leader/facilitator in other capacities. Do you have a "tent of meeting" you go to each day? A special place where you meet with God? It doesn't matter where, it simply matters that you're there. As a leader, you have an extra responsibility to carry out God's will, not just for your own sake but for the sake of those you are leading.

Lord, I want to hear from You. I need Your direction and guidance. Help me to be still long enough to hear You speak to me. Make me into the leader that You created me to be.

Let the word of Christ richly dwell within you, with all wisdom teaching and admonishing one another with psalms and hymns and spiritual songs, singing with thankfulness in your hearts to God. (Colossians 3:16)

I read about a mother who sings to her children. Their house is always filled with music. She uses songs to teach and to correct them. She will make up funny lyrics to teach them about manners or help them to remember the letters of the alphabet. She sings verses of the Bible to help them memorize Scripture. She claims that if she sings while telling them they are going to be disciplined, it helps her keep her emotions from elevating to the point of anger. In short, it helps her not to yell at them!

This is a great picture of how the Bible tells us to teach and admonish. It says to do so with "psalms and hymns and spiritual songs." What a fun way to learn! I have tried this as a method of teaching with my children and they love it. They laugh and giggle and begin to repeat the song.

The entire book of Psalms is filled with beautiful lyrics which were written as songs. Some are songs of praise, some of thankfulness, some of despair, some of a call for God's help. All are meaningful and have great value in learning more about God. The psalmists themselves were passionate people, close to God and in touch with their feelings. Try writing a song or poem of your own to God. It can be a good way of sharing your innermost thoughts. Sing a prayer of thanks to Him. And, if you need some new ways to teach and admonish your children, try singing to them. The results may be music to your ears—and theirs.

Lord, I sing praises to Your name! You are my God, my Savior, my Teacher. Show me how to sing a new song. May we make beautiful music in our house unto You.

When he puts forth all his own, he goes before them, and the sheep follow him because they know his voice. (John 10:4)

The relationship that a shepherd has with his sheep is an amazing thing. A shepherd spends so much time with his sheep that they begin to identify him by his smell and even the sound of his voice. In the darkness, a sheep that has wandered from the flock will respond to his shepherd's voice when it hears the shepherd calling for him. It will follow the sound of its master's voice until it has located him. If the sheep has been injured and cannot move, it will cry out in response to its shepherd's voice until the shepherd finds it. If intruders try to steal from the flock, sheep have an internal alarm system that goes off when they detect the unfamiliar smells and sounds of the one who is trying to lure them away. They will begin to make noise, and lots of it, until they hear or smell their own shepherd.

The Bible often refers to Jesus as the Good Shepherd and to us, His followers, as the sheep of His pasture. We can only learn the sound of His voice by spending time with Him. If we study His Word, we will better understand His voice and its characteristics. If we are intimately familiar with Him, then we can take assurance in knowing that we will recognize His voice even in the midst of the cloudy confusion that may be surrounding us. When we have wandered into a bad situation, the Good Shepherd is out looking for us, calling our name, wanting to carry us home. Do you know the voice of your Good Shepherd?

Good Shepherd, thank You for your loving care. I pray that I will become so familiar with You that I recognize the sound of Your voice even in the most dismal conditions of life and can follow it all the way back into Your arms.

But not so with you, but let him who is the greatest among you become as the youngest, and the leader as the servant. (Luke 22:26)

All truly great leaders are even greater servants. All presidents are servants to their countries. All governors are servants to their states. All mayors are servants to their townspeople. All pastors are servants to their congregations. Even Jesus, the greatest Leader, was a servant to God. Leading isn't about putting ourselves first. A good leader puts the interests of others before his own. Leadership can be difficult. It is tough to make all of the people happy all of the time. Many people don't like to lead a group of any size because of that stigma. Jesus didn't worry about that, though.

Jesus wasn't trying to win a popularity contest. He was merely doing the will of His Father—the one whom He served. He was constantly making people angry, especially the Pharisees. But Jesus just kept spreading the truth and trusting that God would make a way for Him to continue doing it as long as it was part of the plan. Jesus led people to the truth, no matter what the cost. Even the cost of His very life.

Some of the decisions we make in leading our children will not be popular with them. They might not be happy about our television monitoring, early curfews or dating restrictions. But if we are truly acting in the best interest of those whom we serve—our children in this case—then God will continue to make a way for us to lead them. We have to trust Him that He will protect our children and help us to make the right decisions regarding their welfare.

Lord, help me to lead my children in the right direction, constantly steering them toward You and Your righteousness. May I follow in the example of Your leadership and speak the truth, doing what is right for my children at all times, regardless of the cost.

Then Samuel took the horn of oil and anointed him in the midst of his brothers; and the Spirit of the LORD came mightily upon David from that day forward. . . . (1 Samuel 16:13)

Samuel had a very special job. God entrusted him to go to Bethlehem and anoint the man whom the Lord would raise up as the future king of Israel. The extraordinary thing about the event in today's Scripture is that the man whom Samuel was about to anoint and bless in the name of the Lord was a mere shepherd boy.

David was the youngest of eight sons. In the world's eyes, he was the least likely to become a king because he was not in the right position. Most men didn't go from the field to the throne. But in the Lord's eyes, David was the most likely, because his heart was in the right place—this is made clear in First Samuel 16:7. David embodied the qualities that God needed in the king of Israel. He was both gentle and strong. Tenderhearted and lion-hearted. Compassionate and mighty. He had the right balance of gentleness and strength. Most of all, David loved God.

Stay-at-home moms can learn from David's life. Caring for sheep is like caring for children. It can be thankless, tiring and just plain hard work. Sheep stray from the fold into dangerous terrain much like children stray from the right path. In spite of the low-profile job of a shepherd, David was faithful and he found joy in it! How? By keeping his focus on God.

As we go about our day-to-day tasks such as vacuuming, folding the laundry, helping with homework and other details of caring for children, we too can find joy in such seeming monotony. We need only to focus on God and His purpose for having us in our current role. Like David, we may be surprised how, once we find peace in our humble positions, God brings us to a position of great strength and influence.

Lord, thank You for the example of David. I pray that I might have a heart like his—one that desires to serve and please You. Teach me to be content where You have placed me.

October 16

---

*But as many as received Him, to them He gave the right to become
children of God, even to those who believe in His name." John 1:12*

*D*id you know that when you become a Christian, you become roy-
alty? It's true! When we ask Christ to be our Savior and Lord, He
comes to live in us and we become "children of God." Since Jesus is the
King of kings and Lord of lords, that makes anyone who is His child a
member of the royal family. That makes you a daughter of the King—a
princess!

When you are knee-deep in dirty diapers and piles of laundry, it is tough
to feel like a princess. Regardless of how I feel, the truth remains the same:
I am a daughter of the King. When we ask Christ to make His home in our
hearts, we are transformed into a new creation—into a princess, and we are
worth everything based on who our heavenly Father is, not on who we are
or what we do.

Shortly after I gave up my lucrative corporate career to become a
stay-at-home mom, my son became very ill. As I was cleaning up the re-
mains of his recycled dinner from all over the floor, I began to cry. I was
tired and I didn't feel like a princess there on my hands and knees. I had felt
like a princess when I was wearing business suits, changing sales plans and
dining at expensive restaurants where someone else cleaned up after me!
God reminded me in that moment on my hands and knees to rely on the
truth of His Word rather than my feelings. Changing my mind-set helped
me get through the night.

The world's definition of royalty encompassed being served; God's roy-
alty includes those who are the servants. I'd much rather be a daughter of
the King of kings, who will live forever, than the daughter of a king of this
world, whose power and glory will fade with the passing of time.

> *Lord, I thank You that Your Word says I am Your child. Live in
> my life so powerfully that I radiate like royalty even when I am
> washing the dishes.*

October 17

But if any one does not provide for his own, and especially for those of his household, he has denied the faith, and is worse than an unbeliever. (1 Timothy 5:8)

Today's Scripture contains strong words. Sometimes God's Word is hard to swallow. When a woman becomes a mother, she has an obligation to provide for her child. Provision is more than just physical care. Unfortunately, many parents believe that if they provide the physical, they have done their job.

Children have emotional needs that can only be met by mom and dad. All human beings have a need to feel loved. Children who feel secure in their parents' love grow up to be secure and self-confident adults. Those who are never absolutely sure of that love grow up insecure and generally have poor self-esteem. Those feelings of insecurity are carried into every relationship that adult enters, including marriage, friendships and parenthood.

My husband's parents were divorced when he was two years old and he had several stepfathers. There wasn't a lot of hugging or words of affection exchanged in his home during his early years. Lacking needed physical and verbal reinforcement, he never felt sure that he was completely loved.

Fortunately, God can fill those voids in our lives when we ask Him to. If you grew up in a home where love was not communicated openly, you may have feelings of insecurity. Give those feelings to God and ask Him to fill the voids. Children need to know they are loved unconditionally by mom and dad. And they need to know that God loves them too. You can break the cycle of the past by choosing to show and tell your children how much you love them. Provide for all of their needs and you will produce healthy, confident little beings.

Lord, show me how to provide for my children's needs: physical, emotional and spiritual. May I show them an abundance of love and affection; both Yours and mine.

Not returning evil for evil, or insult for insult, but giving a bless-
ing instead; for you were called for the very purpose that you might
inherit a blessing. (1 Peter 3:9)

Our oldest son went through a stage as a preschooler where he solved his frustration by hitting. For a few months, we battled his compulsion to hit, trying to teach him to exercise self-control. We begged, we pleaded, we punished, we reasoned, we insisted; but nothing seemed to help him gain control of his hitting. I didn't want to get together with other moms and their kids to play because I was afraid that Seth would hit one of them.

One day after some friends left and Seth was isolated on his bed again for hitting, I said, "You know it's wrong to hit." Sad blue eyes returned my gaze, "Yes, Mommy." OK. Admission of guilt. "Then why do you do it?" I asked. He sighed heavily, "Well, I just get fwastwated (translated—frustrated) when other kids are mean to me." Understanding and compassion for my "fwastwated" preschooler began to formulate into an idea. He had to have an alternative outlet for his frustration.

I explained to Seth that the Bible says we should not repay evil for evil; instead when others treat us wrongly, we should give them a blessing. I suggested that the next time another kid was mean to him that he shout, "Bless you!" as loud as he could and walk away. "Can you do that, Seth?" His big smile answered my question. "Hey Mom," he jumped up. "Let's practice right now. You pretend to be mean to me and I'll practice shouting, 'Bless you!'" I laughed at his new enthusiasm. I think he liked the idea of having permission to shout something more than anything else.

Seth's struggle with self-control prompted me to assess my own response to frustration. *How do I respond when someone wrongs me? Do I return insult for insult, or do I send them a blessing?*

> *Lord, give me the self-control to respond in love when I am*
> *wronged, sending out a blessing.*

——————— ❧✿❧ ———————

*We shall know by this that we are of the truth, and shall assure
our heart before Him, in whatever our heart condemns us; for God
is greater than our heart, and knows all things. (1 John 3:19-20)*

*Y*ou will know that you are growing in your relationship with God
when you learn to live above your feelings. Or sometimes in spite
of them. When we are driven by our feelings or emotions, we often make
foolish choices. A popular saying in today's culture is to "follow your
heart." The problem with that theory is that our hearts are driven by our
feelings and our feelings are often contrary to God's Word. Jeremiah 17:9
says, "The heart is more deceitful than all else and is desperately sick"!
Why would we want to follow our hearts? Our hearts lie to us and the en-
emy can use our own feelings against us, to try to steer us off of God's
course for our lives and onto His. When we begin to live according to the
truth of God's Word, and not according to the feelings of our heart, we will
avoid many disasters.

Sadly, many Christian marriages dissolve because people put more faith
in their feelings than they do in God. I don't always feel incredible love to-
ward my husband, especially if he has treated me unkindly or spoken to me
harshly. But, regardless of my feelings, I am committed to him.

I don't always feel like getting out of bed in the morning to take care of
my children. But the truth of God's Word says I am responsible to care for
them. If I acted on my feelings, my boys would be the victims of neglect.
My four-year-old doesn't always feel like picking up his toys, but he knows
he has to do it because Mommy said to. And God's Word tells children to
obey their parents. Teaching him such principles even at a young age will
begin to prepare him for a life of living according to God's truth, instead of
his feelings—a lesson we can all learn.

*Lord, guide me away from the deceitfulness of my own heart and
toward the righteousness of Your truth. May I live according to
that truth and not according to my feelings.*

The fear of the LORD is the beginning of wisdom. . . . (Proverbs 9:10)

My older son has a fascination with the garbage truck. At around age two, when he heard it, he would stop whatever he was doing and just remain still. Then, as the big truck's hissing and rumbling faded away, he would return to his previous activity.

By age three, he began venturing toward the living room window when he heard the truck approaching. He would climb up on the window seat where he could get a clear view of the street and the ominous noise-making machine. He would stare in fixed fascination until it was out of sight. As he neared four years of age, he began to shout, "Mom, hurry, here comes the garbage truck. Open the door so I can see." Seth would back away from the open door as the noise blew in and cling to the safety of my leg.

One Monday morning, anticipating the garbage truck's arrival, I suggested to Seth that we sit on the window seat and wait for it to come. He was thrilled.

As we watched the garbage truck roll down our street that Monday, I thought about Seth's reaction, one of both awe and trepidation toward this powerful machine. His fascination was a sort of reverent fear, similar to how I feel toward God. I respect Him because of His power and might, just as Seth respects the garbage truck's powerful abilities. He stopped what he was doing so he could draw close to the truck and be involved in its activity. In the same way, I desire to draw near to God and I often drop what I am doing to spend time with Him. Yet I view Him with reverence and respect because of His omnipotent power.

We honor, respect, awe and fear Him all at the same time. And as we do, He clears out the garbage in our lives.

> *Lord, I pray that I will always hold You in your rightful place in my life—on the throne and in control. May I treat You with respect and honor You.*

Know that the LORD Himself is God;
It is He who has made us, and not we ourselves;
We are His people and the sheep of His pasture. (Psalm 100:3)

The Bible is full of references of Jesus or God as the Good Shepherd and we, the Christians on earth, as His flock of sheep. According to Scripture, when someone becomes a leader of any group of people, God classifies him as a shepherd. For instance, in Second Samuel 5:2, God chose David to reign as king over Israel and the Lord said, "You will shepherd My people Israel, and you will be a ruler over Israel." To shepherd means to lead, guide or guard. Pastors and leaders within the church are often referred to as shepherds.

When a woman becomes a mother, she also becomes a shepherd. Her flock is her children. God has appointed every mother to lead, guide and guard her children. In addition, if you are in any leadership capacity, you are shepherding another flock or group of people. It is interesting to me that God chose a common man such as David, a shepherd, to become a future king. Obviously, God believed David's experience as a shepherd would enhance his ability to lead a nation. Similarly, our experience as mothers may someday serve to enhance our abilities in other leadership roles. God may be developing qualities in you right now that will strengthen your capacity to lead. Take this time to ready yourself for service. Whatever flock He entrusts in your care, you want to look to the Good Shepherd for guidance in all you do.

Good Shepherd, keep me and my family under Your watch care daily. Prepare me to be a shepherd to whatever flocks need guidance toward You.

———— ❧✿❧ ————

"As one whom his mother comforts, so I will comfort you. . . ."
(Isaiah 66:13)

"Mom!" Came the anxious cry from my four-year-old's room. By the panic in his voice, I knew this was not a cry for water or some other excuse to get out of bed. "I need you to hold me in the rocking chair," he sniffled. The fear in his eyes told me he needed some comfort. I held my son close to my chest, stroking his golden hair. The room was dark and silent as we rocked back and forth. After a few minutes, I asked Seth what had frightened him, and he revealed that it was a bad dream, complete with spiders chasing him! After a while, he lifted his head and softly declared that he was ready to go back to bed. As I tucked him under the covers, he smiled and said, "Thank you for holding me, Mom. I feel much better."

No one has the ability to comfort a child like his mother. For Seth, being held in the rocking chair provided comfort. There is a well-worn path on the carpet from those wooden slats as, over the years, that chair has rocked back and forth giving comfort.

There are days when I desperately need the comfort that loving arms can provide. When life is overwhelming and the demands on me have taken their toll, I seek that comfort in the arms of my heavenly Father. He promises to bring comfort to those who seek Him. So I close my eyes and picture God seated in a big rocking chair. Then I visualize myself crawling up on His lap and sinking deep into His broad chest. Those same arms that carried the cross to His own death encircle me and bring me peace. He can bring you comfort too. Just close your eyes and climb up. There is plenty of room.

Lord, thank You for promising to bring me comfort the way I comfort my children. When the burdens of this world drive me to tears, I pray that they would also drive me into Your arms of love.

October 23

Anxiety in the heart of a man weighs it down,
But a good word makes it glad. (Proverbs 12:25)

My friend Kellie recently took on the burden of caring for two very sick in-laws in her home. She had two young children at the time, ages five and eleven, and her house was fairly cozy with her family of four. Caring for two children was a full-time job already, and now she found herself bathing, feeding and meeting the needs of two adults as well.

The demands on Kellie were taxing. A few days into the ordeal, I called Kellie to find out how she was holding up. She sounded exhausted. Her usual cheery nature was replaced with fatigue and discouragement. The next day I cooked a meal for her family and delivered it. I wrapped my arms around my friend and we wept. I stayed for a while to talk with her and shared what I hoped would be some encouraging words and some hope-building Scripture passages. Before leaving, I prayed with her and gave her one last hug.

I talked with Kellie often during the five weeks her in-laws remained in her care. When I asked what else I could to help, her answer remained the same: "Keep praying for me and keep giving me those encouraging words."

Many times when a friend is hurting, we want to do something to help, but don't know how. Often, the best way is simply to encourage them with our love. Sometimes that means saying positive things to help them stay focused on God instead of on their negative circumstances. Comfort can be the most heartfelt in a hug, a meal in the freezer or being available when your friend is ready to talk. When the time comes, be sure you are ready with a "good word."

> *Lord, keep me focused on those around me, stepping up in times of need and giving good words that will bring hope and encouragement. May I teach my children to do the same.*

To sum up, let all be harmonious, sympathetic, brotherly, kind-hearted, and humble in spirit. (1 Peter 3:8)

I stood in the shower holding myself up against the wall, cool water running down my back and tears streaming down my face. "Please God," I moaned. "Make it stop hurting."

Poison ivy. It had been years since I had contracted the itchy rash, and I didn't remember it being so painful.

I had to be inventive so I could properly care for my two boys. I wore turtlenecks to cover the rash on my arms and neck so that the baby couldn't agitate it. I turned the air-conditioning way up. It was July, and 110 degrees in the shade. But once inside my house, you'd have thought you stepped into the Arctic zone. I draped myself with cool washcloths and slathered on the calamine lotion. My husband did all he could as soon as he came home from work.

As I lay soaking in an oatmeal bath about five days into the ordeal, I began reflecting on my health in general, thanking God that illness was not the norm for me. I was thanking God for giving me such a great husband when my thoughts drifted to how many times I had taken care of him when he was ill. There was the flu at Thanksgiving, the chicken pox at Christmas, the head cold on Valentine's Day. I realized that I generally tended to his needs, but begrudgingly. I had silently fumed that another holiday was ruined. I swallowed hard and resolved to show more compassion in the future.

Sometimes the only way we will learn to be more sensitive and caring toward others is to be the recipient of such compassion ourselves.

Lord, thank You for teaching me compassion in the midst of my pain. I pray that I will always care for my husband and children with the same sensitivity and love that I desire.

Do you not know that those who run in a race all run, but only one receives the prize? Run in such a way that you may win. (1 Corinthians 9:24)

Val was the anchor runner on his high school track relay team. He was a devoted athlete and had the utmost respect for his coach. During one meet, his relay team was scheduled for the final event, and anticipation mounted. Val's team got off to a great start. They maintained the lead until the baton pass to Val—somehow it was dropped. Val scrambled to pick up the baton, but the other runners sped past. Still, he pressed on, his confidence bruised but not broken. The other runners finished the race and cleared the track, but Val continued to run. With the meet officially over, the lights on the track began to flick off, one by one. Still, Val continued to run. Both astonished and touched by his persistence, Val's coach and teammates stood along the sidelines cheering. Racing through the dark now, Val had but one thought in his mind: Coach always says to finish. Val finished what he had started. And his teammates were there at the finish line to greet him.

As a stay-at-home mom, I long for that kind of perseverance. Do you? There will be times when we may limp along in the dark while everyone else seems to pass us by, but we need to "finish" what we have started—the training of our children. We need to pace ourselves as we prepare to pass along the baton of faith to our kids. Once we pass it to them, we must understand that they may drop it. The lights may go down on them. It is then that we need to be prepared to run alongside them, cheering them on. They may not take first prize, but if they give their best that is all that matters. And when they cross the finish line, Jesus will be waiting for them.

Lord, help me to pace myself as I run the race of faith, holding tightly to Your baton of truth until it is time to pass it to my kids. Show me how to cheer them on.

—◆❧✿❧◆—

The next day he saw Jesus coming to him, and said, "Behold, the Lamb of God who takes away the sin of the world!" (John 1:29)

"Ifyou cannot learn to respond to Mommy's voice," I told Seth, as I waited for him to obey, "I will take away the TV." Seth's eyes were now transfixed on me in a thoughtful gaze. He stood, turned off the television and said, "OK, Mommy, but if you take the TV away you better be careful, because I think it's too heavy for you." He sauntered off to do as I had asked.

Children take everything literally. Taking away the television had nothing to do with the privilege of watching it in Seth's mind; he pictured a blank space where it used to be and me with a sore back if he didn't do as he was told. It was faith in the simplicity of life. A childlike faith. The kind that Jesus talks about in His Word.

I closed my eyes and pictured John the Baptist by the river's edge, pointing to the approaching Jesus in the Scripture passage above, exclaiming, "Behold, the Lamb of God who takes away the sin of the world." Sometimes the next step up in our walks with Christ is actually a step back—back to where our faith began. Think about the moment when you first accepted Christ as your Savior, when you trusted Him to remove the guilt of sin. That is childlike faith.

If you have never made the decision to receive Christ as your Savior, you can right now. Ask Him to be Lord of your life. Admit that you are a sinner, as we all are, and that you need His forgiveness. His death on the cross bridged the gap between your sin and heaven. Accept the price that He paid for your sin and give up control of your life to Him. Follow Him and live by spending time daily reading the Bible and by talking to Him in prayer. Tell a friend who is a Christian about your decision. As you grow, keep your childlike faith!

> *Lord, thank You for reminding me that childlike faith in You is what brings me closest to You. Help me to take You literally at Your Word, trusting that whatever You say is true.*

Just as a father has compassion on his children,
  So the LORD has compassion on those who fear Him. (Psalm 103:13)

I watched silently from the kitchen window as my husband tenderly held our four-year-old and comforted him. His father had warned him not to run on the wet pavement, but he had not heeded that instruction. Now he was paying the natural price of his disobedience. Yet his father had not given him a callous "I told you so" as he watched his son crash to the ground. Rather, he moved swiftly to gather Seth in his arms and shower him with compassion the moment he heard the cry, "Daddy!"

God is the Author of compassion. He is our Source, and all that we give in tenderness flows from Him. God already knows that we will fail to heed His instructions over and over. He does not stand coldly by and wave a knowing finger at us when we miss the mark. He is ready to meet us with compassion every time, waiting patiently and listening for our cry, "Father!" When we have reconciled with Him, there is an understanding that passes between Father and child, an admonition, drawn from His devotion to us, to try harder, and a promise stemming from our admiration of Him to give our best.

> *Lord, time and again I fail in my efforts as a mother, and yet I know that You are waiting for me with open arms. Give me the same intense compassion for my children that You have for me.*

October 28

Then the men of Gibeon sent word to Joshua to the camp at Gilgal, saying, "Do not abandon your servants; come up to us quickly and save us and help us. . . ." (Joshua 10:6)

Life is hard. We all need help making it through some of the tough times. I, however, am not very good at asking for help. I feel that if I ask for help, I am admitting my own shortcomings. Yet there is an element to admitting our own weaknesses that truly brings out our strengths.

Several years ago I got really sick and could not care for my two young children on my own. The doctor informed me that the only way I would recover from my illness was to spend a few days in bed. "And who is going to take care of my kids?" I scoffed at him. My husband's job was too demanding at the time for him to even think about staying home. The doctor looked at me and said, "Get some help! You got any friends?" I hung my head, slinking out the door. Driving home, I mocked the situation. *Well, sure, I have friends, but they are all too busy. Who wants to take care of two extra kids all day?* I tried to ignore the severity of the situation, but the pain shooting down my arms and neck jolted me into reality. I felt God's gentle voice: "You have not because you ask not."

Suddenly I remembered Joshua. His men were off fighting the good fight for him, and as far as he knew they were doing fine. If he didn't hear anything, it was presumed all was going well. Now what do you suppose would have happened to those men when they realized they were in trouble and needed reinforcements but felt guilty about asking for help so decided to just tough it out on their own? They would have gotten slaughtered! When Joshua received word that his men needed him, he was there in a flash, with plenty of help. And they defeated the enemy.

Lord, give me the sensitivity to see when others need my help and the heart to freely give it. Give me the wisdom to know when I need help and the humility to ask for it.

"For I was hungry, and you gave Me something to eat; I was thirsty, and you gave Me drink; I was a stranger, and you invited Me in." (Matthew 25:35)

We live in one of those "gateway" towns. You know, the kind that everyone drives through on his way to somewhere else. Consequently, our home has become a stopover for many weary travelers. I enjoy entertaining, yet there are times that I have been more anxious than excited over the guests God has brought to my doorstep. It is one thing to give when you are prepared; it is another to give when you are not.

I remember one such occasion when some friends came to town on business. They showed up with an unexpected guest, another business partner who had traveled to town with them and was too weary to drive the 180 miles home. I had a smile on my face when I invited him in, but in my head, I was panicking.

I felt so unprepared for this one extra guest, yet I listened and watched in amazement at the gratitude that he displayed. After spending the night on the couch, he expressed that he was touched and truly thankful for our willingness to take a stranger into our home. It may not seem like much, but it was one of the biggest compliments I have ever received.

Freely opening up our home to others has been a biblical model for our children to learn about hospitality. Jesus says, "Truly I say to you, to the extent that you did it to one of these brothers of Mine, even the least of them, you did it to Me." When we invite guests, expected or unexpected, into our home, we may be inviting the Savior Himself. I certainly don't mind if He sleeps on my couch.

Lord, everything we have comes from You. Help us to share our resources and comforts with others. May we never turn down someone in need when we can help.

———— ❧✿❧ ————

Let every person be in subjection to the governing authorities. For there is no authority except from God, and those which exist are established by God. (Romans 13:1)

*R*ules and laws are set for our safety and protection. Many of us see rules as a nuisance and often ignore them if we find them inconvenient. We do so at our own risk.

Shelley took her three-year-old son to a large public indoor play place. Upon entering the play area, Shelley noticed a sign that restricted outside food and drink. She looked down at the super-size soda she had just purchased minutes before and then looked up at the blazing summer sun. She decided there would be no harm in ignoring the warning.

Her son played happily until he discovered he couldn't see her. "Mommmmmmy!" His voice was filled with fear. He was at the top of the climbing equipment, inside one of the tubes. Shelley still could not see him, but she followed his voice and tried to coax him down. But he didn't budge. Shelley decided to go in after him. She grabbed her designer handbag and her soda. Needing her hands free to climb, she shoved the soda into her purse. She was almost upon him when she stumbled and fell backward. The lid from the soda cup popped off and its contents tipped into her purse. She shrieked; her son cried. All eyes in the play place upon them, Shelley and Tanner emerged at the bottom of the slide sticky and dripping.

My friend said her experience taught her the value of following the rules, even the ones that seem silly. When we show respect for the authority that has been placed over us in every situation, we are in turn showing respect for God and His system of law and order.

Lord, help me to abide by all rules. Forgive me when I pick and choose. I pray that my submission will be an example to my children and anyone else who may be watching.

———— ❧◈❧ ————

. . . {G}row in the grace and knowledge of our Lord and Savior Jesus Christ. . . . (2 Peter 3:18)

Being a mother can be so all-consuming that it is easy to get lost in the job. As parents, we sacrifice consistently. Putting our children's needs first becomes so much a part of our lives that we can plow through life so steadily focused on our children's advancements that we become oblivious to the fact that we are losing ourselves in the process. Don't misunderstand—being a parent does require great sacrifice, and we need to accept that as part of the job. But we also need to protect our own identity as we seek to form that of our children.

Growing as a parent doesn't equal dying as a person. Growing in the grace and knowledge of the Lord includes understanding who you are and who God created you to be—in all aspects of life. It is a fullness of purpose that entails all He wants us to become. Many of us may be a lot of things, but most of us are not all we could be.

Partake in activities that you enjoy and which further your personal growth: a painting class one night a week, a women's Bible study, a college course, an exercise class or a bubble bath. Just as you strive to provide an environment for your children that stimulates their growth in every dimension, you need to do the same for yourself. The next step up for you may be to step out and replant yourself for optimum growth. Go and grow . . . in the grace and knowledge of our Lord Jesus and all He wants you to become.

Lord, thank You for showing me that You have plans for my life that include, but extend beyond the confines of motherhood. Help me to make time for activities that will stimulate my personal growth emotionally, intellectually and spiritually.

November:
Job Security

What do you mean I'm not replaceable if I decide to quit?

Motherhood is the most secure job in the world. Once you become a mother, you never lose the job. No one can fire you and no one can replace you. No one is a mother to your children but you. That makes you unique and incredibly special. It also makes you irreplaceable. The one who spends the most time with your kids will know them the best. It should be you.

If you are a mom who is struggling with what to do—to work outside the home or stay home with your kids—then know that as I write this I am praying for God to speak to your heart this month. You may be struggling with staying at home because you don't feel you're gifted at being a home-maker. I don't believe I am particularly gifted. I hate to clean. I like to cook, but I despise doing dishes. I'm not very patient. Yet I know that because I am right where God wants me to be, I don't have to be gifted. I just have to be willing. He can equip me to do what's necessary. Author and motivational speaker Zig Ziglar says, "Failure is an event, not a person." God, in His grace, is big enough to cover all of my failed events. He is big enough to cover yours too.

Take time this month to truly appreciate your family. Let your husband and each one of your children know why you are thankful for him or her. Plan some special family activi-ties to strengthen your bond as a family unit. And don't for-get to thank God for all of your blessings—especially for your family.

". . . {D}o not fear, for I have redeemed you; I have called you by name; you are Mine!" (Isaiah 43:1)

A friend of mine formerly ran a day care in her home. Kellie cared for the young children of working mothers nine to ten hours a day. Consequently, they spent more time with Kellie than their mothers. That made her the primary caregiver.

In the hearts and minds of small children, the one who cares for them is their mother. This may not be true biologically, but emotionally it is. The primary caregiver is forced into the role of nurturer, disciplinarian, trainer, provider and comforter. One little girl Kellie cared for from three months of age until nearly two years frequently cried when her mother came to pick her up. By the time she was thirteen months, she protested daily when it was time to go home with mom. She wanted to stay with Kellie.

My friend never wanted to take the place of that young child's mother. But because of the hours the child was left in Kellie's care, she was forced into that role, like it or not. That little girl even began calling Kellie "mama" when she could talk.

God knows each one of us and calls us by name. We teach our children to call us "mom." Is that who we really are in the eyes of our children? The biological truth isn't as crucial as the emotional truth. The trust that is established between parent and child is what shapes the hearts and minds of our kids. That will be determined by the primary caregiver, whoever it may be.

> *Lord, show me how to be more available for my kids. I pray they will trust me as they grow and that we will develop a bond that can never be broken, neither by time nor distance. Impress upon my heart the critical aspect of spending time—and lots of it—with my kids.*

And that from childhood you have known the sacred writings which are able to give you the wisdom that leads to salvation through faith which is in Christ Jesus. (2 Timothy 3:15)

Our greatest responsibility to our children as parents is to teach them about Jesus Christ. I know many parents who have led their own children to salvation. My parents are just one example. They led both of my brothers and me to trust Christ as Savior. My parents made sure that we each understood the commitment we were making at the time of our individual decisions.

A recent nationwide statistic reveals that eighty-five percent of all Christians receive Christ as Savior before the age of eighteen. This illustrates that parental influence is enormous! We have a huge responsibility to share the gospel with our kids. Although many teens come to know Christ through outside influences like Young Life, Campus Crusade for Christ or a church-affiliated youth group, some never connect with such groups. Your child's best chance at finding Christ is through your guidance.

Don't drop the ball in this area of your children's lives. Don't quit teaching them about Christ. If you don't feel educated enough or comfortable teaching your kids about a personal relationship with God, then seek help from your pastor. They are a good resource for information on how to best communicate biblical truths to kids. From experience, I have learned one important principle I call "KISS": Keep It Short and Simple. Kids want to hear the truth in simple terms they can understand and apply to everyday life. If you make Christianity practical and relevant to their lives, they will be interested!

Lord, guide me as I seek to teach my children about You. I pray that each of them will make the decision to trust You as Lord and Savior at a young age and serve You all the days of their lives.

Blessed be the God . . . who comforts us in all our affliction that we may be able to comfort those who are in any affliction with the comfort with which we ourselves are comforted by God. (2 Corinthians 1:3-4)

We went on a houseboat trip for a week with some friends. When you live in close quarters, you learn some things about each other you may not have previously known. Sometime after that vacation, I was talking with one of my girlfriends who went on the trip with us about my three-year-old and his unwillingness to allow his father to console him when he was upset. She told me that she noticed on our houseboat trip that my son came to me for comfort. He went to his daddy when he wanted to go fishing or play tag.

That observation caused me to reflect on my role as a mother in a new light. I had never seen myself as a big "nurturer," but to my son, that was an important part of my job description. It's not that his father couldn't comfort him, but for whatever reason, Seth felt better about coming to me when he needed reassurance.

When I am hurting and need comfort, I go to God. He is my ultimate Sustainer and Comforter. His Word says He is the "Father of mercies." When we feel comforted by God, we are then able to comfort others. We also learn to give mercy and comfort when we receive it from other people. My mother was a big nurturer, so I suppose I learned to comfort by her example.

There are some roles in a child's life, such as "comforter" that no one will be able to fill except for you.

Lord, thank You for being my Comforter. Show me how to best comfort my children and teach them how to ultimately look to You for comfort. Guide me in the specific roles that only I can fill.

Thou art my hiding place; Thou dost preserve me from trouble;
Thou dost surround me with songs of deliverance. (Psalm 32:7)

J was not having a good day. The baby wasn't feeling well and he had been crying off and on for hours. My three-year-old had been begging all morning to "play with me." The telephone continued to ring off the hook. The dirty laundry was still in the same heap I had left it. To make matters worse, it was noon and I hadn't even taken a shower yet! I wanted to bury my head in my hands and cry. I wanted to run away and hide. Instead, I took a few deep breaths, put the baby in his playpen, involved my three-year-old in blowing bubbles and made a run for the bathroom. After a quick shower, I checked on the baby—asleep at last. I checked on his brother—busy chasing bubbles. I grabbed my Bible and buried my head in God's hands. Twenty minutes later I felt like a new woman. I now knew I could make it through this day.

Your family needs you. Sometimes the pressure those needs create, however, can be overwhelming. When you feel as if you want to run and hide, run to God instead of running away. Allow Him to be your hiding place. You will return to your family refreshed and renewed every time. Through Him, you will always find the strength to make it through another day.

Lord, thank You for being my hiding place. May I always run to You, rather than away from You in times of trouble. Strengthen and equip me to stand by my family no matter how tough things get.

O LORD, the God of our fathers, art Thou not God in the heavens? And art Thou not ruler over all the kingdoms of the nations? Power and might are in Thy hand so that no one can stand against Thee. (2 Chronicles 20:6)

Today as I write, it is the end of voting day, and the American people have once again made their choice for governing ruler of this nation. The man who was elected president of the United States of America today was not who I voted for. He stands against most of the values that I stand for. As I sat on my living room couch listening to his acceptance speech, I began to weep.

As I sat wallowing in my sorrow, God quietly reminded me that He is still in control. This man is president because God allowed him to be. Nothing happens on this earth that is not under the watchful eye of our Creator. Men may work diligently against the things God stands for, but they will not triumph. God will be victorious. God can save our nation from moral decline.

You may not be able to change the entire country, but change begins one heart at a time. Start with yours. Then work on your family. If every mother in America would concentrate on turning her family's hearts toward God, our nation would be saved from its perilous condition. The president of the United States will change, but God will always be God, and mom will always be mom.

> *Lord, thank You for reminding me that You are the sovereign Ruler of all the world. You are in control of all our nation's governing authorities. I pray for the leaders of our country today, Lord, that You will pierce their hearts with Your truth. I pray for a great spiritual awakening to rock our nation. Start today, Lord, with me and my family.*

"And those on the rocky soil are those who, when they hear, receive the word with joy; and these have no firm root; they believe for a while, and in time of temptation fall away." (Luke 8:13)

Take a minute to read Luke 8:11-15. Jesus used parables often in His teaching. In this parable of the sower, Jesus is specifically referring to Christians who either fall away from their faith or grow fruitfully in it.

This illustration speaks to us as mothers. There are many new mothers who hear the concept of being a stay-at-home mom, see its biblical validity and get all excited. They jump into the role full force. A short time later, however, many of these once-zealous moms have fallen, depressed and defeated, by the wayside. They wave the white flag in surrender and give up their quest for perfection in parenting, returning to the outside workforce.

Why does this happen? Like many new Christians, new mothers often have unrealistic expectations. Then, when their expectations don't line up with reality, discouragement mounts and, if left unresolved, turns into feelings of defeat. Many moms give up simply because they don't understand the complexity of the job—and they don't understand the help they have in accomplishing the task. God is able to get us through the most difficult days on the job.

The terrain of motherhood can be rough. The job is rocky and often filled with thorny thickets. But if we stay committed to our faith and our families, we will take firm root in the hearts of our children.

Lord, help my roots and my family's to grow strong as I plant myself in a relationship with You.

But let it be the hidden person of the heart, with the imperishable quality of a gentle and quiet spirit, which is precious in the sight of God. (1 Peter 3:4)

She breezed around the room effortlessly, greeting each person with a warm smile and a hug. As usual, she was perfectly put together: every hair in place, makeup flawless and the latest clothing fashions adorning her trim figure. She ushered her perfectly groomed children to their Sunday school classes with little effort. She spoke only a word and they obeyed immediately. She was the envy of every woman. But appearances can be deceiving.

Many people didn't know this woman was miserable. Her marriage was in trouble and her kids weren't as well-behaved as they appeared. She, like her life, was meaningless. Everything was staged for the benefit of appearances. She felt it was important to keep up the image of a perfect Christian life. She hoped if she lived it long enough, it would become reality.

Who are you when no one is looking? Are you the same woman in private as you are in public? Do you speak kindly to your children in the presence of others, but scream at them when no one is around? Are you smiling all the time when someone is watching, but crying all the time when you are alone? Do you live in harmony with your husband for the benefit of those who see you together, but behind closed doors, fight and argue nonstop? You may be able to hide from everyone else, but Christ knows your true condition. Christ can bring life to you. He can also bring joy and peace. Spend some time with God right now and ask Him to show you who you are on the inside.

Lord, help me to be real with You. Guard me from false appearances. Take charge of my heart.

He who conceals his transgressions will not prosper,
  But he who confesses and forsakes them will find compassion.
(Proverbs 28:13)

On New Year's Day, 1919, Georgia Tech played the University of California in the Rose Bowl. That game is one of the most famous in history. Here's why: Shortly before halftime, a player named Roy Riegels recovered a fumble for UC. Somehow he became confused and started running in the wrong direction. He made it sixty-five yards before a teammate tackled him just before he would have scored for the opposing team. When UC attempted to punt, GT blocked the kick and scored a safety. As the buzzer sounded signaling the end of the first half, both teams headed off the field, into their locker rooms. As the UC team members sat on the locker room benches, Riegels put his face in hands and cried like a baby. Coach Nibbs Price was silent. Everyone else sat in silence as well. When the timekeeper announced three minutes until playing time, Coach Price looked at the team and said, "Men, the same team that played the first half will start the second."

All the players got up and started back out of the locker room, except for Riegels. The coach went over to Riegels and said, "Roy, didn't you hear me? The same team starts the second half!" Riegels looked up and said, "Coach, I can't do it! I've ruined you!" Coach Price put his hand on Riegel's shoulder and said, "Roy, get up and go back. THE GAME IS ONLY HALF OVER!"

Roy Riegels went back, and everyone who saw that famous game said it was the greatest half of football a player ever had.

Sometimes, as mothers, we run in the wrong direction with our children. We make mistakes as parents and get discouraged, thinking we have ruined our kids for life. But God's Word tells us to confess our mistakes, forget about them and go on.

Lord, I admit that I am not perfect. Help me to lean on Your wisdom as I train my children.

November 9

> *"And I have led you forty years in the wilderness; your clothes have not worn out on you, and your sandal has not worn out on your foot. You have not eaten bread, nor have you drunk wine or strong drink, in order that you might know that I am the LORD your God." (Deuteronomy 29:5-6)*

The Israelites' journey through the wilderness was a long one. God left them in the wilderness for so many years because that's how long it took them to completely trust God. The books of Exodus, Leviticus, Numbers and Deuteronomy record the Israelites' long journey. Throughout the chronicles, their disbelief and lack of trust in God and His provision is exposed again and again. Those forty years were tough.

God takes all of us to a wilderness place in our walk with Him. Not because He is mean and wants to see us suffer, but sometimes He has to take us to a point in life where we feel all alone, before we will come to Him. It is when we enter a place of barren emptiness that our faith is really tested. The wilderness is a different place for each person. It is the place where you struggle to trust God. It is the place of discontent in your life where you don't want to be. It is the place where you have the tendency to be the most unhappy and demonstrate the least faith.

Are you in the wilderness, wandering around looking for answers? Stop walking in circles and looking in all directions. Get on your knees, turn your face toward heaven and tell God you trust Him. He will show you the way out.

> *I thank You, Lord God, for the wilderness experiences of life that teach me to trust You completely. Help me to keep my eyes focused on You, that I might stay on the path You have marked for me.*

For the grace of God has appeared . . . instructing us to deny ungodliness and worldly desires and to live sensibly, righteously and godly in the present age. (Titus 2:11-12)

Sometimes when we give in to our children's desires, we are simultaneously giving up our influence on them as well, without even realizing it. Take television, for example. It is probably the single most overused form of entertainment in homes today. Activities, meals and entire schedules are planned around favorite television shows. Commercials bombard our children.

Most of the characters in the cartoons and children's videos today have disrespectful attitudes, are engaged in some immoral activity, display open defiance and disobedience toward authority and are preoccupied with some kind of "superpower" other than God. The worst part is that most of these things are woven into the story line so subtly that they are hard to see. The wrong behavior is laced with humor so it is easily passed off as "cute."

I noticed a change in behavior in my preschooler within just a few days of purchasing a popular new children's video. After just six days, I noticed that his behavior closely mirrored the one character in the movie who was rebellious, defiant and disobedient. This little rebel wasn't even the central character.

I decided to take control of this area before it took control of my kids. My husband and I began collecting videos that promote righteousness and godliness rather than those that enslave our children to ungodly passions and desires.

Seek God and talk to your spouse about how much control television and videos have in your home. If you discover things are off-balance, here's your chance to get things back on track.

Lord, help me to take control of the television viewing habits in our home. Give me discernment in placing restrictions and give me the courage to do the right thing.

November 11

A generation goes and a generation comes, But the earth remains forever. (Ecclesiastes 1:4)

From the beginning of time, each generation of children raised into adulthood has had a unique set of advantages and disadvantages. Every generation has its opportunity to leave its contribution to society, its mark on the world. Each generation builds upon the discoveries and accomplishments of the last, bringing constant change and new innovation to life—some good, some not so good. Regardless of the cycle of life, God's creation remains intact.

God says "the earth remains forever." He is ultimately in control of its condition. The same hand that created the world, can destroy it in one fell swoop. Yet we give too much credit to the supposed "experts" of our day who predict certain doom soon. We need to be good stewards of what God has entrusted to us (the earth) but not at the expense of the human heart.

One of our jobs in parenting this next generation of children who will soon be managing the businesses, controlling the media and running for office is to educate them to the causes that really matter. Everyone today has a "cause." Most of them are about things that don't last. A tree's life may be cut short by a zealous lumberjack trying to make a buck, but that tree is not as important as a living, breathing human being. The tree does not have a soul that will spend eternity either in heaven or hell.

God has entrusted us to take good care of the world we live in, but not at the expense of the ones who live in it. We need to teach our kids that they can make a difference in life by making a difference in the lives of others.

Lord, show me how to instill in my children a love and value for human life that supercedes any other passions or causes the world promotes, making an eternal difference in the lives of others.

November 12

And he got up and came to his father. But while he was still a long way off, his father saw him, and felt compassion for him, and ran and embraced him, and kissed him. (Luke 15:20)

Most of us are familiar with the story of the prodigal son. (Read Luke 15:11-32.) This has always been one of my favorite parables because it is such a good example of how Jesus wants us to be as parents.

When this man's youngest son went off to a distant country and squandered his share of the family inheritance on immoral living, the father continued to pray and wait for his son to return. He never gave up on him because of his poor choices. How this father's heart must have ached for his son's return home. When the young prodigal finally came to his senses, his father's reaction to his son's homecoming is remarkable. He didn't lecture or judge or hold back compassion. He celebrated!

You may have a prodigal son who has "quit" on you. Perhaps he has left home and is living a lifestyle that you don't approve of. Your responsibility as that child's mother is to love him unconditionally. You must pray for your child and wait expectantly for his return. Be patient.

When we sin, we wander away from our place in God's kingdom. But God never turns His back on us—we may leave His heart, but He never leaves ours.

> *Lord, thank You for Your unconditional love and for the way You are waiting to receive me with open arms when I return to You. Keep my children close to Your heart, always. If they should wander, keep me steadfastly trusting in Your promises for my prodigal. Give me Your love.*

And even when I am old and gray, O God, do not forsake me,
Until I declare Thy strength to this generation,
Thy power to all who are to come. (Psalm 71:18)

ome days I watch my children, and think, *Oh Lord, I have so much training to do—please don't let anything happen to me until the job is finished!* My plea is much like this psalmist prayer.

Once a child is school age, he begins to learn a myriad of scholastic concepts. Sometimes the stimulation and challenge can seem overwhelming. A child's frustration over a homework assignment he is struggling with may give way to a desire to quit. That is where your encouragement and assistance with the homework comes in and helps the child to get through the exercise. Persistence soon pays off, and the child does learn.

Similarly, we need to be diligent in training our children in biblical concepts and instruction for living. They may get frustrated at first because they don't understand all of the spiritual concepts you are introducing, but if you are consistent, they will soon be practicing the spiritual truths you are teaching.

As with anything taught, you must introduce concepts on an age-appropriate level. Just as you do not allow your children to quit school because they are frustrated with learning at times, you do not want to quit teaching God's school of thought to them even if they get flustered in the learning process. Take it slow, and make learning God's Word fun. Encourage your children to learn spiritual truths on their own as well. Some children will acquire a spiritual discipline quicker than others. Just plan on declaring God's Word to your kids until you are old and gray, and that should cover it!

Give me the time and the energy, Lord, to complete the task of instructing my children in Your ways. May I never run out of enthusiasm for Your Word, and may my children never run out of the desire to learn it.

For I have told him that I am about to judge his house forever for the iniquity which he knew, because his sons brought a curse on themselves and he did not rebuke them. (1 Samuel 3:13)

*I*f there is any doubt in your mind that you are responsible for the choices your children make while they are under your supervision, this Scripture should clear it up. Eli was a priest and a good man who loved God. He had two sons, however, who chose to turn their backs on God. Scripture describes them as "worthless" in First Samuel 2:12. Their father knew of their ungodly lifestyles but apparently did nothing to steer them toward God. He did not use his position of authority as their father to insist that they turn from their sin while they were still living under his roof. Because of Eli's decision to look the other way, God judged his entire household severely. His judgment included taking the lives of Eli's sons.

It is our responsibility as parents to train our children in biblical living and then hold them to that standard. We are responsible for the choices they make as long as they are living in our house. God will hold us accountable for our attempt to hold our children accountable to the standards we set. Don't misunderstand me—we cannot make our children behave a certain way, but we can train them in the proper behavior and then hold them accountable in the form of consequences and discipline if they choose wrong behavior.

Don't let your household be judged as Eli's was. Be involved in your children's lives and make it a point to know what they are doing. Making their business your business may save all of your lives.

Lord, I pray that You will help me to take my responsibility as my children's guardian seriously. Give me eyes to see what my children are doing and ears to hear what they are saying. Give me the wisdom and courage to force them to face their sin rather than turning my back on it.

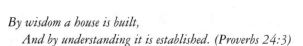

By wisdom a house is built,
  And by understanding it is established. (Proverbs 24:3)

The parents of babies and parents of teenagers have something in common: They both spend a lot of time trying to get their kids to talk to them! When their children are young and just developing their vocal skills, the child is trying to learn the parents' language. But as the child matures and grows, the parents often end up trying to learn their teenager's language. Don't give up! Your teenager needs you just as much as he did when he was a helpless infant—he just won't admit it. As a baby, he needed your support as he learned physical skills such as sitting, crawling, walking and running. Now he needs your support in the emotional skill of making it through life.

There are many seasons we go through in parenthood. When your baby was beginning to make noise, you couldn't wait for him to speak his first word. Then he became a curious preschooler full of questions, and you couldn't wait for him to be quiet. As the parent of a teenager, you come full cycle and are back playing the waiting game again—waiting for him to talk to you.

We can help keep lines of communication open by treating children with dignity and understanding as they face an expanding and changing world. Things like the first day of school, riding the bus, braces, puberty, a first crush, not making the team, acne and school social events are potential threats to our kids. We need to be sensitive to their fears. Make your home a refuge where your child can find solace and acceptance. In the early years, by demonstrating wisdom in your parenting practices, you will build a strong family. In the later years, by demonstrating understanding in your parenting practices, you will establish a mighty fortress.

Lord, may I acquire wisdom and understanding at the proper times as I parent my children through the various seasons of life. May our home be a mighty fortress—secure from the storms of life.

Then Jacob summoned his sons and said, "Assemble yourselves that I may tell you what shall befall you in the days to come." (Genesis 49:1)

*J*n the days of our forefathers, the responsibility of preparing one's children for the future was taken very seriously. Many households had regular family meetings where the children, especially the sons, were briefed on upcoming events and then trained and equipped to handle them. It may have been something as small as the weekly chores and as large as a raging war on the horizon. Whatever the challenges ahead, the family unit in the early years was one that represented a sense of pride. The battlegrounds our children face today are more emotional and spiritual than they are physical. Still, our children will be left bruised by the enemy if we do not properly equip them to handle life and all of its adversities. We need to warn them of "what shall befall [them] in the days to come," and then equip them to be victorious.

Training your children for the future can be fun. Use the past to help. Spend time doing a family tree; research your descendants and make a record of who they were and what they were like. Enlist the help of older family members. Use the opportunity to build pride in your family unit, pointing out to your kids how what they do with their lives and who they become will impact the family hundreds of years from now. Come up with a motto or slogan that your children can adopt to help them understand they're part of a team. In our family, we give the thumbs-up sign, and it translates, "We're Rileys and we do what's right!" Teams work together. Each man standing alone cannot accomplish as much as the unit as a whole. The same is true for a family.

Lord, help me as I seek to adequately equip my children to face their futures. Show me how to build a sense of family pride and loyalty that will bridge the gap for generations to come.

November 17

For Thou didst form my inward parts;
Thou didst weave me in my mother's womb.
I will give thanks to Thee, for I am fearfully and wonderfully
made. . . . (Psalm 139:13-14)

e went through a series of medical problems with my oldest son
when he was about eighteen months old. The endless doctor visits,
medical bills and sleepless nights took a toll on our whole family. Seeing
my son suffer and endure so much pain was very difficult for me.

My first reaction when we detected Seth's problems was to ask God,
"Why my child?" But Psalm 139 changed my perspective. I realized that
God, who formed Seth within my womb, had His hand on every part of my
son's body. When I was pregnant with Seth, I used to pray for each body
part that was forming every month, for God to bless each stage of his devel-
opment. I remembered this in the middle of my crisis as I was reading
Psalm 139 and made a decision to trust God instead of question Him. The
Father had His hand on Seth as he developed and Seth was "fearfully and
wonderfully made" by God. To me, that means his body is perfect in God's
eyes. Seth is exactly what God formed him to be. God knew from the mo-
ment of conception who this baby was and what he would become.

Each one of us is exactly the way God wants us to be. We may think our
legs are too short or our nose is too big, but to criticize ourselves in such a
way is to criticize what God made! I have learned to be thankful for my
body and my children's bodies just as they are.

Lord, thank You for making each of us "fearfully and wonder-
fully," with such care and individual character. Keep Your hand
upon my family and sustain us during the times when our physical
bodies do not hold out as well as others.

November 18

> *"For My thoughts are not your thoughts,*
> *Neither are your ways My ways," declares the LORD.*
> *"For as the heavens are higher than the earth,*
> *So are My ways higher than your ways,*
> *And My thoughts than your thoughts." (Isaiah 55:8-9)*

Have you noticed that God does things so much better than we ever could? We cruise through life thinking we are all together and in control, and then wham! A trial hits us: The kids get sick, your husband gets laid off, the car breaks down. Suddenly, we don't feel so in control. That's what God wants. Because when we don't feel in control, then we allow Him to be in control.

A friend was frustrated and fed up. They had just moved from Tucson to Yuma, Arizona, and they had decided to keep their house in Tucson and rent it out. They already owned a house in Yuma but weren't planning on moving into it because it was too small. It had been a rental property and the last tenant had completely ransacked the place, requiring costly repairs and repelling prospective tenants. After months of no prospects, two mortgages and current cramped living conditions, Missy became very discouraged.

She was a worrier by nature. For her, making a conscious decision not to worry and to trust God was a big step of faith. From the moment that Missy gave her worries to God, He worked quickly. Her husband received a lucrative job offer with a large firm in another state. They sold all properties and moved! They are now in the best financial state they have ever been.

God thinks differently than we do. He can see the whole big picture, when we can't see past today. Truly, His ways are better than ours. Trust God with all the details of your life—don't give up! Nothing is too difficult for Him.

> *Lord, help me to trust You with every detail of my life. Give me*
> *Your perspective on my situations.*

———— ❧❀❧ ————

I am the way, and the truth, and the life. . . . (John 14:6)

I have learned some spiritual principles that have helped me to deal with frustrating circumstances. Sometimes our circumstances can even seem hopeless, but when we have Christ in our lives, we always have hope.

The first principle I implement for dealing with negative circumstances in life is to cement in my mind the fact that God demonstrated His absolute and complete love for me on the cross. That love will never change—ever. When I lean on that knowledge, it helps me to see my situation more clearly.

Another principle is to never attempt to understand what God is like from the middle of my circumstances. If I try to figure out what God is like when things in my life are not going my way, I have a skewed and inaccurate perspective of God. Job is a good example. From boils to Bildad, Job was tested. Still, he clung to what he knew to be true about God, that God loved him absolutely.

A third principle to get through bad circumstances is to go to God in prayer and ask Him to help me see His perspective. My perspective is always affected by my circumstances. I have learned that I will not know the truth of my circumstances until I know the truth of God. I must then wait on the Holy Spirit to reveal God's truth to me. Sometimes reading the Bible can help me understand the truth of my circumstances. His Word says He is the truth. The truth is that He loves me in spite of my circumstances. Can you see how all of this fits together? One principle builds upon another to give you rock-solid faith in times of turmoil. Try applying these spiritual principles to your life the next time you find yourself in the middle of some bad circumstances.

> *Lord, give me Your perspective on my situation. Show me how to view my circumstances in light of Your truth. May I rest in the constant of Your love in the midst of a changing world.*

For it is God who is at work in you, both to will and to work for His good pleasure. (Philippians 2:13)

Making decisions that concern the welfare of our children can be difficult. We always want to do what's best for them, but sometimes we don't have all of the information we need to make the best decision. I believe God has given women an instinctive knowledge when it comes to knowing what is best for their children. This instinct can put out a red flashing "warning" signal within us when something just doesn't feel right. I have learned to trust this instinct with the help and guidance of the Holy Spirit. The Bible says that "it is God who is at work in you," so I know that if I ask for God's guidance when I'm trying to make the right decision concerning my kids, He will guide that inner instinct. I would not, however, advise relying on that female instinct alone, because sometimes our feelings can be guided by our emotions. Check those feelings against God's Word. God never leads us to do things that are contrary to His Word.

There have been many times in our marriage when my husband and I have prayed about a decision we needed to make and I end up saying to Jimmy: "Honey, I just don't feel comfortable with doing this. I feel a warning signal going off in my spirit, although I can't rationally explain it." My husband has learned to trust that check that God has placed within me and has honored my opinion in those situations. We almost always later discover why God had placed that uncomfortable feeling within me—there was a reason why He didn't want us to do something.

Don't make rash decisions concerning your kids' welfare. Take the time to pray, read God's Word and wait on His reply. He is at work in you!

Work within me, Lord, to guide me in the right direction concerning my children.

My sorrow is beyond healing,
My heart is faint within me! (Jeremiah 8:18)

I stood studying the sea of faces: men and women of all ages and ethnic backgrounds. We were all there for the same purpose: to pay homage to someone who had not experienced hope, to give support to the husband and two daughters she had left behind. A sadness overwhelmed me as I watched the deceased's eight-year-old daughter. Did she understand that her mother would never again tuck her in at night, never again kiss a boo-boo, never again be there to greet her at the door when she arrived home from school?

The funeral service commenced and tears flowed as we listened to the words of the older daughter as she read a love letter to her mother: "I love you, Mom. You are the best mother anyone could ever have. I regret that you are gone and never again will I hold you. I regret that you will never see me marry and never hold my children in your arms."

The mother's death had shocked the community because she had chosen to take her own life. For some reason, she had decided her sorrow was beyond hope, beyond healing.

Don't think for a minute that your choices do not affect your family. They do, especially the choice to check out. No matter how bad things may seem, if you have Jesus in your life, you are never without hope. If you have not made the decision to ask Jesus to come into your life, then invite Him to take control of your life. God will be your Help and your Guide, your Source and your Strength. No sorrow you bear will be too great for Him to carry.

Lord Jesus, Healer of sorrows, thank You for loving me enough to die on the cross for my sins. Bring me fullness of life with You in control and heal the hurts that have kept me from living a joy-filled life. May I always remember that my choices do affect my children. Fill me with hope.

November 22

---❖❖❖---

*"If a man makes a vow to the LORD, or takes an oath to bind himself
with a binding obligation, he shall not violate his word; he shall do
according to all that proceeds out of his mouth." (Numbers 30:2)*

am shocked at headlines that tell of yet another child abandoned
by his mother. Some are tossed into trash cans immediately after
birth. Some are left in gutters, and the recent horrifying headline was of a
young girl chained to a toilet for days while her mother was out "partying."
The truth of the matter is that more children are abandoned by their par-
ents than are ever discovered. Many parents find themselves unable to han-
dle the enormous pressures of raising a child—it is not an easy job. So they
take the easy way out—they quit. Whatever happened to commitment?

Once we give birth, we have made a commitment to raise another hu-
man being. We are responsible to love, nurture, train, discipline and guide
that child through life until he is able to handle life on his own. That does
not happen at the age of six weeks, six months or six years. Parenting is a
commitment. That means you are bound to your children for as long as it
takes to raise them.

We are all God's children, and He doesn't quit on us when He doesn't
feel like caring for us. He is always near, loving us, disciplining us and
training us in righteousness. Once we enter into a relationship with God,
He vows to love and protect us at all costs. It cost Him the life of His only
Son. Our commitment should be the same to our children—at all costs.

*Lord, be with the many children whose mothers have abandoned
them. Protect them and bring them to safety. Help them to find
homes with loving parents who will care for them.*

And we proclaim Him, admonishing every man and teaching every man with all wisdom, that we may present every man complete in Christ. (Colossians 1:28)

As believers in Christ, one of our responsibilities is to proclaim Christ as our Savior. That doesn't mean go out on the nearest street corner and begin shouting your faith to all. It does mean that whenever presented with the opportunity to share our faith in Christ, we should do it. Some opportunities to share Christ are obvious, such as when a friend or acquaintance asks, "What religion are you?" I like to say that my relationship with Christ is not a religion, but a way of life.

The best way to share our faith is to live it out by our words, attitudes and actions. One mother I know was asked by another mother, after observing her with her children on various occasions, how she managed to have so much patience with her children. That curiosity opened the door for her to share how her relationship with Christ made all the difference in her patience level, as well as many other areas of her life.

Part of our job as mothers is to teach our children about God and to instruct them in how to have a relationship with Him. That is what it means to present someone as "complete in Christ." Complete doesn't mean perfect. It simply means saved from sin. It means we are a work in progress. It means we are forgiven.

Lord, my prayer today is that I would proclaim You to my children, that I would admonish them and teach them with all wisdom that I may someday present them complete in Christ.

And the tongue is a fire, the very world of iniquity; the tongue is set among our members as that which defiles the entire body, and sets on fire the course of our life, and is set on fire by hell. (James 3:6)

Ouch! A tongue that is out of control can do a lot of damage. When I am angry, words fly off of my tongue that I always regret later. If not carefully guarded, our speech can rip people apart. I am amazed at the kids who speak disrespectfully to adults and get away with it. We must teach our children self-control in their speech. The best way to teach it is to model it. A wrong action can often be corrected, but harsh words can leave permanent scars.

A teenage girl that is close to our family was deeply hurt one stormy night by the damaging words of her father. When she was eight years old, she discovered that the man who had been her father since infancy was not her birth father, as she had always thought, but her adopted father. In the heat of an argument with his wife, this man pointed his finger at this little girl and screamed, "I don't care if I see her. She's not even my daughter." That one swift act of his tongue "[set] on fire the course of {her} life" and has been the cause of immeasurable pain, fear and insecurities in this young lady's life.

Don't underestimate the power of your words. The old childhood rhyme, "Sticks and stones will break my bones, but names will never hurt me," is not true. In the heat of an argument with your spouse, has one of you ever heard yourself say something like, "I wish I'd never married you"? Even if you don't mean what you say, you cannot erase such lethal words. Stop them from flying off of your tongue before it's too late.

Think carefully before you speak. Ask God to take control of your thoughts and words before they take control of you.

Lord, give me control of my tongue. Help me to speak words that build up, not words that tear down my children. Give me discernment and sensitivity as I speak, always choosing words that would be pleasing to You.

For Thou art my hope; O Lord God,
Thou art my confidence from my youth. (Psalm 71:5)

We took a trip to Colorado to visit some of my husband's family when our two boys were three-and-a-half and nine months old. We spent much of the four days just relaxing and visiting our relatives. The majority of them we see only once a year or even once every couple of years. Our oldest son can be challenging, and my husband and I have worked diligently to train him. It has been a struggle because of his temperament. Sometimes God gives us a boost just when we need it the most.

On this particular trip, we spent an entire day at my husband's aunt's house, where all of the relatives had gathered. My sister-in-law, who had not seen Seth since he was eighteen months old, spent a considerable amount of time playing with him. I could see she was really enjoying him, and it pleased me very much. What really pleased me, however, was a comment that she made after spending an entire day with him. She told my husband that she was "amazed at how well-behaved and well-mannered he was for a three-year-old." She noted that he "obeyed right away." How thrilling for us to hear that our extensive training of his heart was showing up after all!

Sometimes as mothers, we are too close to our children to see all of the good come out that we have worked so hard to put in. We often need others to point it out to us. My sister-in-law also told us that she observed Seth to be "very confident in himself and his abilities, and with parents like us who clearly loved and supported him he would grow up with a healthy self-esteem." Wow! Such a nice prediction! Those are the kinds of comments parents love to hear, aren't they?

Lord, remind me daily how special each one of my children is. Show me how to help build in each one a healthy self-esteem and confidence that comes from knowing of You and Your love.

Now I urge you brethren, keep your eye on those who cause dissensions and hindrances contrary to the teaching which you learned, and turn away from them. (Romans 16:17)

A friend of mine was a stay-at-home mom for three years and then had to "quit" and return to work outside the home because her husband returned to school. She was to be the sole source of income for two years while he furthered his education. They had one preschool-age daughter who went from spending all day with mom to spending all day with strangers. Gradually, the preschool teachers and day care workers became the center of influence in this little girl's life.

The mother tried to spend time with her daughter in the evenings training her in biblical values, but she noticed a slow-forming resistance against these things. This mom tried to pass off her daughter's new disinterest in spiritual things as "just a phase." In time, however, she could not ignore the behavior and attitude patterns that were also now evolving in her daughter's character. She had become increasingly whiny, clingy, argumentative and demanding in her behavior. My friend admitted that returning to work and letting someone else care for her daughter full-time had been a mistake.

You never know what the output is going to be when you are no longer responsible for the input. Thankfully, my friend was able to return to her job as a stay-at-home mom when her husband completed his schooling. Her daughter was young enough that she could "undo" the damage.

> *Lord, thank You for reminding me how invaluable my job is as a stay-at-home mom. Show me how to protect my children against the false teachings and antibiblical values that the world promotes.*

"But I say to you, love your enemies, and pray for those who perse-cute you." (Matthew 5:44)

$\mathcal{I}$was sitting at the kitchen table with my preschooler one morning when, through a mouthful of cereal, he mumbled, "If bad guys come to our house, we should shoot 'em, right, Mom?"

"Well, Seth, not necessarily . . ." my voice trailed off. I wondered where he came up with these ideas. I knew that my son's line of thinking was fairly typical for a preschooler. I didn't want my boys to do the "typical" thing; I wanted them to do the right thing, and in today's world that means you're different. "You know, Seth," I said, "What we should do is pray for the bad guys, because God can help them. He can make them good. The Bible tells us to pray for our enemies, and that includes all the bad guys."

His eyes grew wide, "I didn't know that! Can you show me, Mommy?" The cereal was left to grow soggy as we cuddled up on the couch and spent the next twenty minutes reading and talking. I read the story of Joseph and his "mean" brothers, and we talked about how God turned a bad situation into a good one. Joseph had been praying for his family, in this case, the "bad guys," and he treated them with kindness, even though they didn't deserve it.

Opportunities like these cannot be calculated. They are precious mo-ments that God gives us to shape our children's thinking and values. The beauty of being home with your children is that you will more than likely be the one who captures and shapes many of these moments. Don't miss them!

Lord, show me how to pray for those who persecute me and how to love those who are unkind to me.

For I am convinced that neither death, nor life, nor angels, nor principalities, nor things present, nor things to come, nor powers, nor height, nor depth, nor any other created thing, shall be able to separate us from the love of God which is in Christ Jesus our Lord. (Romans 8:38-39)

Although I grew up in a Christian home, I was a rebellious teen-ager. As a result of my reckless behavior, I was in a car accident one night that should have ended my life. It was my car, but I was in the passenger seat. The friend driving was intoxicated and lost control. The car flipped end over end and slid down an embankment, coming to a halt at the base of a large pine tree. The police officers stated that it was a miracle anyone of us was alive. We all walked away with scrapes and bruises.

I knew I had to contact my parents, and let them know what had happened. Nervously, I picked up the phone and dialed. When my mother answered, I tried to talk, but the only sound was that of me choking on my tears. "Laura! What's wrong?" my mom said. "Whatever it is, just tell me. I'm your mother. I love you." That made me cry even harder.

With both of my parents on the line now, I managed to tell them the details. Silence. I winced as I waited for their anger. But their reaction was not what I expected. They didn't lecture or scold me. Instead, they told me they loved me. They also told me they were disappointed in the choices I had made, but they reinforced their love for me in spite of my decisions. I had to live with the consequences of my actions and go without a car for the rest of the school year. But my actions had not cut me off from their love.

For the first time in my life, I understood the love of a parent. In the same way, God loves us unconditionally.

Lord, thank You for Your unconditional love. I blow it often, and yet I know that You still love me. Thank You for my parents' deep love as well. Keep me as committed to my own children.

And He had said to me, "My grace is sufficient for you, for power is perfected in weakness." (2 Corinthians 12:9)

My community was rocked with shock and disbelief when a churchgoing family faced the sudden death of their newborn baby. How could God let something so bad happen to such a good family? Why do bad things happen to good people? That question is complex; the answer, simple. Tragedy entered the world when sin entered the world back in the Garden of Eden. Because we live in the middle of a sinful existence, even when we are following God, we may still fall victim to the sin that surrounds us. Once we accept misfortune as a part of life, we can deal with it in a simple way.

We must trust God and rely on His grace to get us through. (I said simple, not easy!) When something bad happens to us, our first reaction is to whine or demand to know why. It is not about why, as we just discovered. We know why bad things happen—because of sin. The question should be, "What are we going to do to get through it?" We have two choices when disaster strikes. We can either learn from it or run from it. Running doesn't do any good, because the world is full of sin and sickness and death no matter where we go. There is no escape. If we try to find comfort in other people or things, we will only feel better temporarily. God is the mender of broken hearts.

He mended the hearts of the parents whose baby daughter died. They chose to trust in God and lean on His grace rather than to question Him. The key to their recovery is in the first part of Second Corinthians 12:9, "My grace is sufficient for you."

I thank You, Lord, that Your grace is sufficient for me. Make that truth a reality in my life.

November 30

*At my first defense no one supported me, but all deserted me; may it
not be counted against them. (2 Timothy 4:16)*

Children are abandoned and abused; the statistics are shocking. I was
struck with grief and disbelief one evening as I watched the late
news. While attending her high school prom, a nineteen-year-old girl went
to the rest room, gave birth to a baby and then dumped the infant in a trash
can and returned to the dance.

A custodian found the baby in the trash can sometime later in the eve-
ning. Attempts were made to revive the baby, but they were unsuccessful.
"What could have been going on in the girl's mind?" I wondered aloud.
"How could she do that?" I was incensed. The story grew more compelling
as the news anchor announced that supposedly no one knew she was preg-
nant; her family, her friends, even her boyfriend and father of the child
were clueless.

I don't understand the sense of desperation that drives a person to make
the decision to take a child's life. Feeling a sense of loss, I bowed my head
and shed a tear for the little boy who began his life in a bathroom stall. I
prayed for his mother's heart to be changed. I prayed that God would bring
her to repentance and not hold her insidious act against her.

When I hear of tragic circumstances surrounding a child's life, I feel
compelled to do something. Every single time God reminds me that the
most significant difference I will ever make will be in the life of my own
children.

> *Lord, please forgive the thousands of women who take their babies'
> lives. Bring them to repentance and restoration in You. Change the
> hearts of women in our society who are unwilling to face their role
> as mothers.*

December:
The Boss

OK, I'll take the job—who's my supervisor?

Every job has one, like it or not—a boss. The big cheese. The chief Indian. The guy in charge. When you are a stay-at-home mom, you work for the greatest boss in the world. You work for the King of kings—what position could be more exalted than that? There is certainly nothing lowly about working for a king!

This month, we celebrate the birthday of our Boss. Let's ponder His mother for a moment. Mary was an ordinary girl from an average family. She was a simple woman who loved God and was willing to obey Him. She sacrificed her reputation, her future and her place in society to accomplish God's will. Her obedience brought salvation into the world by the hand of God.

Amidst the hustle and bustle of shopping, baking, wrapping and decorating, pause now and again to think about the sacrifices that Mary made. As you ponder what to give to your loved ones to unwrap on Christmas morning, consider the greatest gift ever given; the gift of salvation through Jesus Christ. The greatest gift you can give your family is yourself. Equally, the greatest gift you can give to God is yourself. Allow Him to be "the Boss."

———— ❧🌹❧ ————

Again therefore Jesus spoke to them, saying, "I am the light of the world; he who follows Me shall not walk in the darkness, but shall have the light of life." (John 8:12)

Christmas is such a fun time of year to be a parent! I remember the Christmas our oldest was two-and-a-half years old. He was enthralled with Christmas lights. Each time we got in the car after dark or took an evening walk he would stare in wonder at the colorful lights.

Seeing Seth's fascination and appreciation of the lights, we took that opportunity to draw a parallel and explain to him how Jesus was the Light of the world. Just as all the lights on the houses lit up the neighborhood, Jesus could light up our lives if we allowed Him into our hearts. We began the annual tradition of packing everyone into the car and driving through countless neighborhoods on Christmas Eve to look at lights. Our children love this. We explain the significance of Christmas lights, painting a visual picture of Christ as Light of the world.

Christmas is full of symbols that parents can use to teach children about Christ. The evergreen of the Christmas tree, for instance, symbolizes everlasting life. The lights on the tree symbolize Jesus as the Light of the world. The star atop the tree symbolizes the Bethlehem star that the shepherds followed the night Jesus was born. And the gifts that surround the Christmas tree symbolize the celebration of the greatest Gift ever given—Jesus. Take time this month to use the teachable moments of the Christmas season.

> *Lord, thank You for the beauty of Christmas lights. May they be a reminder to us that You are the light of the world. Help me to use the teachable moments during the holidays to teach my kids about You.*

O LORD, my heart is not proud, nor my eyes haughty;
Nor do I involve myself in great matters,
Or in things too difficult for me. (Psalm 131:1)

My husband and I had been married for nine years and he had never hung a strand of lights on our property—except for the Christmas tree in our living room. I never made an issue out of it—until that one year.

We were driving home the first weekend of December, when Seth asked, "Mom, can we puts lights on our house?"

"Well, honey, you'll have to ask Daddy."

"Pleasssseee?" came the response from the backseat.

That night, after Seth was in bed, I asked, "So when are you and Seth going to hang up some lights?" Jimmy's reply was not what I expected. "We're not. I told him we'd buy lights when they're on sale and hang them up next year, and that was fine with him." What followed was an all-out battle and I lost.

The next morning, still angry, I decided to do the job myself. Seth was thrilled. Too bad he wasn't old enough to help me do it! It took five hours, a lot of staples, another trip to the store, a few broken nails and a very sore neck and back, but I did it. And boy, was I proud of myself.!

The next evening when I went to plug in the lights, they blinked on, then shorted out. I begrudgingly realized that the job was beyond my expertise. Later that night I asked Jimmy if he would figure out what I had done wrong. He found the problem and fixed it. It took him two hours! Jimmy never said a word about my error. I learned an age-old lesson that December: Pride does go before the fall!

Gracious Lord, forgive me for the times when I allow pride or anger to control my actions. Help me to humble myself enough to admit when I'm wrong. May I walk in humility in all that I do.

———— ❧✿❧ ————

"Call to Me, and I will answer you, and I will tell you great and mighty things, which you do not know." (Jeremiah 33:3)

Everyone loves candy canes, and yet most people do not know that there is a spiritual meaning to the candy cane.

A Candymaker's Witness

A candymaker wanted to make a candy that would be a witness, so he made the Christmas candy cane. He began with a stick of pure white, hard candy. White to symbolize the virgin birth and the sinless nature of Jesus and hard to symbolize the solid rock, the foundation of the Church, and firmness of the promises of God. The candymaker made the candy in the form of a "J" to represent the precious name of Jesus. It could also represent the staff of the Good Shepherd with which He reaches down into the ditches of the world to lift the fallen lambs who have gone astray. The candymaker stained it with red stripes. He used three small stripes to show the stripes of the scourging Jesus received, by which we are healed. The large red stripe was for the blood shed by Christ on the cross so that we could have the promise of eternal life.

Every December we give candy canes with "A Candymaker's Witness" tag attached by a bright ribbon to whomever comes to our door. It is a simple yet beautiful way to share the message of Christ's love, even if you don't have the gift of evangelism! I have found that people are generally more open to spiritual things during the Christmas season. I have never had anyone refuse a candy cane.

> *Lord, thank You for giving someone the insight a long time ago to create a candy that pays tribute to You. Show me how I can help to spread the Christmas message to those who may not know You.*

But lay up for yourselves treasures in heaven, where neither moth nor rust destroys, and where thieves do not break in or steal; for where your treasure is, there will your heart be also. (Matthew 6:20-21)

Memories are one of those precious things in life that no one can ever take from you. Time is the commodity needed to make memories, not money. The Christmas season is a great time to create some wonderful memories for children. Interaction among families is at an all-time high during the holiday season, so we have a natural environment for filling our kids with meaningful memories. Memories are often made from family traditions and the holiday season is a great time to start some.

We started some holiday traditions when our kids were just toddlers that we count on year after year to bring peace and focus to the often hectic pace of the holidays for us. After church on the first Sunday of advent, the whole family goes together to select our Christmas tree, and then we spend the afternoon decorating it. It is a fun time, filled with laughter and singing. We always make popcorn and play Christmas music while we decorate. The advent wreath is carefully placed at the center of our kitchen table, where we gather for meals. Every evening throughout the month of December, until Christmas Eve when the center Christ candle is lit, we light the appropriate candle(s) and have a special devotional during our evening meal. This helps us to keep our focus on Christ during the entire holiday season.

Lord, thank You for the things in my life that can never be taken or destroyed: my salvation, my love for my family, my memories. Help me to create meaningful memories for my children and keep us focused on the true meaning of Christmas.

December 5

But if any of you lacks wisdom, let him ask of God, who gives to all men generously and without reproach, and it will be given to him. (James 1:5)

Watching children progress through the stages of physical and emotional development is exciting and sometimes frustrating. I remember my oldest when he began asserting his independence at the ripe old age of three. It was as if he woke up one day and decided he wanted to do everything himself, everything from fastening his pants to fastening his seat belt.

Making mistakes is part of the learning process. That is how we fine-tune our skills. I was happy to teach Seth new skills, but he would often prematurely decide he was ready to do it himself. I knew he wasn't, but I would let him try and then wait in the wings until he needed me. One day after he insisted on tying his shoes himself, he hung his head and sighed, "Mommy, do it," leaving me to untie the mess he had made of his laces and start over again.

Isn't that just like our relationship with God? We decide we want to do something and so we do it our way, saying resolutely, "I'll do it!" When all the while, God is probably watching in frustration, knowing there is a better way. He waits and watches patiently, allowing us to make mistakes and learn from them. Then we finally come to Him, head often hung in defeat, whispering, "God, will You please do it?" He happily scoops us up in His arms, dusts us off and cleans up the mess we have made of our lives, helping us to start over again.

The Boss has the answers we are looking for—He is just watching, waiting for us to ask for His help.

Lord, thank You for being patient with me when I venture off on my own, and thank You for picking me up and dusting me off when I fail time and time again. May I never be to proud to ask for help.

December 6

For you know the grace of our Lord Jesus Christ, that though He was rich, yet for your sake He became poor, that you through His poverty might become rich. (2 Corinthians 8:9)

Sometimes being a stay-at-home mom means making some adjustments and some sacrifices. Without a second income, we usually have to give up some material extras. But unless we make a big deal about not having everything we want, our children don't miss these things. The holiday season can be difficult because there are so many things we'd like to put under the Christmas tree for our children but cannot afford. If you find yourself slipping into the self-pity pit when you see others buying expensive gifts you cannot afford, consider that you really are rich.

That's right—you are rich! You have wealth beyond measure; however, it is not a system of wealth that the world validates. You are a child of the King, and you have inherited all eternity. Consider giving your children the gift of eternal life this Christmas by teaching them about Jesus. Nothing is worth more.

When you make a decision to follow God, you will have to make adjustments. One of them may be the adjustment from working full-time outside the home to working full-time at home. For many women, this is the most difficult decision they will make as a believer.

The Bible is full of examples of God's people making adjustments in their lives in order to follow God. God's own Son even had to make some major adjustments. Whenever I begin feeling as if I have to give up "so much" to be a stay-at-home mom, I think about Jesus and everything He gave up for me. There's no comparison, so I have no more complaints.

Lord Jesus, You have given up so much for me. Forgive me when I pity myself, thinking that I have to sacrifice too much to follow You. Help me to make the necessary adjustments in my life to be totally devoted to You.

The sacrifices of God are a broken spirit; A broken and a contrite heart, O God, Thou wilt not despise. (Psalm 51:17)

The following story, taken from *God's Little Devotional Book for Moms*, paints a vivid illustration of sacrifice for the sake of our children:

A number of years ago, a young mother was making her way on foot across the hills of South Wales, carrying her tiny baby in her arms. The wintry winds were stronger than she anticipated and her journey took much longer than planned. Eventually, she was overtaken by a blinding blizzard. The woman never reached her destination. When the blizzard had subsided, those expecting her arrival went in search of her. After hours of searching, they finally found her body underneath a mound of snow. As they shoveled the snow away from her frozen corpse, they were amazed to see that she had taken off her outer clothing. When they finally lifted her body away from the ground, they discovered the reason why. This brave and self-sacrificing young mother had wrapped her own cloak and scarf around her baby and then huddled over her child. When the searchers unwrapped the child, they found to their great surprise and joy that he was alive and well! Years later, that child, David Lloyd George, became Prime Minister of Great Britain, and is regarded as one of England's greatest statesmen."

There is no greater sacrifice than that of life itself. David Lloyd George's mother was willing to give up her life to save her child's. And yet, there are mothers all across America who aren't willing to give up a bigger house, a newer car or better furniture to save their children. God rewards those who sacrifice what their heart desires in order to do what His heart desires.

Lord, help me to sacrifice willingly for the sake of my children. May I submit to Your authority, even when the sacrifice hurts. Transform my heart's desires to meet those of Your heart.

. . . {I}t is more blessed to give than to receive. (Acts 20:35)

The holiday season has always reflected the spirit of giving. Jesus Himself modeled this by giving the greatest gift of all—His life. My husband and I have tried to model the joy of giving for our children in various ways. One way is to give a gift to someone who cannot give one to you. A great way to do this is through a ministry called "Project Angel Tree." This ministry delivers gifts to children whose parents are in prison.

The Christmas that our oldest son was three, he helped us pick an angel tag from the tree at church. He and his dad chose a little boy named Steve, who was also three years old. The afternoon that we were to go shopping for little Steve's gift, my husband sat Seth on his lap and carefully explained that Steve's parents were in prison and they couldn't buy any Christmas presents for Steve, so we were going to help by purchasing some presents for him. He told Seth what the Bible says about giving and why it is good to share with others what God has blessed us with. Seth sat silently, listening intently to his father's words. Jimmy asked Seth what he thought we should get for Steve. The room was silent for a long moment. Finally, Seth said, "I think we should get him a new mommy and daddy."

My eyes welled with tears as I saw the concern on Seth's face, concern for little Steve, who had no mom or dad to buy him a Christmas present. In his young mind, it was the gift that made the most sense, a gift of love that would keep on giving. When we explained to Seth why we couldn't accommodate his request, his next suggestion was a "drum." Seth didn't know it, but he gave something to his daddy and me that Christmas too: He gave us great joy in being his parents.

> *Lord, teach me how to give joyfully. As I seek out opportunities to bless others during this holiday season, open my eyes to those around me in need. May I respond with love and generosity.*

". . . {N}ot by might nor by power, but by My Spirit," says the
*L*ORD *of hosts. (Zechariah 4:6)*

Our church decided to host a Christmas party for our local women's shelter. When our women's ministry coordinator approached me in November and asked me to head it up, I gave an enthusiastic, "You bet!"

A few weeks later, the project turned out to be a migraine headache. Only three women agreed to help, but I needed twice that many. Everyone was too busy with the holidays to help. All of the women at the shelter were really looking forward to the party. I knew I was doing what God wanted me to do. But why was it not coming together this time?

Over the next few days, as I went to God in prayer, I heard His still, small voice speak to my spirit. He did not want this event to come together by my energies or efforts, but by His grace and love. I released it all to Him and did the best I could. The day before the party, the women's ministry director and I were the only ones who came to set up. We did all we could, but there was still much to be done.

I was so tired that I did not hear the alarm the next morning. "O, Lord," I whimpered as I showered and dressed quickly, "How could You let me oversleep?" With tear-filled eyes and an anxious heart, I drove to the church and ran into the activity center. I couldn't believe my eyes. Everything was done. "What happened?" I asked my friend Shelley.

"I don't know," she said, "women just showed up early to help. Pretty great, huh?" Great was the word, all right. The party was great and the women from the shelter had a great time. But the greatest part was how the Lord pulled it off.

> *Lord, thank You for choosing to display Your power when I need it*
> *most. When things get too overwhelming, remind me to rely on*
> *Your strength, not mine.*

"Let your heart therefore be wholly devoted to the LORD our God, to walk in His statutes and to keep His commandments, as at this day." (1 Kings 8:61)

One of my favorite things about Christmas is decorating. One of the best investments we ever made was a beautifully painted nativity set. All of the pieces are made of wood and are large and sturdy. We purchased it when the boys were small because we wanted something they could handle without fear of breakage. They love to help set out the nativity each Christmas and they often play with the pieces, as they imitate how things might have been on that night long ago.

Another way we emphasize Christ's birth is by making a special dessert in His honor. After Christmas dinner, we have a birthday cake for Jesus. We light a single candle, and everyone gathers around the cake, singing "Happy Birthday" to Jesus. This is a great way to share Christ's love with friends and neighbors, whom you might invite over for Christmas dinner or even dessert! We talk about Jesus' birthday all month long so that by the time Christmas arrives, they know exactly what they are celebrating. Santa Claus is an added bonus, but not the focus.

With all of the commercialism surrounding us today, we have to try harder at Christmas to keep the focus on Jesus. Most people have more company than usual during the month of December, and placing visual reminders throughout your home of the Reason for the season is a great way to witness. Be wholly devoted to Him as you decorate; after all, He is the Reason for the season.

Precious Jesus, may You be mirrored in my home this month as I decorate for the celebration of Christmas. May I keep the focus on Your birth in every part of the holiday season. I pray it will be evident to all who enter my home this month that I am wholly devoted to You.

December 11

". . . {T}he Father abiding in Me does His works." (John 14:10)

When I was a sales coordinator for a big cosmetic corporation years ago, I remember feeling a sense of pride when sales were up and things were going well in my district. People succeed in the business world based on their achievements. I was praised when my stores performed well.

The problem with this barometer of success is that all of the responsibility for good or bad lies in the person's abilities alone to do the job. Either you have it or you don't. There is no room for God's grace to take over when you rely on your own abilities. True, God has gifted us with talents and abilities, but when we operate on those talents and abilities alone, we can become prideful.

When I made the decision to be a stay-at-home mom, my first feelings were that of fear. I feared I didn't have what it takes to be a good mother. It wasn't something that came "naturally" to me. In time, I learned to put my faith in God and His abilities, not mine. He is my Boss, my Source, my Provider. He equips and trains me to accomplish all I need to do through His power and strength, not my own. When I ask God to give me patience with my children, He doesn't just give me patience, He gives me Himself, so His patience becomes my patience. And His supply is endless, whereas mine runs out daily.

God's power is an untapped resource for many frustrated moms. He has every quality we desire. When Jesus comes into our lives, He does the needed work—if we allow Him to. Thankfully, with the Father, we are not rated based on performance or achievements, we are simply loved and valued as we are.

> *Lord, I give You thanks for all of the ways You have helped me to be a good mother to my children. Forgive me when I lean on my own abilities instead of Your grace.*

December 12

But sanctify Christ as Lord in your hearts, always being ready to make a defense to everyone who asks you to give an account for the hope that is in you. (1 Peter 3:15)

I was having coffee with a friend one day while our children played nearby. We were enjoying refreshments when the children began to quarrel. We defused the argument, and off they went to play again happily, until another disagreement arose. This pattern continued on and off throughout the morning. After an hour or so, my friend asked, "How do you keep it together so well? My daughter's defiance is pushing me over the edge!"

I had the privilege of sharing my "secret" with my friend who was not a believer. I explained that Christ is the one who gives the hope, patience and wisdom I need to deal with my children. I invited her to a women's Bible study at our church. She accepted. A few months later, she and her husband joined us in a parenting class, also offered at our church. I watched her raging frustration transform into gentle assurance as she began to understand the principles of God's Word. As she began to sanctify, or respect Christ, she made a place in her heart for Him to become Lord.

Don't think for a second that if you choose to be a stay-at-home mom, God can't use you to make a difference in a life besides your children's. People will notice a difference in the way you parent, in the way you treat your spouse and in the way you handle everyday life. They will ask what your secret is, and you will have an open door to share Christ's love.

You are my Lord and Master, Jesus. Keep me willing to share with others the hope that You can give. Give me the right words at the right time. Use me to bring others to Your saving grace.

In those days there was no king in Israel; every man did what was right in his own eyes. (Judges 17:6)

Can you imagine life with no laws, no rules, no standards, no absolutes, no order? That is not the way God set things up, but that is the way many people today live their lives. In the Old Testament book of Judges, a time such as this is recorded. The standard of right and wrong was all relative; there were no moral absolutes and people did whatever they wanted with no consequences for their behavior. It was anarchy. Sin ran rampant and no one classified ungodly actions as "sin" during that time because there was no standard by which to measure anyone's actions. The book goes on to document the peace that developed as law and order was finally established.

Our world is gravitating today toward this type of old-world anarchy. Our children face pressure by their peers to succumb to the notion of "If it feels good, do it!" The abstract standard of feelings is become the driving force of our culture, rather than the concrete standard of God's Word.

Imagine what your home would be like if you didn't have any rules; the children could decide what was right for them and govern their actions according to their own personal standard. What if none of your kids had to pick up their toys, eat their dinner, brush their teeth, do their homework, help with the household chores or be in bed by a specific time? They'd be in horrible health; physically, intellectually and emotionally! You have rules for your children because you care about them. Similarly, we need rules to protect the spiritual health of our children. Living by God's rules brings freedom from anarchy.

Lord, help me to live my life and teach my children to live theirs according to the standard of Your Holy Word. May You be at the center of our home as the driving force to do what's right.

Let each one do just as he has purposed in his heart; not grudgingly or under compulsion; for God loves a cheerful giver. (2 Corinthians 9:7)

One evening I was doing some errands when I glanced at my watch and discovered that it was no longer on my wrist. I scanned the ground around me and then began a hurried backtrack of my route around the store. I checked my car. I went back inside the store and left a description and my telephone number with Lost and Found just in case.

As I started the car, I prayed, "God, please help me find that watch. You know how much it means to me." It had been a Christmas gift from my husband. The value to me was in the giver, not the gift. I drove to the church, where I had been earlier for my meeting and, shining the headlights onto the sidewalk, began to search the ground. Something glinted. As I bent for a closer look I saw my watch! I shouted "Praise God" right there in the middle of the street!

As I was driving home, I thought about the value of that watch. For a moment, I believe I caught a glimpse of the value God places on the gifts we give to Him, gifts not just of our money, but of our time and energy. The value is not in the gift itself, but in the heart of the giver. If we give to Him begrudgingly, the gift is meaningless; but if we give cheerfully, then the gift, no matter how small, is priceless to God. What is your heart attitude when you give to God? What is your heart attitude when you give to others at Christmas and any time of the year? God loves a cheerful giver.

Thank You for all of the gifts You give to me, Lord. All I have comes from You. Search my heart and show me if there is any reluctance when I give back to You. Purge me of any selfishness and pour Your joy into my heart.

And your ears will hear a word behind you, "This is the way, walk in it," whenever you turn to the right or to the left. (Isaiah 30:21)

*I*n a parenting class my husband and I enrolled in at our church, I learned a wonderful principle called the "moral warehouse." It is based upon the idea that our heart is a type of moral warehouse where basic values are stored, and then later used in life. Look up Psalm 119:11. Here's how it works. There are two aspects to the human conscience; the primary conscience and the moral conscience. The primary conscience is something we are all born with. It consists of a basic sense of right and wrong and an innate awareness that God exists. The moral conscience is the trainable portion of man's conscience. Just as easily as the moral conscience can be trained correctly, can it be trained incorrectly.

Picture a huge warehouse with rows of shelves from floor to ceiling. On each of those shelves are various values and character qualities. In the first years of our children's lives, we stock our children's shelves with virtues: honesty, self-control, patience, kindness, gentleness, faithfulness, respect, honor and fairness. Picture your child running up and down the aisles, looking for a value to apply when he needs to make a decision. Have you stocked the shelves?

(For more information about the moral warehouse, read *Growing Kids God's Way* by Gary and Anne Marie Ezzo.)

> *Lord, give me wisdom and discipline to correctly train the hearts of my children and to stock the shelves of their moral warehouses with the values that will rightly reflect You.*

Thanks be to God for His indescribable gift! (2 Corinthians 9:15)

"Only nine more shopping days until Christmas," the speaker blared out as I went from one department to another trying to find the right gifts. Knee-deep in men's ties and a bad attitude, I sighed. I didn't want to give my brother a tie again. Did I give him a tie last year or the year before? I couldn't remember. I threw the ties on the counter in disgust and waved a halfhearted thanks but no thanks to the yawning salesgirl. I loved giving gifts, but I wanted them to be special. On my way out to the car I cried, "Help me, Lord!"

Once home, I settled into a comfortable chair to sort through the mail. A catalog caught my eye. It was a merchandise catalog by a Christian publishing house. To my surprise, I found much more than books. There were calendars, tapes, games, videos, clothing items, home decor items and even a children's section with age-appropriate books and games. Suddenly, I knew what I wanted to do: I wanted to give Christmas gifts that encourage growth in a relationship with Jesus.

That year was the beginning of a new tradition. Each Christmas I seek out a gift for every person on my list that will in some way build them up spiritually. Giving a gift that communicates Christ's love is the most meaningful gift I can give—meaning I can't find at the tie counter!

Thank You, Lord, for sending the greatest Gift of all—Your Son to be the Savior to the world. Help me to be a reflection of Your message of hope and love by the gifts I give this Christmas.

❧❀❧

. . . {J}ust as the Son of Man did not come to be served, but to serve, and to give His life a ransom for many. (Matthew 20:28)

There are days when I am sure that if I look up the word "mother" in the dictionary, the definition will be "servant." Do you ever feel that way? Between the cooking, the cleaning, the laundry, the errands, the ironing and the chauffeuring, I often feel like a servant. At first, my feelings about serving were not favorable. I would grumble and complain as I bent over to pick up my children's toys and my husband's socks. I failed to see anything glorious about cleaning up someone else's mess. However, over time, I began stumbling upon verses in the Bible about servanthood, and God began to change my perspective. I discovered that God's view of serving was very different than mine.

Jesus spent most of His time helping. He did a lot of clean-up, particularly of people's lives! Once I understood that Jesus, the King of kings, was more a Servant than anything else, I had a greater appreciation for the role.

As a mother, I spend a great deal of time helping, teaching, guiding, training and cleaning up. I have come to realize that as I serve my family, I serve God as well. He has placed me in the role of motherhood and I have an opportunity to glorify Him as I serve my family. That includes scrubbing toilets! Every year at Christmastime, God reminds me to be humble and desire the role of a servant. Because as I serve, I become more like Christ.

From His life as a servant, emerged a Savior. Out of His humility came glory and honor and power. At the very least, I can give Him my heart, and I guess I can pick up a few socks too.

> *Lord, help me to clothe myself in humility as You did so long ago. Remind me that serving is an honor and is highly esteemed in Your eyes. Give me joy in serving my family in all of the daily tasks that motherhood brings.*

And Abraham said to his young men, "Stay here with the donkey, and I and the lad will go yonder; and we will worship and return to you." (Genesis 22:5)

The first time I read the story of Abraham and Isaac, I had to go back and read it again. God wanted Abraham to do what? God's request of Abraham to sacrifice his only son made no sense to me. Maybe I could understand if Abraham was the kind of guy who only listened to God when he really felt like it, who only followed God when it was convenient for him, and God was trying to teach him a lesson. But this wasn't the case.

After reading the story several times (Genesis 22:1-18), I realized Abraham didn't seem to be questioning God the way I was. He simply gathered up his son, a few servants and some wood and headed for the mountains. Once he arrived, he made the statement in the above verse: "I and the lad will go yonder; and we will worship and return to you." Did you catch that? Abraham didn't say, "I will return to you." He said, "we"! His unwavering trust in God is found in a two-letter word. Yet his actions said he was willing to go through with the sacrifice. And his obedience brought forth an entire nation.

Wow! What a lesson in faith! Abraham knew his duty was to obey God first, whatever the cost. Sometimes being a mom means following God even at great personal cost. It may mean doing things that don't make sense. It definitely means times of sacrifice. Yet, as illustrated through the story of Abraham and Isaac, it always means great reward.

Father of Abraham, You are a God who is worthy to be held in the highest regard. Forgive me for the times I dishonor You by disobeying You. Give me the faith of Abraham, that I might have the same allegiance to You as he did. Give me eyes to see You as he did, and ears to hear You as he did, and a heart so full of trust that it follows You without question, just as he did.

December 19

"Peace I leave with you; My peace I give to you; not as the world gives, do I give to you. Let not your heart be troubled, nor let it be fearful." (John 14:27)

Seth started to cry. The only thing that was going to quiet him was some sleep, in his own bed, in his own house.

Peace—now that was a concept to be pondered. Our household had been anything but peaceful the past few weeks. Aside from all of the normal seasonal preparations like baking, shopping, wrapping and decorating; there were lots of invitations to holiday parties and events. And I wanted to do it all. I'm the kind of person who doesn't like to miss out on anything fun! But that night my conscience was telling me I had overloaded my toddler and that I needed to pass on this party and get him to bed. He was asleep before I had even driven a block.

At home, I tucked him into his crib and stood there for a while watching his deep, even breathing. He was getting some peace now. I thought about the past few weeks and how hard it had been on him. I had been going a million miles an hour, requiring that he follow suit. His schedule had been thrown way off and any sense of normalcy or routine that he was accustomed to had vanished once the tinsel and lights appeared.

As I bent down to kiss his baby-soft cheek, I promised myself that as long as I was the mother of young children, I would limit my activities during the holiday season. Consider limiting your families activities during the holidays to maintain peace in your home.

Help me, Prince of Peace, to do what's right concerning my children. Keep me focused on their best even when I get caught up in the excitement of the Christmas season.

December 20

"But when you give alms, do not let your left hand know what your right hand is doing that your alms may be in secret; and your Father who sees in secret will repay you." (Matthew 6:3-4)

When my husband and I were newly married and young in our faith, we attended a small but dynamic church in a big city. The members of this church were warm, sincere, kind and thoughtful, but most importantly, their love for God was evident. If anyone within the body was in need, everyone pitched in to help. No questions asked. No judgment passed.

Just before the holiday season, John, a regular attendee, was laid off from his job. The burden of supporting the family rested on his wife Linda's shoulders. The income from her part-time job wouldn't pay all of the bills. As Christmas drew closer, Linda began to be concerned over whether or not they would be able to purchase any Christmas presents for their two daughters. Determined not to worry, she gave the matter to God and waited for His provision. But nothing happened. Two days before Christmas, she and John decided to tell the girls the next day not to expect any gifts.

The next morning, Linda decided to check her mail before talking with the children. To her great surprise, she found a large sum of money in her mailbox with a note saying simply, "Merry Christmas—Love, Santa Claus." It was in a plain white envelope and there were no markings that would identify the giver.

John and Linda were able to provide their girls with gifts that Christmas because of the generosity of someone who discovered their need and responded to it. The giver remained anonymous because he wanted God to have the glory, not himself.

Lord, thank You for those who are living examples of Your love. Show me how to see the needs of others around me. Teach me how to give without desire for recognition or gratitude, but merely for the sake of seeing You be glorified.

December 21

"*Do not fear, for I am with you;*
   Do not anxiously look about you, for I am your God.
I will strengthen you, surely I will help you,
   Surely I will uphold you with My righteous right hand."
(*Isaiah 41:10*)

looked anxiously at the clock and turned to do a rush job on my makeup. Giving my husband and son a hurried hug on my way out the door, I grabbed my costume for the Christmas program. On the drive to church I began to make a mental list of everything I needed to get done in the next two days before our out-of-town company arrived.

By the time I arrived at the church I was fighting back tears. When we gathered in small groups to pray for the people who would be attending the program that evening, our leader asked if anyone had any personal prayer requests. My pent-up frustration found an outlet and I burst into tears, rambling about everything I had to do. "When did Christmas turn into a burden, instead of a blessing?" I blubbered. "This is not the way it's supposed to be."

After some supportive hugs and prayer from my group, we talked about all of the preparations I had scheduled. "Is it that big a deal if you only bake one kind of cookie instead of your traditional three?" one friend challenged. "Would your guests really be offended and leave if your house is not spotless?" another friend inquired. Their questions made me think. Perhaps I had turned Christmas into a burden. If the blessing was gone, it was my doing.

I learned a lot that first holiday as a parent. I learned to slow down and enjoy the season. I now look forward to it instead of anxiously at it. And there have been many Christmases now as a mother that I only have time to bake one kind of cookie, and amazingly, no one has ever complained!

Lord, keep me wrapped in the simplicity of the Christmas season by focusing on You.

And we know that God causes all things to work together for good to those who love God, to those who are called according to His purpose. (Romans 8:28)

Three days before Christmas my husband called to me from the bathroom with an urgency in his voice, "Honey, please come tell me what this is on my arm!"

"Looks like you've got chicken pox." I said.

"Great," he moaned. "Just in time for Christmas!"

We had been counting the days and holding our breath, hoping that Jimmy would not contract chicken pox from our preschooler. As an adult, they could be very serious and very painful. I called the airlines to cancel our flight to Colorado and called the doctor to get a prescription. Within a few hours, chicken pox were covering his body and the virus began attacking his nervous system. The pain was almost unbearable. We prayed specifically that he would be well enough by Christmas to enjoy the day with the children. The next two days were very difficult for Jimmy. He commented that the boils Job suffered (Job 2:7) must have been chicken pox!

By Christmas morning Jimmy was out of bed and opening presents with the rest of us. The rest of the week was an unexpected blessing. Jimmy felt well enough to be out of bed but he was still in the contagious stage so he couldn't go to work. He spent time with our boys. They played and laughed and laughed and played. I enjoyed myself just watching them. There was no agenda, no schedule to meet, no expectations, just time.

Sometimes as parents we get so caught up in the day-to-day routine that even our days "off" become scheduled. We don't leave time to just "be" with our kids.

Thank You, Lord, for always doing what is best for me, even when I don't. I know that You will work out all of the things in my life for good if I will just trust You.

> *And they came into the house and saw the Child with Mary His mother; and they fell down and worshiped Him; and opening their treasures they presented to Him gifts of gold and frankincense and myrrh. (Matthew 2:11)*

Christmas with young children can be very eye-opening to the misconception that more is better. When Seth was two, we were really looking forward to Christmas with him. With great anticipation, we awoke that Christmas morning and had our traditional cinnamon roll breakfast before entering the living room, where the gifts were piled in huge stacks underneath the tree. We got out the video camera and the still camera, poising ourselves for the look of joy we just knew would be on Seth's face when he made his grand entrance. Instead, we got a lot of pictures of a frustrated toddler looking very distraught. He just stood in front of the tree, looking dumbfounded.

Finally, when he got over the shock of it all, he began to play with one of the toys. Then he began a mad flurry of running from toy to toy. When we began to open presents, he ripped his open as fast as he could, not even bothering to look at the contents. Then he fell back in an exhausted heap on the floor. The poor child was completely overwhelmed!

We learned a valuable lesson that Christmas: Less is more! And it led to a new tradition in our home. We limit our gift-giving to our children to three gifts each, following the model that Jesus received only three gifts, one from each of the wise men. It has improved the quality of our Christmas experience tremendously. It teaches the kids to be more disciplined in their desires, and it teaches us to be more disciplined in our spending! Our kids now portray the look of gratitude and excitement on Christmas morning that we prefer to capture on film!

> *Lord, thank You for teaching me that the joy of Christmas can be lost when we endlessly heap gifts under the tree. Help me to keep my family focused on the greatest Gift of all—Jesus.*

But now you are light in the Lord; walk as children of light.
(Ephesians 5:8)

stared at the Christmas tree lights in the quiet living room. Everyone was asleep and the house was dark—except for the light from the tree. My eyes fell to the gifts. The wrappings and ribbons shimmered in the tree lights. By this time tomorrow, it would be bare once again underneath the big fir.

My thoughts wandered to the significance of the tree, an evergreen: a symbol of new life; the lights reminding us that Jesus is the Light of the world and the gifts representing the greatest Gift of all.

I paused to thank God for bringing the true meaning of Christmas into our lives. I was so thankful that when I looked at our Christmas tree, I could see its deeper meaning. I saddened for a moment as I thought about the many people who didn't know about Jesus; I prayed that I would be a child of light.

I knew from Christmases past that the gifts my boys would open tomorrow would hold great joy—for a while. But in time, some of the gifts would break, lose their appeal or sit forgotten on a closet shelf. But the gift of knowing Jesus was a treasure that would never lose its luster.

That Christmas Eve in the still of the night, I prayed that my children would one day open their hearts to the greatest gift of all: knowing Jesus as their Lord and Savior. Then I asked God for the only gift I really wanted: to be a mother who leads my children into His light. I knew it was the best gift I could give them—this Christmas or any other.

> *Lord, thank You for bringing Your Son to earth to be my Savior. As I celebrate the birth of Jesus tomorrow, help me to spread the light of Your truth to my children and many others.*

December 25

For today in the city of David there has been born for you a Savior, who is Christ the Lord. . . . But Mary treasured up all these things, pondering them in her heart. (Luke 2:11, 19)

Merry Christmas! And Happy Birthday, Jesus! Have you ever reflected on what it must be like to be the mother of the Savior of this world? What an honor! It is difficult to imagine the pride and excitement Mary must have felt on that first Christmas morning. The Scriptures only give us a glimpse of her emotions—"But Mary treasured up all these things, pondering them in her heart." Mary probably glowed with pride, just as every mother does after giving birth. But her first moments had to have been different—they were on a level that we, as mothers, will never quite comprehend. Jesus was in a class all His own! That puts His mother in a class all her own as well.

As she treasured those early minutes alone, holding her sweet Baby in her arms and staring into His soft, trusting eyes, I'm sure it must have been impossible for her to envision the life that was about to enfold for them all. Jesus was a public figure even before He was born. Many were already anticipating His coming, spreading the news quickly as Jesus arrived. How could Mary know the whirlwind life she was entering?

As you enjoy this joyous celebration of our Savior's birth today, take a few quiet moments to reflect on Mary's first quiet moments with her Son. Let your mother's heart imagine how she must have treasured that time. Treasure your time with your own children today and be sure to give thanks to God for the gifts He has given you in them. Have a blessed Christmas!

Thank You, God, for sending Your Son to be my Savior so long ago. Help me today to treasure my children and all of the good gifts you have given to me.

Unless the LORD builds the house, they labor in vain who build it. . . . (Psalm 127:1)

When my boys were one and four years old, my husband and I had the opportunity to get away for a few days on a business trip. My parents took care of the children for us for three days and three nights. By the last night Seth really missed us. Seth said to his grandpa, "Papa Jim, I like your home, but I like my home the best."

That was a preschooler's way of saying, "I'm homesick, I'd like to go home now, please!" I noticed that Seth used the word "home" instead of "house." A house is just a building, but a home is a sanctuary. It is a place where children should find security, peace, comfort and love, all necessary for healthy emotional development.

We, as mothers, have a responsibility and an opportunity to make our homes a place where our children want to be, where they love to be more than anywhere else. A dwelling place built on the foundation of Jesus Christ and anchored in a parent's love will become a home; without either of those things, it will only be a house. Natural disasters such as flood, fire, hurricane or tornado can destroy a house, but none of nature's toughest forces can tear apart a home. A house is built with hands, but a home is built with hearts.

Lord, I thank You that our home is built solidly upon the founda-tion of Your Word and love. Help me to make my home the place that my children like best, even as they grow. May they always find unconditional love and acceptance within these walls.

For there is no partiality with God. (Romans 2:11)

We are all equal in God's eyes. His Word is clear that we are all created in God's image and He has an abundance of love for every human being. White or black, short or tall, man or woman, stay-at-home mom or not, He loves us all the same.

I am passionate about the importance of being a stay-at-home mom. But unbridled passion can run wild and lead to disaster. I have to be careful to give my opinion only when asked (You asked for it when you picked up this book!) and then in love and grace accept the decisions that other moms make. That doesn't mean I have to agree with a friend who chooses to go back to work outside the home full-time and put her baby in day care. But I do have to love her, in spite of our differing choices. God has not called us to sit in judgment of each other. (See Matthew 7:1.) He has called us only to love each other. He does not love the stay-at-home mom more than He loves the mom who works outside her home. Our actions do not determine His degree of love for each of us. There is no partiality with God.

I hope that this book has given you a better insight into the role that God intended for us as mothers. I pray that it has taken you on a journey of discovering God's very best for you, and that you will choose to walk in obedience. You may have a new excitement about being a stay-at-home mom after scouring these pages, and in your zeal, you may be tempted to tell all of your friends why they need to stay at home with their kids too. Don't do it. Walk in humility. If you rush into the lives of others, giving unsolicited advice with great enthusiasm, your well-meaning words will most likely be misconstrued as judgmental. You don't always know all of the circumstances surrounding others' decisions. We are each accountable to God, not each other, for our choices!

> *Lord, help me not to sit in judgment of women who have chosen to work outside the home. Give me your compassion and impartiality for those who choose differently than I.*

You, however, continue in the things you have learned and become convinced of, knowing from whom you have learned them. (2 Timothy 3:14)

Growing is a process. Physically, emotionally and spiritually, maturation takes time. It is easy for us to accept the fact that patience is required when it comes to physical and emotional growth. Why then do so many of us expect to become super Christians or super moms overnight? Just as babies learn to roll over, then crawl, then walk and run; so we progress in our faith—one step at a time. All too often, I grow impatient with myself, getting aggravated when I make a mistake or don't feel that I'm progressing quickly enough in my relationship with God or in my role as a mother.

The key is in looking to God as our Source. Time and experience are great confidence builders, but the best there is comes from the truth of God's Word. When I take the time to start my day by reading my Bible and praying, I am inviting God to be in control of my life and all circumstances of that day. Then I can focus on God and not my situation. If I continue to practice the things I have learned from God's Word in every area of my life, soon confidence and trust in God will outweigh my propensity to get frustrated.

One of my favorite sayings is, "The only failures are those who have failed to try." Trying does not mean I will be perfect. It just means I have perseverance. Perseverance is a quality that will serve us well in all aspects of life. As I grow in the knowledge of God's Word, I will grow in my abilities as a mother. I am being trained by the greatest parent of all, so why can't I be the greatest mom ever? I can, and so can you! One step at a time.

Lord, You are my Source and my Strength. Give me the daily discipline to continue the habit of spending time in Your Word. Teach me how to be the kind of mom you want me to be. Give me confidence in my parenting as I grow in my relationship with You.

December 29

". . . {F}or my house will be called a house of prayer for all the peoples." (Isaiah 56:7)

aking down Christmas decorations every year is the only part of the holiday that I do not look forward to. The house always looks so bare after being filled with shining lights and glittering tinsel. There is a certain drabness that seems to reappear every January as each bulb is taken off the now-sagging tree.

I was lingering over the basket of Christmas cards sent from friends and relatives, reading them one last time before depositing them in the trash. *It seems such a waste to throw these away,* I thought. *This is the only time of year I hear from some of these people and I feel so disconnected from them once I throw these cards away.* Hand poised over the kitchen garbage can, I suddenly remembered an idea I had heard from a woman who kept her Christmas cards all year long and then prayed for the people who sent them. All I needed were the cards and a basket.

That is how our prayer basket began. Each year as we take down our lights and tinsel, we put out our prayer basket filled with Christmas cards that we received the previous season. Each Sunday we pick a new card from the basket and pray all week long for the one(s) who sent it. We make it a family event, and mealtime is a good time for everyone to participate. As we pray for the sender of each card, we are reminded of Christ's birth and its significance in our lives all year. Sometimes, we even send a short note at the week's end, letting the person or family know that we prayed for them for an entire week. The response can be heartwarming. And it's a wonderful way to keep Christ's love burning in our hearts all year.

Lord, thank You for showing me that I can be reminded of the gift of Your love all year by a simple basket of cards. May I be diligent in praying for those who touch our lives by written word.

Jesus Christ is the same yesterday and today, yes and forever.
(Hebrews 13:8)

One of the things that I am discovering as I grow in my role as a mother is that things change constantly. Our children grow and change at a rapid pace. They go from babies to toddlers, from preschoolers to adolescents and finally to adults. Each of these stages represents a "season" in our parenting. Each season brings different conditions, circumstances and needs. Our children must be treated differently at each stage of their development. We, as mothers, must grow and change with them in order to accommodate their current "season."

Growing up is hard, and we can help our children get through their own struggles and frustrations with their ever-changing bodies and minds by teaching them to rely on the constancy of Jesus. In the frequent turmoil and inevitable disappointments that come with maturation, especially in adolescence and the teenage years, our kids will find comfort in the stability we provide. You can help by giving them a stable and loving home environment and by pointing them to Jesus as the One constant in life.

During anxious moments, when I find myself questioning my abilities as a mom, it is then that God reminds me to lean on Him. He will lead me through the process, one step at a time. He is the One constant in life. He is forever faithful, always merciful, completely sovereign, continually gracious and perpetually wise. When the winds of change are blowing about me, and I am struggling to figure things out, Jesus is the solid Rock upon which I can stand steady in the gale.

> *Lord, thank You for being the One constant in my life. Bring me*
> *stability through Your faithfulness as I walk with my children*
> *through the different seasons of growing up.*

"I have fought the good fight, I have finished the course, I have kept the faith." II Timothy 4:7

*B*eing a mother is the hardest job any woman will ever have. It is also the most rewarding. I think the poem "Continue On" by Roy Lessin says it best:

A woman once fretted over the usefulness of her life.
She feared she was wasting her potential being
  a devoted wife and mother.
She wondered if the time and energy she invested in her husband and children
would make a difference. At times she got discouraged because so much of what she
did seemed to go unnoticed and unappreciated.
"Is it worth it?" she often wondered.
  "Is there something better that I could be doing with my time?"
It was during one of these moments of questioning that she heard the still small
voice of her heavenly Father speak to her heart.
"You are a wife and mother because that is what I have called you to be.
Much of what you do is hidden from the public eye.
But I notice. Most of what you give is done without remuneration.
But I am your reward.
Your husband cannot be the man I have called him to be without your support.
Your influence upon him is greater than you think and more
  powerful than you will ever know.
I bless him through your service and honor him through your love.
Your children are precious to Me.
Even more precious than they are to you. I have entrusted them to
  your care to raise for Me.
What you invest in them is an offering to Me.
You may never be in the public spotlight. But your obedience
  shines as a bright light before Me.
Continue On.
Remember you are My servant.
Do all to please Me."

Stay focused. Keep the faith. Continue on, fellow Mom.

Heavenly Father, may I seek to please only You.

Closing Comments

My heart is full. I cannot begin to tell you the many ways in which God has enriched my life during the writing of this book. He has brought me immeasurable joy as I have attempted to share my heart with you. What used to be a burden for a generation of women who need encouragement and inspiration to answer the call God has placed on our hearts is now a practical resource. I give all of the glory to God for the product you now hold in your hands. It was made possible only by Him. He brought me time to write when I thought there was no time, when the demands of raising a family were too overwhelming. He brought enlightenment when I felt empty, when my ideas were all used up. He brought strength when I was weak, when I didn't think I could write another word. And in His generosity and grace, He brought me the beautiful gift of a husband who believed in me, encouraged me and empowered me when no one else could.

My sincere desire is that the words on these pages have illuminated your life with truth and girded you with strength. My prayer for you is Ephesians 1:18-19: "I pray that the eyes of your heart may be enlightened, so that you may know what is the hope of His calling, what are the riches of the glory of His inheritance in the saints, and what is the surpassing greatness of His power toward us who believe."

I believe in the God who believes in you, who walks with us side by side, day by day, down the road of life. I pray that you too will walk with Him hand-in-hand down the road He has marked for you to travel. I'll see you on the other side.

-Laura Sabin Riley-

---

*L*aura Sabin Riley is a committed wife, mother, author and speaker. While her first ministry is her family, Laura loves to write and her short stories and articles have appeared in numerous Christian publications. She also loves to travel, speaking to various groups on those topics which she is most passionate about: faith, family and friends.

Laura believes that life is a gift to be embraced and enjoyed, and that relationships are the only real lasting investment. In her presentations, she practically and powerfully equips her audience with tools for getting the most out of life. She is a graduate of CLASS (Christian Leaders, Authors and Speakers Seminars).

To inquire about having Laura speak at your next meeting, conference or retreat, contact her at P.O. Box 1150, Yuma, Arizona 85366. Or e-mail her at RileysRanch@juno.com.